S0-BRK-617

THE AMERICAN CONDITION

Richard N. Goodwin

THE
AMERICAN
CONDITION

DOUBLEDAY & COMPANY, INC., GARDEN CITY, NEW YORK, 1974

A substantial portion of this book appeared originally in *The New Yorker*, Copyright © 1974, in somewhat different form.

ISBN: 0-385-00424-9
Library of Congress Catalog Card Number 72–94757

To Sandra, whom I love

And to the living—
Richard, the heir
Michael, the witness

CONTENTS

This book is an essay on the human and material circumstances responsible for the condition of life in modern America. Although divided into sections and chapters, the work is one argument.

It begins with a brief description of freedom as a standard against which to measure society—to gauge the extent of our failure to make society a means toward the fulfillment of human existence. The meaning of freedom, along with the process of alienation which obstructs freedom, is further elaborated in Part II; and the general themes of freedom and alienation recur throughout the book.

Part II examines the evolution of the modern consciousness of individualism. Beginning as a struggle for individual assertion, that evolution has led in our time to the destruction of those social bonds through which individuals could express and exercise authority over the circumstances of social life. We then turn specifically to the dissolution of community, shared social consciousness, and moral authority, finding ourselves amid a fragmentation so complete that the isolated individual, man alone, is driven to seek new authority, a binding force made more coercive because, lacking inward roots, it must be imposed.

The last half of this book examines the coercive structures of modern society—in particular, the bureaucratic institutions of the economy and the political process which, by their nature, sustain the dominant sources of private power. The analysis proceeds to the mechanism and techniques of institutional control over social existence.

The description is of a process, in which all causes are also consequences. The major categories of analysis, such as fragmentation and coercion, are intended to describe relationships which tell us something, but not all, of the ways in which that process functions. It is, as the epilogue points out, necessary to understand the sources and nature of oppression before liberating change can become a possibility.

Kingfield, Maine   *Richard N. Goodwin*
October 1973

THE AMERICAN CONDITION

PROLOGUE

And though your very flesh and blood
Be what your eagle eats and drinks,
You'll praise him for the best of birds,
Not knowing what the eagle thinks.

Edwin Arlington Robinson

Resigning his commission after Yorktown, George Washington wrote:

> The Citizens of America . . . are, from this period, to be considered the Actors on a most conspicuous Theatre, which seems to be peculiarly designed by Providence for the display of human greatness and felicity; . . . surrounded with every thing which can contribute to the completion of private and domestic enjoyment . . . (with) a fairer opportunity for political happiness than any other Nation has ever been favored with. . . . Treasures of knowledge . . . are laid open for our uses and their collected wisdom may be happily applied in the Establishment of our forms of government, the free cultivation of letters, the unbounded extension of commerce, the progressive refinement of manners, the growing liberality of sentiment . . . if (our) citizens should not be completely free and happy, the fault will be entirely their own.

The implicit confidence that human will can master the human condition characterizes those rare and short-lived historical flourishings of shared human creativity exemplified by Renaissance Florence, Elizabethan England and the America of the Founding Fathers. The condition of our more uneasy time confirms Washington's narration of American advantages and justifies his unwillingness to promise that within this "most conspicuous Theatre," we would be "completely free and happy."

Washington spoke toward the close of a century in which the seeds of Galileo, having germinated for more than a hundred years, had begun to fissure the foundation of society: The time of the French Revolution and the steam engine; the American Revolution, the cotton gin and the principle of interchangeable parts, the emerging possibility of monumentally ascending wealth and proliferating goods. Questions of property and its distribution began to move toward the center of thought, and during the nineteenth century a group of utopians diverged from traditional concern with the forms of the state and concentrated on the elimination of material necessity. The most compelling promise of Marx, his predecessors and progeny, was not the elimination of private property, a very old idea, but the abolition of material necessity, freeing the mass of mankind from toil and poverty. Through the just and rational organization of the productive forces the energy needed to sustain life might be reduced, liberating individuals to fulfill the more expansive possibilities of their humanity. "The realm of freedom only begins." Marx explained, "where that labour which is determined by need and external purposes, ceases. . . . Nevertheless this [a socialist economy] always remains a realm of necessity. Beyond it begins that development of human potentiality for its own sake, the true realm of freedom, which however can only flourish upon that realm of necessity as its basis. The shortening of the working day is its fundamental prerequisite."

This Marxist vision had many antecedents, among them the idea of America. Preindustrial in origin, the American idea had focused on political liberty, the rule of law and human equality. Men whose liberties were assured, inhabiting a social order charged with preventing unjust privilege, would be liberated to construct their own "realm of freedom" from the abundant material of a new continent.

During the Federal Convention of 1787, the conservative Charles Pinckney of South Carolina outlined the economic foundation for American freedom: ". . . the people of the United States are more equal in their circumstances than the people of any other Country —that they have very few rich men among them,—by rich men I mean those whose riches may have a dangerous influence, or such as are esteemed rich in Europe . . . that vast extent of unpeopled territory which opens to the frugal and industrious a sure road to competency and independence will effectually prevent for a considerable time the increase of the poor and discontented, and be the means of preserving the equality of condition which so eminently distinguishes us . . ."

Whether, like Hamilton, the early Americans believed in economic growth through industry and commerce or, like Jefferson, in the almost universal ownership of productive land, the assumption of American freedom was that all citizens would have the chance to secure a decent material standard; that there would be no great inequalities, no powerful exploiters and no mass of the exploited. There was no need for the state to provide access to abundance when God had already done so.

Liberty, self-government and access to material sufficiency were the means to an end. That end was not stated in the analytical or "scientific" terms later used by uncongenial thinkers from central Europe. The American word was "happiness." The Declaration of Independence modified the traditional trio of rights by substituting "pursuit of happiness" for property. Pinckney, in the speech quoted above, explained that a free society with such material possibilities was "capable of making them [the people] happy at home. This is the great end of Republican Establishments." For Jefferson, America was a "chosen country," a nation whose political structure and economic prospects would eventually liberate citizens to pursue the arts and the refinement of manners. Almost one hundred years later a contemporary of Marx, Walt Whitman, although more doubtful than those who had lived amid the powerful innocence of our beginnings, nevertheless conceded that "our New World democracy [has been a] . . . success in uplifting the masses out of their sloughs, in materialistic development." Yet: "I say democracy is only of use that it may pass on and come to its flower and fruits in manners, in the highest form of interaction between men and their beliefs . . ."

For the moment we are not concerned with the historical corruptions of these utopian premises, the narratives of exploitation, poverty, slavery and oppression. Neither is this the place to analyze the parallel corruptions of socialist reality, nor the awesome horrors which flowed from that secular mysticism which placed its faith neither in liberty nor production, but in the state itself.

Our investigation begins from the similarity between the Marxist utopia and the American dream: The belief that the entire body of citizens had a right to share in material abundance; and that from this necessary base people would enter the "realm of freedom," develop "human potentiality" or "pursue happiness." A society which could provide its members with a decent standard of material life, justly distributed, and based on a diminishing necessity for labor, would lead, almost inevitably, almost in the nature of things, to the enlargement of human freedom in its fullest sense.

> So then, to every man his chance—
> To every man, regardless of his birth,
> His shining, golden opportunity—
> To every man the right to live,
> To work, to be himself,
> And to become
> Whatever thing his manhood and his vision
> Can combine to make him—
> This, seeker,
> Is the promise of America.

Thomas Wolfe

. . . in communist society . . . each can become accomplished in any branch he wishes, society regulates the general production and thus makes it possible for me to do one thing today and another tomorrow, to hunt in the morning, fish in the afternoon, rear cattle in the evening, criticize after dinner, just as I have a mind, without ever becoming hunter, fisherman, shepherd or critic.

Karl Marx

These were the guiding assumptions of the most humane and progressive thought during almost two centuries of socialist idealism and American liberalism. They have now been overturned. Amidst unparalleled productive power, freedom is being eroded and confined. The golden prospect, the material liberator, seems metamorphosed into a spreading affliction that menaces the values and

the relationships among men which are the basis of human fulfillment, the stuff of freedom. It is like the story of Jack who marveled
at his unexpected beanstalk only to glimpse, as he neared the top,
the ominous form of a disturbed giant. Modern confusion and distress now reveal themselves as a consequence, not of human evil,
but of the process which provides material abundance. That process
has assumed a vitality and form of its own. Partially independent
of human will, its necessities of ideology, value and organization
impose themselves on the social order, and thereby define and
construct our social existence. The moment of liberation recedes
as the "realm of necessity" continually expands, while the ideology
and institutions devised to create the apparatus of abundance have
so fused with our environment, life styles, values and thought that
it is no longer possible to know who is the instrument of the other's
purpose.

PART I

I muse upon my country's ills—
The tempest bursting from the waste of Time
. . . .
With shouts the torrents down the gorges go,
And storms are formed behind the storm we feel:
The hemlock shakes in the rafter, the oak in the driving keel

                                    Herman Melville

CHAPTER 1

Much of this book discusses American circumstances and institutions, especially those called "economic." It is not, however, a general survey of American life. Its descriptions are employed to reveal the magnitude and sources of modern oppression or, in terms once congenial to American public thought, to the denial of our possibilities for happiness.

Appraisal requires some criterion against which present realities can be measured, a standard by which to judge and understand the influence of American society on the quality of our existence, the extent to which, in Washington's words, it discharges its "essential purposes"—"the liberties and happiness of the people of the United States . . ."

The standard for appraisal is "freedom." Freedom as a social precept is intended in a particular and definable sense, one which derives from the time men first began to think about the ideal state. It corresponds to Plato's "justice," to Marx's "return of man to himself" and to the pursuit of happiness of the Founding Fathers. It incorporates themes which have come to dominate the modern search for an alternative to an order prescribed by divine will. These historic judgments are fortified by what we have since learned of human nature and by our own intuitions. The desirability of freedom as a standard and ideal cannot be scientifically demonstrated. But it is self-evident.

Freedom constitutes the argument of this book. Subsequent discussion will elaborate its meaning and its relationships to the dominant structures of American society, so that which now appears as unnecessarily abstract or as bare assertion will, hopefully, gain in content from later chapters.

We can begin to define freedom by describing it as: *The use and fulfillment of our humanity—its powers and wants—to the outer limits fixed by the material conditions and capacity of the time.* This statement, and the elaboration it will require, diverges somewhat from those earlier descriptions of social purpose in which it is rooted. This is necessarily so. For freedom is not the creation of some ideal social order inhabited by a transfigured humanity. It is a statement of historical possibility, and, as such, its content is influenced by the material conditions and understanding of the age. The present time, for example, cannot share Plato's tacit assumption of unchanging material realities, nor Marx's faith that imposed changes in economic relationship would, of themselves, set society on an inalterable course toward freedom.

Although this brief abstraction does not take us very far toward a definition of freedom, it does prescribe a direction for inquiry. It states that freedom consists of the relationship between the human being and the material capacities of his society; and requires that material possibilities be fully exploited and totally devoted to the enrichment of human life.

Let us postpone consideration of what is meant by "the fulfillment of our humanity," to look at that aspect of freedom contained in the phrase "the outer limits fixed by the material conditions and capacity of the time." To take a simple example: American society has the capacity to provide every citizen with the necessities of a tolerable existence. The failure to do so is a denial of freedom, made all the more oppressive by the fact this could be accomplished within the existing social structure and without any sacrifice of wealth or productive power. In many earlier societies no form of social organization could have provided the mass of people with such a standard of life. Within such societies, therefore, freedom could be consistent with poverty, although perhaps not with inequality and bondage. To deny this, is to maintain that in such a period men could not be free; transforming freedom from a de-

scription of human potential to a construct of theology or utopian thought.*

This does not mean that the "outer limits" of material capacity
are fixed by present achievements, by what we now produce or
could produce within the present economic structure. Were that so,
freedom would be a problem of just distribution. We must distinguish between *present ability* and *capacity* as a description of potential ability. Capacity is what could be accomplished with the
resources, technology and knowledge now available—were society
structured and devoted to the enhancement of human existence.

Capacity so understood cannot be liberated simply by changing
the division of production, by the creation of greater wealth as
wealth is now defined, or by allocating resources to different objectives. Although capacity is material it cannot be expressed in calculations of national product or income. As we shall see, these
categories are themselves consequence and justification of the present economic structure. The purpose of capacity is the creation of
"social wealth," i.e., those additions to production which, in the
context of the economic structure as a whole, enhance the well-
being of the members of society, which serve as the material basis
for freedom. Social wealth may be increased, for example, by decreasing the hours of labor rather than the volume of production.
Capacity also includes the ability to alter the manner in which
wealth is produced—the "relations of production"—so that life is
enhanced not only by received benefits, but by the nature of individual participation in the social process.

Capacity does not have a material existence; that is, we cannot
point to it or sketch its contours with indisputable logic. Since it
can only be liberated by a radically changed social structure, any
description must contain assertion and prophecy. Yet these un-

* Marx seemed to believe that freedom must await the development of productive
forces powerful enough to permit a virtual end to the division of labor and to reduce,
if not eliminate, the necessity of labor. His rejection of the Hegelian world spirit did
not permit a complete escape from Hegel's progression—where each synthesis, each
stage of development, moved humanity closer to some ideal. The examination of
historical societies and comparison among existing societies fails to validate this progressive view. The way in which wealth is produced—the relationships of the economic process—sets the limits to *actual* freedom. Productive powers determine the
historical *possibilities* of freedom. But the capacity to produce large social wealth is
not a necessary condition for the *existence* of freedom. Indeed, only men who were
already free, or rapidly progressing toward freedom, could hope to create the economic relations which constitute the final stages of communist society.

certainties begin only when we try to establish the measure of disparity. In Part III we shall examine evidence of a capacity far more expansive than our present achievements. That gulf between historical possibilities and present realities is both a source and measure of our oppression.

It should now be apparent that the "material conditions and capacity of the time" are not just a measure of our potential ability to satisfy wants, a description of means. Capacity also contains a conception of purpose. It is capacity *for*. Thus, we cannot know the full dimensions of those "material conditions and capacity" which enter into the definition of freedom until we also understand what is meant by the "fulfillment of our humanity."

D. H. Lawrence writes, "Men are not free when they are doing just what they like. . . . Men are only free when they are doing what the deepest self likes. And there is getting down to the deepest self! It takes some digging." The barrier to the "deepest self" is not inadequate introspection or psychic repression, surmountable by obedience to the admonition of Socrates and Freud to "know thyself." It consists of that subjection to external authority which is alienation.

The subject of alienation has dominated all serious social thought and philosophy, along with much of literature, for almost two centuries. Subsequent parts of this book discuss the general properties of alienation as a theme of social existence, and the specific forms which are given to modern alienation by American institution and relationships. It is introduced here to clarify the meaning of freedom. Freedom requires the overcoming of alienation, the elimination of that process whereby the individual transfers, i.e., alienates, a portion of his own existence—of his will or powers—to an autonomous authority. That authority need not be human, e.g., a slaveowner or capitalist; it can also be an object, a process or an institution. Once it seemed that all alienation ultimately referred to human authority; those, for example, who owned the factories, railroads and other instruments of production. "The alienated character of work for the worker," writes Marx, "appears in the fact that it is not his work but work for someone else, that in work he does not belong to himself but to another person." But the individual who does not belong to himself need not belong to another. The principal source of today's alienation is not a ruling class, but a social process dominated by bureaucratic institutions which have, as we shall see, transcended traditional concepts of ownership—which are unowned.

In order to gain access to the deepest self and its wants, it is necessary to eliminate external coercion and recapture alienated existence, the condition for the "fulfillment of our humanity" is an end to alienation. This is not a truism of the order, let us say, that the prisoners must escape from their cells. To eliminate alienation would require a transformation of the entire social process, a redirection of the social forces and institutions which constitute the subject matter of this entire work.

Although the nature of modern alienation can only be revealed by examining the tangible institutions and operation of contemporary society, awareness of its dominating role allows us to formulate a preliminary and incomplete statement about freedom: *The free individual is one who can direct his energies and labor to purposes of his own choosing. He retains mastery over his social existence.* "The just man," writes Plato, "sets in order his own inner life, and is his own master and his own law, and at peace with himself."

These statements seem consistent with the purest kind of individualism. Nevertheless, freedom does not mean the pursuit of private desires, the condition which permits each person to constitute himself a society of one. A society of any complexity cannot be regulated by the fragmented will of isolated individuals. If the members of a society cannot act on the basis of shared purpose and values, then direction must be supplied by some form of external control. If individuals are not controlled by one another, as subjects and objects of a reciprocal authority which is derived from common values and from participation in the structures of a common life, they must be ruled from without; not only by others, but by insensate process, by the necessities of material institutions. The united will which is required to regulate the social process is necessarily transferred, i.e., alienated, to such external authority.

We will next examine the modern ascendancy of the individualism which had its inception in the rebellion against medieval order, and which has culminated in an ideology which equates liberty with the absence of all bonds, commitments and restraints upon individual action. This ideology assumes tangible social form in the dissolution of the human connections traditionally sustained by social institutions such as family, community, common social purpose and accepted moral authority. Our description of this decay is not intended to lament the past or to chronicle changing ways of life, but to illuminate the progressive destruction of a necessary condition of freedom. Such institutions are the means through which individuals in society can join to create and rule themselves. They are the alternative to that anarchy of desires which necessitates and nourishes an increasingly coercive social process whose dominant structures are both the beneficiaries and agents of fragmentation. We may, as many do, view these institutions of a common life as impediments to the free expression of the self and struggle to escape their bonds. But that does not alter the fact that the liberty to pursue wishes which are purely individual is paid for by the relinquishment of control over social existence. The conviction that social wants are constituted of private desires is itself an important aspect of the ideology which sustains oppression. The reduction of freedom to preference and opinion is a sign of advanced social fragmentation and decay. Through the exercise of private liberty we are made to forfeit the possibility of association and intimacy which is the premise of individual power, i.e., of unalienated existence.

Moreover, participation in a common life is more than a condition of freedom, the alternative to external coercion. Intimate association with others is itself an attribute of that humanity we wish to fulfill. It is part of human nature, of biological and evolutionary inheritance. Detachment from others, from shared existence, is diminution of the self, just as if one were deprived of perceptual capacities or outlets for sexual instinct.

This analysis compels us to enlarge and qualify our preliminary statement about freedom: *Not only does the free individual establish his own purposes, but they are consistent with the purposes of his fellows. He seeks his own wants and to cultivate his own faculties in a manner which is consistent with the well-being of others.* "Let us," exhorted Jefferson, "restore to social intercourse that harmony and affection without which liberty and even life itself are but dreary things."

To modern Americans this statement seems more calculated to confuse than to clarify the meaning of freedom. It appears a paradox: If the individual sets his own purposes how, except by chance, can they coincide with those of society; and must not social purposes be imposed by social authority if they are to govern individual behavior? Individual liberty and social responsibility appear as imperatives to be balanced, an increase in one resulting in the diminution of the other.

Yet for much of human history individuals have not looked upon their wants as distinct from those of the social order which they inhabited. In Plato's Republic the greatest good is the "bond of unity," "where there is community of pleasure and pain—where all the citizens are glad or grieved on the same occasions of grief or sorrow." More than two millennia later Nietzsche spoke of a society whose members view "a social order as the goal of the individual." These phrases are not exhortations to self-sacrifice or Christian brotherhood, but descriptions of a social condition wherein the individual experiences common values and shared inclinations as his own. He not only inhabits society, but the society inhabits him; not the individual within the commonwealth, but social man. Within such a "bond of unity" the apparent contradiction in our description of freedom is dissolved. If one exists as part of an organic community, its wants and necessities are not external. The individual who serves social goals is not alienated any more than one is alienated to his own senses and thoughts. The will of the individual contains the social will which is, therefore, an instrument of personal fulfillment rather than of external coercion.

The historical possibilities of our existence, and, therefore, the meaning of freedom, are contained within the same social order whose structures, institutions and ideologies bar us from their realization. We cannot observe this society from without. There is no vantage point beyond the historical circumstances which contain and entrap all existence and all reflection upon existence. This book does not pretend to give an "overview" of the society, to provide a judgment which is "well-balanced" or "evenhanded." It studies from within, the conditions which confine and diminish our human possibility. We can give content to the idea of freedom only by such indirection, by examining the sources and nature of oppression. Oppression is the extent to which we are barred from fulfillment, cut off from our own humanity by the process which comprises society and by our condition within that process. The state of oppression is not subjective; it can coexist with a sense of contentment, even of happiness, within the confines of a limited existence. The instruments of coercion are designed to make us perceive shackles as the objects of desire. But their power to do so is never complete. Always, the buried awareness of larger possibilities strains against settled realities and provokes a general discontent which makes its appearance as unrest, anger or despair.

The varied forms of contemporary discontent, the appearance of grievance without object, help demonstrate that the source of oppression is not simply a fact or condition which can be changed directly. For social fragmentation and oppressive authority, atomization and coercion, are different aspects of the same process, with roots in more than three centuries of Western history.

PART II

EVOLUTION OF THE MODERN
CONSCIOUSNESS—THE FRAGMENTATION
OF AMERICAN SOCIETY

TWO PROPHECIES:

Toscanelli, letter to Columbus, about 1481:

> . . . For the said voyage is not only possible, but it is sure and certain and will bring honor, inestimable gain and the widest renown among all Christians . . . I am not surprised that you, a man of great courage, and all the nation of the Portuguese, who have always been men of courage in all great enterprises, should be seen with heart aflame with great zeal to carry out the said voyage.

Henry Adams, letter to Henry Osborn Taylor, January 17, 1905:

> The assumption of unity which was the mark of human thought in the middle ages has yielded very slowly to the proofs of complexity. The stupor of science before radium is a proof of it. Yet it is quite sure, according to my score of ratios and curves, that, at the accelerated rate of progression shown since 1600, it would not need another century to tip thought upside down. Law, in that case, would disappear as theory of a priori principle, and give way to force. Morality would become police. Explosives would reach cosmic violence. Disintegration would overcome integration.

CHAPTER 1

As the latencies of ruin are contained in the energy of creation, our own condition was implicit in the earliest and most heroic statements of modern man's power, freedom and unity. The centuries of Michelangelo and Columbus, Dante, Cervantes and Da Vinci, Galileo and Shakespeare were labeled the "Renaissance" to express a widespread belief that classical culture had been reborn. From our own more remote and less confident time we can see that it was not a Renaissance, but a creation—the emergence of the modern world. Western man had begun, not to rebuild Athens, Alexandria and Rome, but to draw the plans for London, Berlin, New York and Moscow. This new world was not be be centered on the mild and sensual lands encircling the Mediterranean Lake, but in countries of uncertain and hostile seasons confronting the "ocean sea." Its ideal was not to be man in harmony with the "polis" or the nature of things, but, finally, man alone. And it was not to culminate in the Transcendence of Christ followed by the barbarian invader, but in the rational mysteries of Newton succeeded by inward brutalizations. It was to endure until sometime in the twentieth century.

Almost all the elements of modern civilization can be found scattered through the centuries which preceded the Renaissance, and some of these earlier forces are of special relevance to our own condition. Most influential were the technological advances of the

Middle Ages. Aside from the still unconcluded present, there have been two periods of technological progress which reformed and extended the fundamental possibilities of human life. The first came sometime between the eighth and fourth millennia B.C., when prehistoric geniuses devised ways to grow crops and domesticate animals, making it more productive to stay in one place than to keep moving. The hunter-wanderers were transformed into residents of communities, cities and empires.

The second shaping period for the West occurred during the Middle Ages. New technology had been produced by classical civilization, but though these innovations changed individual lives and the history of states, they did not reshape the basic structure of life for the mass of mankind; that is, they did not greatly modify or enhance the production of wealth. Advances in war and seamanship drew and unstrung nations. Roman roads and Athenian ships helped to concentrate the wealth which nourished power and art. But the foundation—the soil and its produce—went almost untouched by innovation. Classical philosophy and science shattered the limits of earlier thought and still mark the boundaries for much of our own, but the technology of everyday life was virtually ignored. The problem and possibilities simply didn't exist, for they were lying beyond the assumptions and framework of the time. This was partly the case because in elitist societies fueled by slave labor the man of learning and ideas was intellectually and spiritually apart from the world of work. Ancient thought nearly always assumes that the nature and dimensions of necessary labor are permanently fixed, and the search for utopia involves establishing durable relationships between individuals, classes of men and their occupations. It is the possibilities of technology which measure the gap between the communism of Plato and that of Marx, between justice as order and justice as equality, between the state as hierarchy and the nation as change-called-progress. Only when classical societies collapsed into the almost universal poverty of a fragmented and ignorant Europe was the new technology born.

During the Middle Ages, and especially after the tenth century, a stream of anonymous inventions was clearing the way for the modern world. Someone designed an iron plow, others uncovered the enriching possibility of crop rotation. The force of moving wind and water was captured by extended blades which turned wheels to perform varied labors. Clothing and fabric accumulated more rapidly from new looms and spinning wheels. Artisans contrived sophisticated methods to work and shape ancient raw materials such as iron and glass. These and other inventions proved deeply subversive. For the feudal hierarchy was an agrarian order whose parts were linked by a barter economy. At every level, from serf to king, individuals were obligated to make payments in kind to those above and below them in the hierarchy. The serf paid in labor or in the produce of the fields which he worked, and received a right to farm the soil and to be protected from external violence. At higher levels, men were obliged to provide soldiers, horses or equipment for war; or grain to replenish the treasuries of the kingdom.

These obligations were intensely personal, running between man and man. For centuries the concept of private ownership of land was vague or undefined since each man's estate was contingent upon the fulfillment of his own obligations. One held the land only so long as he performed his role and acquitted his duties. This hierarchy was a practical order for a chaotic society of severely limited resources. It would have been difficult, almost impossible, for most individuals to protect and maintain themselves outside these structures. The land, the only source of wealth, had to be worked, and it produced little more than was needed to sustain life, prepare for inevitable violence and provide varied tributes to God. Ordered social hierarchies seem characteristic of civilizations—from Egypt to the Incas—which depend largely on subsistence agriculture. What we might view as oppression was also security; within the severe framework could be found food, a place to exist, a community and some small protection against an ungenerous, uncertain and violent world.

The new technology did not assault the medieval social structure directly, but it did begin to modify the conditions on which it depended. New devices and techniques helped to increase production, creating wealth which was surplus to former necessities, making increased trade inevitable. A surplus of wealth must be translated into goods or the capacity to acquire goods. The excess produce of the land becomes a larger home, dinnerware or a new pair of silver stirrups. The trader and many of those whose occupations touched commerce were separated from the land and, therefore, from the elaborate structure of reciprocal obligations. Both their status and occupations required the use of money. Their ties to producer and consumer were not personal but commercial; and to function effectively they concentrated their enterprise in trading centers, usually on caravan or water routes. All of this required a new class, neither lord nor serf, landholder nor farmer, but people who were—much later—to become known as the bourgeois or middle class.

The new class and urban life grew together, but surplus wealth in the form of money began to corrode the medieval structure far beyond the ports or centers of manufacture. As money took on independent value it became possible to fulfill personal obligations through payment: cash instead of services, gold instead of horses and bowmen. Deeply personal ties which had extruded the consciousness of the age, a mode of thought, and a structure of values and perceptions metamorphosed into commercial bonds. You no longer owed yourself, but money. The spirit of commerce gradually infiltrated extensive regions of social life which had not received the benefits of increasing wealth; ascending beliefs overtook those who were excluded from the new possibilities, still captive within feudal relationships. This invasion came armed with the powerful, liberating idea of value. Once obligations had value, once they could be priced, then the fact of payment overshadowed, and ultimately displaced, the identity of the debtor. The new kind of debt was impersonal and even transferable. Lordship over the land was no longer one of the mingled strands in a web of personal obligations, but something of calculable value whose earnings, in part, could be used to pay taxes rather than homage. But value was not the thing in itself. It implied exchange, and the power to exchange was ownership. The lord who held the land became the landowner. The earth was transmuted into capital—its produce into income, and income into goods—not only to maintain life, but to bring comfort, pleasure, luxury, beauty. The powerful sought ownership in addition to power and, finally, as a source of power. Since "to own" became the authority to exclude, the mass of peasants was steadily denied their right to the land they worked or held in common. Inevitably their discontentments and occasional rebellions were crushed. They were defending the past against the future.

The surplus of wealth and the evolution of new occupations

expanded the possibility of survival outside the agrarian order. There were other ways to make a living and perhaps—for the most ingenious and energetic—to escape from poverty, even to rise in importance and power. It was more than anything else money-and-bourgeois, inseparably linked, then and forever, which made possible, likely or inevitable, a growing individualism, a sense of the power of personality, which was fatally opposed to a hierarchy in which man's consciousness was dominated by *what* he was, rather than by *who* he was. For centuries the values and ideology of personal hierarchy uneasily coexisted with the new ways in continually changing proportion. And never were the old feudal values more intensely proclaimed in art and public loyalty than when they began to go under.

The change came late to England, but, as one would expect, it was conducted there with a high thoroughness. A standard history of that country explains that "in the medieval centuries land was used mainly to produce the means of livelihood for the people who lived upon it. . . . Then . . . English merchants began to look abroad for export opportunities. . . . Men began to invest money in lands in order to be able to grow crops for profit. They were no longer mainly interested in producing agricultural goods merely to make an agrarian economy self-sufficient. They wanted to make money." The new merchant-landlords evicted tenants and combined small holdings. They seized and enclosed open fields and the traditional "common land" surrounding a village. Communism yielded to capitalism.

Because the Renaissance began in Italy, we associate it with that country, but it had a large and influential flowering in England at a time after the Italian Renaissance had already ended and Italy had fallen into the hands of foreign conquerors. Not only were the achievements of Shakespeare and Newton unsurpassed, but those achievements more powerfully formed and reflected the modern temper than did those of their Continental predecessors. And England was to exceed all other nations in realizing the potential wealth and power of the new economy.

Technology was not the sole catalyst for the rise of a commercial culture. Economic progress was not possible to a society continually disrupted and ravaged by foreign invasions. It was not until late in the tenth century that the recurrent waves of barbarian invasions—

raids by Asiatic Magyars and Moslem assaults—began to diminish. In the later Middle Ages, Western Europe—for the first time since the end of Roman rule—was relatively free of violent disruption from without. Although Europeans fought each other, it was with the aim of re-distributing their civilization, not destroying or displacing it. Simultaneously, renewed contact with Byzantine and Arab empires—the repositories of a classical learning which they had enriched with their own advances—brought new and valuable knowledge to Western Europe. Far more importantly, that contact unveiled forgotten possibilities, new dimensions for the exercise of human energy. Henry Bamford Parkes, in *The Divine Order*, writes: "The West acquired a vast mass of theory and information from Eastern civilizations; but in developing its own views of life and forms of expression it reacted against them rather than incorporating them. Contact with an alien culture is often an important factor in arousing a people to creative activities of their own. It was no accident that the French cultural efflorescence of the early Twelfth Century coincided in time with the beginnings of the Crusade."

But it was more than reaction. However intense their hostility, traders and crusaders could not evade the tangible demonstration that the order of the Middle Ages did not contain all social possibility; that men had found other ways to make war, dominate nature, organize and describe the world. This awareness was liberating, striking at the sense of inevitability, of divine will, which helped bind men to feudal society. The process of rejecting Eastern forms required comparison and argument in place of unquestioning acquiescence. (In modern Asia similar contact with an alien civilization has stimulated the Japanese to imitation, while China has moved from defiance of Western culture toward a new sense of Chinese possibility. Analogously, the postwar migration of rural American blacks to the urban North helped to create a new and more intense awareness of black oppression, possibility and identity.)

Shifting economic patterns made change necessary; freedom from barbarian invasions helped make change possible; exposure to alien sophistication intensified a revolutionary awareness. Beyond this point it is difficult to separate cause from consequence, the accidental from the inevitable. One cannot, for example, fit the "black death" into any theory of social change. Yet in the middle of the fourteenth century the plague killed one third of the population of Europe, introducing a disorder which must have weakened existing structures.

As the conditions of existence changed, men inevitably began to think differently about themselves, each other and the universe. The streams of the material and intellectual soon merged, fortified each other and drowned the past.

CHAPTER 2

Modern thought, the modern vision, took shape in the late Middle Ages and is today, as it was then, compounded of two major elements: mysticism and scientific reason. However different their premises, both mysticism and scientific reason are fatally opposed to social hierarchy and the authority which sustains it. Neither the mystic nor man of scientific reason can permit any institution, any collective and historical authority to mediate between him and the truth. God or the world is the revelation of his own experience and what is revealed may stand in contradiction to the beliefs and perception of the entire race. The true philosophers, says Galileo, "fly, and . . . they fly alone, like eagles, and not in flocks like starlings." To the medieval mystic and devout Christian, Meister Eckhart: "When a free mind is really disinterested, God is compelled to come into it. . . . The soul imbibing God turns into God as the drop becomes the ocean." To experience God directly is to experience uniquely, to contract the community of believers to the self alone.

If logic or observation lead the man of scientific reason to contradict all received knowledge, he has found, nonetheless, the truth, not for himself alone, but for all men. In the early days of modern science, before men had contrived the technical and mathematical language to mask the ambiguities behind scientific thought, the process of reason was more openly empowered by experience.

The most original astronomer of the Renaissance, Johannes Kepler, justifies his advocacy of the Copernican system: "Since I have attested it as true in my deepest soul, and since I contemplate its beauty with incredible and ravishing delight, I should also publicly defend it to my readers with all the force at my command."

Not because of their conclusions, but because of how they reached them, mysticism and scientific reason participated in the slow dismemberment of the medieval order. They allowed one to approach knowledge of the truth through his own experience, senses and thought. The knowledge so attained was not simply a matter of opinion or preference (that evasion was not to appear until the modern decay). It was reality, a description of the spiritual and material world. This manner of thought severed the single mind from a collective consciousness, a community of belief: indeed, was only possible to one already set apart. Man was separated not only from his contemporaries, but from the community of the past whose laboriously constructed code of authority and belief had justified and illuminated human society. The constitution of the universe was opened for revision by anyone brilliant enough or blessed with a guiding inspiration. "I do not wish to be counted as an ignoramus and an ingrate toward Nature and toward God," wrote Galileo, "for if they have given me my senses and my reason, why should I defer such great gifts to the errors of some men." Strike the reference to God, and the assertion carries the same force. Why too should the mystic, in direct communion with God or the infinite, defer to the authority of popes and conclaves, old philosophers and ancient scientists, or to another's interpretation of the Gospels, which finally had to mean the authority of the Gospels themselves? Stripped of authoritative interpretation, the Bible becomes a document of convenience, a kind of Constitution perpetually awaiting new appointees to the Supreme Court.

The Renaissance man, as he was also heir to the Middle Ages, saw no discontinuity in mingling reason and revelation, mind and spirit, mathematics and magic. Astronomers cast horoscopes while prophets, such as Bruno, invoked the new science as evidence of spiritual insights. Ultimately, however, scientific reason and mysticism were bound to clash, since they often yielded contradictory assertions. It was, for example, the leaders of the Reformation, those fragmenting mystics of the universal church, who first attacked the theories of Copernicus. Almost a century before the Vatican censured Galileo, Luther said: "This fool Copernicus wishes to reverse the entire science of astronomy: but sacred Scripture tells us that Joshua commanded the sun to stand still and not the earth." Calvin scorned: "Who will venture to place the authority of Copernicus above that of the Holy Spirit." The Catholic Church was tardy in its rejection of the new astronomy, not out of tolerance, but because it was unaccustomed to the possibility that philosophical or scientific, i.e., non-theological ideas asserted by an individual could be thought to challenge the divine order. The ideas might be interesting, useful and might even have practical results (as the astronomical observations of Copernicus helped Pope Gregory design his new calendar), but the conclusions of human intelligence could not be supposed to discredit the truth which surpassed all understanding. Only in reaction to the Reformation, as the modern spirit overtook the Catholic Church itself, did the new science seem a threat.

Thus a standard astronomy textbook of 1594, by Thomas Blundeville, said by way of friendly praise that "Copernicus affirmed that the earth turneth about and that the sun standeth still . . . by help of which false supposition he hath made truer demonstrations of the motions and revolutions of the celestial spheres, than ever were made before."

Within a few decades men of science would scorn such timidity. (Although they would also soon prove that most of Copernicus' suppositions had been false, except that the earth did move.) Scientific descriptions became truth—accurate descriptions of the real universe. It was only after the twentieth century departed from the mechanics of Newton that we went part way back to Blundeville; i.e., not true supposition or false supposition, but simply supposition.

Mystic and scientist steadily accumulated followers in the name of freedom, striking at an order and authority newly felt to be oppressive. A new truth was arising from a new reality: from technology and commerce, value and money, exploration and ownership. That new truth materialized a new man. Malraux has said that the art of Renaissance Italy displayed the "honor of being a man." Yet preceding centuries had not thought it dishonorable to be a man. It was simply a fact, an aspect of existence, not the most important. The village of serfs was not merely a community of men and women who tilled the soil, but the tilling of the soil also created the village of serfs. Men were their relationships with others and they existed, were defined by, their function. The self was an atom bound to others by natural law in order to form irreducible units of existence linked with the infinite through space and time in an ordered process. All that men thought or believed could be contained by this same universal pattern, ultimately incomprehensible, approachable finally through faith alone; a design whose earthly manifestation was the hierarchy and authority of the social and spiritual order. All thought was in the service of this order, not as a consequence of coercion but as a matter of necessity. Thinking, believing, feeling man existed only as a fragment of the pattern. How then could the brick defy the building, the thread abjure the fabric?

The common understanding of the Middle Ages had been recurrently illuminated and enlarged by men of unusual spiritual insight and intelligence. Still, they did not regard their logic and understanding, argument and exhortation as the truth itself, but only one path among others toward a revelation both mysterious and complete. We cannot think, or even imagine that we think as did that earlier race, although there are some traces of these ancient values in a few of the most puzzling acts of modern communist states. Heinz Brandt, in his tormented biography, *The Search for a Third Way*, describes how "the first builders of Soviet computers were thrown into jail because Norbert Wiener's theoretical philosophical grounds for his revolutionary discoveries were condemned as 'idealistic-reactionary diversions against Marxism.'" When the Russians deny scientific "facts" or the Chinese defy economic "laws" it is not that such facts and laws are not accurate but, at least in part, that they conflict with a higher truth, that of the social order and its sustaining beliefs. Such denial and defiance do not suit the modern temper, nor do any people or nation seem willing to accept the consequences of subordinating the rational structure of materialism. Indeed, to do so in today's West would be simple tyranny, for we are no longer sustained by a shared order of belief and function. To protect such a shared order can be a defense of freedom; in its absence the same acts are oppressive.

Even the received science of the Renaissance, the physics of

Aristotle, expressed and supported the social order of the Middle Ages. Stones fell to the ground because that was their natural place, it was where they belonged. "Up" was where fire and air went. "Down" was where earth and water tended. Fire that didn't press upward was not fire. Its direction and motion were part of its definition or, in contemporary terms, function and purpose were elements of identity. Place and purpose were distinct "potencies." Existence was a compound of structure and process and function. Once separated from these relationships, no material or human grouping could be said to exist. The encroaching Renaissance loosened these bonds to free different sources of energy. With gathering momentum the fundamental units of human existence began the five-century pilgrimage from necessity to choice. Is water, water? Or is it hydrogen and oxygen? Is hydrogen, hydrogen? Or is it electrons, protons and neutrons? Etcetera. Till death do us part. The Renaissance celebrated man, the individual, in honor of a creation.

Did mysticism and scientific reason, the ideological tools of that creation, lead to an enlargement of freedom? We cannot enter into the mind of medieval man and replicate his consciousness, that conception of one's existence, of what it is to be human, which bounds historical freedom. From within our own consciousness, the end of the feudal and divine orders must be viewed as liberating. So it seemed to the men of the Renaissance. To them the interchanging boundaries of thought were weapons against an authority which obstructed new forces of liberation—the rise of individualism, growth of commerce, dissolution of hierarchy, defiance of supranational authority. The ice-out was at hand. The fissures of the world were one with the fissures of the mind. They could not foresee that shared existence, social man, might shatter into a fragmentation so complete that the isolated individual, man alone, would be driven to seek new authority, a binding force more coercive because lacking inward roots, it must be imposed.

The thought which helped to liberate men from the restraints of medieval order also contained the possibilities of new enslavement. Because the mystic and man of science devised truths not just for themselves but for all men, if such beliefs were joined to power they could be enforced on all. Once the constraints of tradition received authority, and divinely ordained social institutions were dissolved, the potential power of tyranny and enslavement was increased.

Mysticism was more threatening than scientific reason, as we can see from one of its more virulent manifestations—racism. The conclusions of scientific reason were at least subject to analysis, criticism and correction. What could not be challenged, however, was the process of reason itself. Its truths could be disproved, but they could not be refuted by non-rational authority—by Scriptures or sensation, intuition or aesthetic urgencies. Technology, moreover, provided the belief-compelling miracles of scientific reason. It pumped riches from the earth, illuminated the night, carried men into the skies: It worked. This dazzling success was the key to power. The metamorphoses were ready: First, it works; then, if it works it must be true; and finally, if it is true, then it alone must be true.

The very idea of truth, of validity, came to be defined as the product of scientific reason. A statement was valid not because of its content but because of the mental technique used to produce it. The logical process of inferring conclusions from fact, observation or assumption, which we call scientific reason, is not the same as the idea of reason or rational behavior which means to come to terms with the world through use of the intellect. Reason in this sense can include motive, justification, cause or excuse. Although values cannot be prescribed by scientific reason, they can be a product of rational thought. It may be rational to be a pacifist, love your neighbor, exercise compassion and seek love, but it can't be proved. Yet by the nineteenth century many believed that all of existence could be compacted within the framework of scientific reason. And some still believe this.

The claims of scientific reason transcended history, asserting truths and a way toward truth that would be forever valid or a prerogative hitherto reserved for the Bible and its theological elaborators. The power to enforce this claim was not rooted merely in material success. As religious faith helped satisfy primal needs, so scientific reason helped to satiate a primal vanity. For it rests upon a capacity which is the lowest common denominator of intelligence. Almost everyone has some ability to draw logical conclusions—to infer from facts and observation. The great scientists were men of dominant genius, but their intelligence was simply greater than our own and not of a different order. No one but Michelangelo could have carved his Moses, but if Newton had died at birth we would still have had a theory of gravity. There are many who legitimately work to revise and improve Einstein's work, but no sane writer would put his pen to Shakespeare's plays. Even animals and machines are capable of scientific reason, but not of moral or artistic revelation or consciously coming to terms with mystery.

Intellectuals and scholars in every generation have been able to understand, duplicate, refine and advance the calculations of the past; a mediocre student at MIT can work out the proofs of Euclid and Newton. One of history's few certain lessons is that scientific reason is more widely accessible and more easily evoked than other qualities of mind essential to a rational and liberating society. As with all successful faiths, this sense of comprehensible connection contributed to ascendancy. Most could not follow into the outer spheres of mathematical debate, but many could see lunar irregularities through a telescope or observe, with some understanding, the flow of energy from a lamp or engine. Almost every life was invaded by the technological by-products of scientific reason— loaves and fishes—and mixed with wonder was an intuitive understanding that the most difficult calculations were similar, analogous, or the same as the operations of mind which guided an individual in rotating his crops, repairing a cart, designing a guillotine or setting his prices.

All can vicariously share in scientific revelation. And not just one revelation either—a single Sermon on the Mount, a lonely crucifixion, one ill-attended resurrection, but new ones all the time. Almost everyone has experienced, in himself or others, the inexplicable gratification of announcing the latest contrivance of technology, or has felt a muted satisfaction at working out a logical puzzle or even using the tables in *Consumer Reports* to calculate the size of air conditioner needed to cool a room fifteen feet long and nine feet wide with three windows and an easterly exposure. Many, most of us, have experienced an irrational pleasure in solving a puzzle, overcoming a technological challenge as simple as changing a tire or fixing a toaster, or even plugging in a new gadget and watching it run. It fits.

These are no mere mechanic pleasures, and their marginal intensity demonstrates and reflects our participation in the great scheme of thought: What scientific reason does not prove is not true, though all the prophets, poets and madmen of the world proclaim it. We are all scientists. Galileo's message was for all men. Every man, whatever his station or scars, contains a spark of logic, an unextinguished ember of analysis.

Listen even to the student demonstrating that grass or hash harms the body no more than pasteurized milk, when a moment's pause at intuition or experience would reveal absurdity. Our technician of his own body does not feel it necessary to define harm or to ask whether the question is important or even relevant. Similarly, the debate over pornography often centers on the question of personal and social harm; does it tempt one to rape or lure toward masturbation? It is part of our capacity to transform questions of values into medical problems. Drugs and pornography do affect people or no one would want them. (The same is true of alcohol, too much starch and hot baths.)

The question is whether the effect is good or bad for the individual and for society. Does it tend to increase or diminish freedom? Any pastime which reaches large proportions with little effective opposition does not menace the existing order and may even support its repressions. There are no revolutions by acquiescence. When impassioned public rhetoric and stern laws are not followed by strong and successful action we can assume that there is no real threat to the dominant institutions of society. Our experience with Prohibition indicates that it can be far more unsettling to deprive people of their pleasures than to permit them. And few advocate a dry nation even though we know that a regular or systematic drinker is bound to suffer mental and physical damage. Millions already do, but alcoholics do not endanger the system. Heroin is helping to "solve" the problem of the ghettos. Indeed, drugs are becoming a barrier to black freedom second only to the racism which encourages their use.

Scientific reason was necessary to the emerging age of individualism and mass desire. It expressed and justified one and helped satisfy the other. Its simplest litanies evoked the common response and belief requisite for a successful creed. It provided feelings of domination and control necessary to individuals severing life-defining bonds. To calculate was to rule; to understand was to exploit; knowledge was power. To reason about the world was to incorporate it within the mind. Resistance to the emergence of science has sometimes been explained as a reluctance to admit that man did not hold the center of a finite universe, as a proud refusal to be reduced, a defense of mankind's collective ego. On the contrary, the pioneers of scientific reason did not seek to diminish man but to glorify him. Their temper was exultant arrogance rather than humility.

Man's position in the medieval cosmos was the physical counterpart of a material universe subordinate to spiritual powers. In the center of the world the human creation toiled, encompassed by light-festooned spheres, his destiny controlled by a nameless power whose mysteries he might approach or worship, but never question or fully comprehend. "We are owls attempting to see the sun," wrote Nicholas of Cusa, perhaps the greatest medieval mind. Nature itself was not man's environment, the stuff of reality, but a metaphor of the divine poet. Medieval cosmology did not reflect the beliefs of a self-important race, but of a creature struggling to understand, systematize and accept its substantial but subordinate position in the unimaginable scheme of creation and the uncreated.

By the late Middle Ages, men began to look at the world around them with a vision lost since the end of classical civilization. Nature reappeared in art, poetry and thought, not as a symbolic abstraction of the divine, but concrete and vivid, as bounty and challenge. Before this the natural world had existed as evidence of things not seen, as diversion or as guide to the inward gaze. Now history's newly created ruler, man the individual, sought to impose his personality on that which, like himself, had an existence which could be perceived. As a creature compounded of sense and skill, his significance could be no greater than the world he understood and used. That natural world, and no other, was assurance of his own reality and power. The long transition from discovery to conquest to devastation had begun.

A builder who thought his cathedral only a dim and transient translation of divine majesty could not think of himself as a great architect. Nor did Moses pride himself on his engineering abilities when water flowed from the stone. Since men now wished, needed, were compelled to honor themselves, they must necessarily esteem their world and perceive it as concrete, sufficient reality—as the "real world." It was the Irish—the Celts—whose poetry first departed from the medieval vision of nature as symbolic abstraction. In their early rhythms the Homeric sea reappeared as "heavy waves over the glittering ocean." The significance of man and his personal world is the theme that links the paintings of Michelangelo, Da Vinci's inventions, the Portuguese explorations, Kepler's computations and the man of La Mancha. To strip humanity of its focal position in an eternal symmetry, to place it on a tiny circling globe carelessly lodged in endless space, was not exile but liberation. It did not matter where man was located if his brain could contain the universe. If that same universe was infinite, there was no place beyond, no tangible home for a divine or satanic order. We could not be in transition to the infinite if it was already our home. Man was no longer fixed in time and space and possibility. Now he could think of himself as he wished, extend himself as he could.

If the labor of individuals was now to define society, it followed that those of the highest talent were great men. In the Middle Ages the often anonymous artist was important only as the vessel of a collective spirit. The onset of the Renaissance brought the modern idea of a creative genius. The great talents of that age thought of themselves as geniuses, and so do we since our experience is bounded by the same consciousness—then new, now old; then beginning, now ending. In many ways these first modern men have never been surpassed. Their advantage was to see the new world for the first time—ambiguous, amorphous, liquid, its extravagant substance latent with abundant forms.

A man abandoned at birth in a dark cave, raised by some benign spirit of the inner earth, emerging after twenty years, what is the sun to him?—painful fierceness and warmth, lantern to ease his path and disturber of his sleep, the eye of God and the fires of Hell, a distant beacon and encroaching apocalypse. It is all of these, until we know what it is. Then it can never be the same.

In those early days, before received authority became aware that scientific reason did not wish to win God's favor but usurp his kingdom, the new spirit was openly confessed. Johannes Kepler, first to describe the elliptical orbits of the planets, writing of technology's all-time triumph, exulted, "O telescope, instrument of much knowledge, more precious than scepter! Is not he who holds thee in his hand made king and lord of the works of God." The scientific mystic Giordano Bruno—translated into an Aristotelian flame for his theology, and not the Copernican science he mixed it with—asserted that the denial of traditional cosmology "has given freedom to the human spirit and made its knowledge free. It was suffocating in the close air of a narrow prison house whence, but only through chinks, it gazed at the far-off stars. Its wings were clipped, so that it was unable to cleave the veiling clouds or reach the reality beyond." Freedom was not a blessing or a gift of grace, but within reach of intellect and will. One who could describe the circuit of the earth might also extinguish the flaming sword. Galileo, the supreme technician-explorer of the Renaissance, discoverer not of one new world, but thousands, dispensed with metaphors about winged spirits and divine scepters: "To apply oneself to great inventions, starting from the smallest beginnings, and to judge that wonderful arts lie hidden behind trivial and childish things is not for ordinary mortals: these are concepts and ideas for superhuman souls." ("What hath God wrought," asked Samuel Morse of his newly created telegraph, and did not stay for an answer.)

Science was the disguised guerrilla of the medieval order. Intriguing to the leaders of the Middle Ages, they did not regard it as knowledge of the highest order. As an inferior support for the structure of belief it could not menace theology. Though a scientist might amuse his colleagues with his telescopes and numbers he was primarily employed to devise and teach the construction of fortifications, waterworks and other skills useful to rulers. Few, except the poets, were aware that this harmless discipline was shaping a counterideology. While the Church acquiesced, John Donne perceived the presumption. In 1611, the year that Jesuit mathematicians feted Galileo in Rome—twenty-two years before his forced abjuration—Donne writes of "*Galileo* . . . who of late hath summoned the other worlds, the Stars to come nearer to him, and give him an account of themselves. Or . . . *Keppler*, who (as himselfe testifies of himselfe) . . . hath received it into his care, that no new thing should be one in heaven without his knowledge." Later in the same fiction, *Ignatius his Conclave*, the long-dead

Copernicus petitions Lucifer for special treatment: "I am he, which . . . raised both thee and thy prison, the Earth, up into the Heavens. . . . The Sunne have appointed to go into the lowest parts of the world. Shall these gates . . . be shut against me, who have turned the whole frame of the whole, and am thereby almost a new Creator?" But when the guardians of the divine order awoke to the danger it was too late. Copernicus' works were not banned until a century after publication, and when the Pope tried to halt all traffic in Galileo's works they had already been carried to Protestant Europe. It was, said Milton, like trying to "pound in the crows by shutting the park gate." So much for the tale of science's valiant assault on irrational human vanity. Instead, it was the Church which struggled to keep man within manageable proportions.

The defiance and human assertion contained in the origin of scientific reason helps to explain why its progress has been companioned by mysticism—brother and enemy, reflection and shadow. Mysticism is a belief in realities beyond the reach of intellect or of normal perception, but which are accessible to the individual through a process of intuition, communion or heightened experience. From within the medieval Catholic Church, St. Anselm wrote, "He who has not experience cannot understand, for just as the experience of a thing surpasseth the fact of hearing it spoken of, so the knowledge of one who experiences outweighs the understanding of one who only hears." It is a judicious statement. The difference between experience and authority is one of method and degree. For St. Anselm, the religious experience could only confirm and strengthen the true belief. A personal experience was near to the idea of faith, and in the Middle Ages faith was a collective and historical experience, the touchstone to a universal harmony. The idea of faith as experience evolved in order to establish an authority which could not be threatened by rational doubts. As long as the common order was the total reality it would inevitably be verified by experience. Were a medieval man to proclaim a personal revelation that the Gospels had been forged by Satan he would only announce his own madness. In a world where consciousness itself was collective, no sane experience could set the one against the many; it would be as if a ship's timbers demanded relief from the penetration of nails.

(The belief in the unity of thought tempted theologians to their self-destructive effort to reconcile reason and religion, even though such a demonstration was only possible by first accepting the methods of rationalism and thus ensuring failure. As my law school textbook advised the acolytes of justice—if you can frame the question you can win the argument. The attempt to harmonize reason and faith was an expression of an even more chimerical urge to reconcile desire with power.)

To admit experience as a way toward truth was to assume a large and unforeseeable risk. For experience is mated to consciousness, to the way in which one conceives his own experience. As consciousness changed, experience was transformed, providing a common support for both scientific reason and mysticism. Like scientific reason, mysticism served the need to defy collective authority and thrived on the emerging demands of a commercial society. Pretensions to universal authority conflicted with the efficient organization of national power; nor could a creed designed to sustain a society of land and universal poverty be permitted to obstruct ideas necessary to expanding economic possibility. There were new needs. And as reason toiled, the angel of revelation also obliged. Through Luther the authority of the nation state won the blessing of God. After all, explained Cardinal Richelieu, Galileo's contemporary, "The Church is in the state, not the state in the Church," sending off five tubfuls of gold to finance the heretic King of Sweden's depredations against the rest of Catholic Europe. Calvin retranslated the will of God, liberating the conscience of new classes: "Ivory and gold and riches are the good creatures of God, permitted, nay destined, by divine power, for the use of man; nor was it ever forbidden to laugh, or to be full or to add new to old and hereditary possessions, or to be delighted with music or to drink wine." How simple it was. Don't shrink the camel, just widen the eye of the needle. Changing consciousness transformed the unacceptable and the absurd into the self-evident.

Mysticism and scientific reason share not only common origins but, in their purest form, a dangerous possibility, which has reached its most enshrouding fulfillments in our own time. It was analyzed by Nobel laureate Werner Heisenberg, director of Hitler's uranium project, with what would have been irony equal to the best of Swift or Beckett, had he not been sincere. He records his remarks to a scientific colleague as the two men emerged from an air-raid shelter and began the long walk from Berlin's Potsdamer Platz to suburban Dahlem, at the end of an Allied bombing attack: "Perhaps we Germans, of all people, have a special part to play in this area [science] precisely because the absolute exercises so strange a fascination on us. . . . If Germany has made scientific or artistic contributions that have changed the world—we have only to think of Hegel and Marx, of Planck and Einstein, of Beethoven and Schubert—then it was thanks to this love of the absolute, thanks to the pursuit of principles to their ultimate consequences." Suddenly Heisenberg's reflections were interrupted, because "As I was speaking my right shoe had caught fire again, and it took me quite some time to scrape off all the phosphorus." One of the creators of modern physics, the truth at his feet, love of the absolute sputtering and smoking only a sole's width from his own body.

The conclusions, the "truths," of scientific reason and mysticism originate with the individual, but they pretend to universal validity. Both have powerful inclinations toward system, toward a total order, a structure of beliefs or facts which contain and define all of reality. Once this structure is established, opposition can only be perceived as ignorance, superstition or malevolence. And if conviction is mated to power under the right historical circumstances, such opposition must logically be re-educated or suppressed—in the name of truth, on behalf of freedom, to the everlasting benefit of mankind.

The absolute makes its first appearance in commitment to process—logical analysis or mystical communion are the only ways to know reality. Dissent is more readily allowed by scientific reason, but only if it shares the assumptions of the process. If a scientist, addressing a convention of mathematicians, wrote $2+2=5$ on the board, his audience would wait attentively. If he then elaborated a whole new theory of numbers they might burst into argument or even applause, but not if he simply announced, quoting Dostoevsky, "It's true, gentlemen, because I prefer it." A Nazi leader might have announced new discoveries, i.e., revelations, that the Japanese race was superior—purer—to the Jews and Slavs, but not that the Japanese deserved warmth and respect because they were very nice people.

It is tempting to make the journey from process to result, from method to system—to endow the more persuasive and appealing conclusions of thought or revelation with the quality of being absolute. If you have discovered the way toward truth, to reality itself, you are unlikely to doubt what you find at the end of the road. Since Columbus knew you could reach Japan by sailing West, he also knew he had arrived there. Modern history abounds with examples: some defeated, some discarded, others among the rulers of the world. Scientific reason has given us Herbert Spencer's social evolution and Soviet Marxism along with the more fragmented and subtle assumptions which partially dominate our own society. Modern mysticism hinted at its possibilities when Luther supported the bloody suppression of the peasants who, like the Soviet kulaks, stood in the way of history. But Catholic shrine seeking, Protestant poverty pounding and Puritan witch crushing were only previews of the spectacular modern mysticisms of racism, fascism, imperialism and the infinitely durable National Mission-Greatness-Destiny.

Mysticism and scientific reason are forced to share their dominion, not only because they originate in individualism and tend toward the absolute, but because scientific reason opened a gap in the scheme of thought which could only be filled by mysticism. Mythology as religion had connected human life to aspects of reality which scientific reason could not reach. Through mythology we became part of the historical design, worn into the creation of a physical universe whose existence and process could be comprehended, reconciled to mystery through awareness of our limited position in the divine scheme. Such a connection does not require control or even understanding; only that we have a place, an existence, in relation to the universe. Of the many institutions man has contrived to establish his identity, mythology alone gave our existence a dimension in time. Without it, we would be planless fragments, accidental collections of chemicals, spinning through nothing to nowhere. In the Greek legend Prometheus gives man the capacity to reason, to plan, to invent. The modern world originates from these gifts. Yet Prometheus realized this was not enough:

> CHORUS: Did you perhaps go further than you have told us:
> PROMETHEUS: I caused mortals to cease foreseeing doom.
> CHORUS: What cure did you provide them with against that sickness?
> PROMETHEUS: I placed in them blind hopes.
> CHORUS: That was a great gift you gave to men.

Mythologies were the blind hopes of mankind. As mythology was discredited, the human needs remained. The strength to conquer was not the talent to occupy. Only secular mysticism could satisfy the necessity for connection. For a long time that mysticism was restrained by a conviction that advancing knowledge would yield laws and principles for the scientifically reasonable conduct of society and individual life, that scientific reason would provide the links or remove the need of non-rational connection.

In the late nineteenth century history began to dissipate this illusion, leading toward irreversible dissolution amid the absurd trenches of World War I. As always, thought responded to the lessons and facts of history. The certainty and order at the very core of scientific reason, its ability to command the material world, were transformed into doubt, speculation and even the denial of order. The more intently our scientific agents scrutinized the world the less sure one could be of what was there. The increasing and justified apprehension that scientific reason had destroyed forms of order which it could not replace opened new frontiers for mysticism.

Some forms of secular mysticism are relatively benign, like humanism of all sizes and shapes, organic gardening and Reverence for Life. But other manifestations of secular mysticism contained unparalleled possibilities for repression and control. Earlier leaders —popes, priests and kings—were compelled to justify their deeds by obedience to a divine will and nature as set forth in holy books, and to act within a large and complicated institution. They were constitutional dictators. And even though human ingenuity was capable of outrageous constructions, the divine constitution was a restraint (as our own Constitution, despite great changes of meaning, has given us a great deal of protection against the willful use of power). At the very least, to flaunt the general understanding increased the danger of rebellion. No pope, for example, could use the Church for purely personal goals, disregarding the prerogatives of cardinals and conclaves, without endangering the foundation of his own power. Once divine authority was displaced, many of these restraints disappeared. New creeds could establish their own morality, goals and institutions. If religion had been the opiate of the people, non-religious mysticism became their loco weed. Moreover, modern mysticisms were able to strengthen their hold by incorporating elements of the scientific faith. If a revelation also claimed scientific support it was doubly true, viz., the demonstrations of Nordic or Teutonic supremacy. So too was scientific Marxism blended with Russian destiny.

Wilhelm Reich regarded mysticism as a product of sexual repression. Some connection is self-evident, but can it be said that the society of the twentieth and nineteenth centuries with its many triumphant mysticisms has been more repressive—patriarchal—than that of the two preceding centuries? It is doubtful. Reich seems to regard scientific reason as the adversary of mysticism, more the product of sexual liberation. Yet the two have grown together and in the same societies. For all his important discoveries, when Reich's ideas are applied to society as a whole we get another system, a sexual absolute. At Organon, in Rangeley, Maine, Reich's house is as he left it before he died, luxuriously redecorated for an expected visit by President Eisenhower, his imagined protector. He was insane by then, partly as a consequence of brutal and unjust harassments, slander and persecutions. Yet there is a metaphor. When systematic thought is mated to power the result is madness.

The alliance of mysticism and science also took more subtle but very effective forms. Given the mystical premise, e.g., the British Empire, defense of freedom, or American self-interest, scientific reason could then be used to prove that certain policies and actions were required. However, the rational pursuit of a mystical idea is not rational and, if carried far enough, loses whatever reason it once contained. The war in Vietnam is an instructive example.

That war began as the rational pursuit of an unexamined, i.e., mystical premise: It was in our national interest to help any government threatened by any group which was known or suspected to think of itself as communist. Why? . . . Because. This premise seemed to be, but was not, related to an entirely different policy of containing Russia and China. We can see the lack of relationship in the absence of any felt necessity to demonstrate that a communist government in Guatemala or Cuba or Indochina would, in fact, increase Soviet or Chinese reach. There was almost no important debate over precisely this issue. In retrospect, none should reasonably have been expected. Just as one would not have expected Winston Churchill to compare the economic benefits of maintaining the empire with its cost; or ask a priest to submit a communion wafer for laboratory analysis.

In the early stages of escalation, in 1965, a principal assistant to the Secretary of Defense was asked, in a private conversation, how we could justify the killing of South Vietnamese civilians in the course of protecting them. The question did not faze him, for he had been provided an answer by his more philosophically inclined superiors: "Better the death of the body, than the death of the spirit under communism." Torquemada was alive and well in suburban Virginia.

The policy in Vietnam was "given," i.e., it conformed to a reality which was apprehended neither by logic nor the senses, conforming to the definition of mysticism. At some point, probably during late 1965 or 1966, our acts in Vietnam exceeded even their own internal logic. The rational superstructure crumbled, and the conduct of the war became the irrational pursuit of a mystical premise. Confronted by the fact that military victory in the classical sense was impossible (our leaders even admitted the fact: Why not? What difference did it make?), we stepped up the fighting. Knowing that South Vietnam could only survive as a stable society under a politically skilled and broadly based government, we installed corrupt military dictators and helped them to suppress and destroy all the vital political forces of the country. Once faced with the inevitability of our withdrawal, we widened the conflict to include Laos and Cambodia, making it likely that our total departure would result in the collapse of three countries rather than one. If it was necessary in order to prove the theory, we would set the dominoes up by ourselves. As the war took such an enormous toll of American spirit and economic well-being that no rational process could discern any conceivable outcome that would be of greater benefit to America than a withdrawal, we still kept on. The advocates and leaders of the war were undergoing a classical mystical experience. The war for Vietnam was the war for America. South Vietnam was America, their America, them. All the rest—domestic turbulence, economic decline, the decay of shared social purposes—was incidental, an annoyance, or a subversive obstacle to the pursuit of a compelling destiny across the Pacific.

And just as it seemed we had reached the outer limits of imagination, the story soared into a further fantasy. The chambers of power-clutched debated the chambers of power-longed-for over the time and method of surrender. The great question of world policy became how many more people should be killed before we release Indochina to its inhabitants? How high a price should we pay for their victory?

To the future, the war in Vietnam will probably seem as transforming a period to the second American century as the Civil War was to the first—symbolizing, accompanying and evoking shifts in the substructure of society. It is discussed here as a partial illustration of the way in which reason can become unreason, step by logical step. A logical structure built on faulty premises can be rational. It may even be brilliant. Sir Isaac Newton, the combined St. Peter and George Washington of the scientific hagiarchy, assumed an absolute space and time and the separate conservation of matter and energy. Yet rejection of these premises by modern science does not lessen the rational qualities of the most influential text in the history of scientific reason. But when premises themselves are contradicted or are ignored when found contrary to desired conclusions, then reason becomes something else, retaining the skin of language which we tend to associate with rational thinking.

A TO B: We must get to the other side of this turnpike. Let's walk across.

B TO A: We'll be killed. It's jammed with traffic coming around a blind curve at seventy-five miles an hour.

A TO B: Look (*patiently*), the only way to cross is to walk. The Indians would still own the country if the pioneers thought like you, and Hitler would have conquered the world. Let's go!

Even if crossing the turnpike is worth any conceivable risk, A is either deranged, terribly confused or a mystic.

If A had said: "Don't worry, it's our destiny to make it" or "God will see us through," it would quickly be apparent that we were not confronting faulty logic, but a different kind of thinking altogether. Of course, if a rare visual defect prevented A from seeing the cars, or if a wildly secluded upbringing left him uninformed about an automobile's power, we would simply be faced with faulty reasoning due to inadequate data. This is true so long as he is ignorant of his ignorance. But when a person purports to reason on the basis of information he knows to be inadequate, then he moves toward non-rational or mystical thought. It is a question of degree. When we know the most crucial information and/or we are willing to deal in probabilities, our conclusions or acts can be rational even if wrong. If your car radiator overheats, it is logical to put water into it, even if it later turns out that a blowfish of uncommon vagility has swollen to plug a connecting pipe. On the other hand, if we lack knowledge of basic information, are aware of that lack and proceed to reason from what we do know, then we are not reasoning at all. This is what happens every time a deer hunter fires at movement or the sound of trampled leaves, thus sacrificing a fellow sportsman to humanity's blind hopes.

As late as 1966, one of the highest officials in the American government remarked that it might be a good idea if some person who understood the Vietnamese people and their culture were asked to attend the meetings where the struggle to win "men's hearts and minds" was being plotted. This man knew he didn't know the most important facts of all, and yet his confident recommendations were asserted as logical and even necessary. But it was pure magic. Even had he been right it still would have been magic.

Just as they originate from a common impulse, scientific reason and mysticism can finally merge: not the blending of distinct substances to produce a third, but a biological mating whose structure is determined by the dominant mystical genes. This transformation into mysticism is latent in the process of scientific reason itself. Wherever it expands its claim of authority to include the social process, and is then carried to its "logical" conclusion, scientific reason becomes a form of secular mysticism. We have given the mysticism bred of these unlikely parents a special name. It is called ideology. The term is usually reserved for "systematic ideologies," those which assert a "science" of society complete with laws; coeval, historical and inexorable. Marxism and its variants are the most prosperous modern examples. Since mysticism qua ideology has had only a limited appeal west of Germany and east of the Formosa Straits, in these lands metamorphosed reason has usually had narrower pretensions: e.g., theories of constitutional structure, division of authority, comprehensive legal codes and, most recently, the missionary struggle by the sages of economics to justify, order and prescribe our getting and spending. Indeed, a resident economist or two is as necessary to a modern head of state as a private confessor once was to the king and both have been equally generous in justifying their wayward rulers.

Ideologies, social theories and even economics often contain much that is true and useful, as do the Bible, the Dialogues of Plato and the Wittenberg theses. Yet these ideological mysticisms have even greater potential for repression than did supernatural beliefs. Exclusively concerned with the affairs of this world, their commitment to control tends to be total and exclusive. Their assumptions are usually obscure or unstated, not candidly set forth in a book of relevations, and the theoretical superstructure is often complex and difficult. It takes far more sophistication to disagree than it once did to disbelieve. No one is likely to descend a mountain bearing the created refutation of a modern ideology or even a graven disproof of Keynesian economics. Indeed, dissent is not permissible unless it is based on the process of scientific reason; just as Christian theologians once had the power to confine all dispute to the interpretation of holy texts whose validity was beyond question.

It is for this reason that the intellectual issues of the Reformation often seem trivial from our perspective. They prayed to the same God and from the same book. But the clash which generated debate was not sham; the germinating future could not be reconciled with the obstructing past. The Catholic Church might have moved faster, but that would have not only required changes in creed and practice, but decentralization of authority—the establishment of a federal system. Although that appears theoretically possible it was practically, i.e., historically and psychically, impossible. Since the conflict was primary to the participants we must accept it as such. To conclude otherwise is simply to impose our own standards and beliefs on the past and on its finest and most creative minds: It is not difficult to imagine a future commentator describing the clash between "communism" and "free enterprise" as economic systems: "They both believed in production, technology, mass consumption, economic growth and the control of large economic units by paid managers. The most passionate division seems to have occurred over the question of ownership, even though in both communist and capitalist countries those who owned major economic units (i.e., some of the people or all of the people) did not control them. (Surprisingly, judging from contemporary works, they even realized this.) It is undeniable that one system may have been more efficient than the other in allocating capital resources, but that alone is not enough to explain the almost religious fury of debate. (See the valuable work *Pre-Modern Economic Rituals*, programmed and printed by IBM #7, especially the chapters on 'May Day Parades' and 'Stockholder Meetings.' An intriguing appendix contains reproductions of an ancient share of stock in General Motors along with a ballot used in Russian elections of the same period.)"

Would this view be right? No more than our own. Certainly it would be superficial. We need a kind of temporal anthropology, a method of viewing past societies within the frame of their own assumptions and awareness, so that we can be as generous to St. Paul and Alexander the Great as we are to the headhunters of New Guinea.

The transformation of scientific reason into mysticism is a fact of historical experience. Perhaps, however, some true science of society is fragilely suspended from the branches of time awaiting its Newton. Hundreds of academic bureaucracies, equipped with brain-stretching computers and instruments worldly enough to measure and even photograph the gulp of an exultant vagina and the oscillations of a voiding penis, toil in anticipation. The church is built, hierarchy constructed, priests trained, believers conditioned. Why doesn't it come?

We know so little about the process and structure of society, of human associations on a large scale, that any effort to construct a rational structure must either assume or ignore much fundamental data. As we have seen, the belief in a system based on the unperceived is faith. Nor can this obstacle be eliminated through study and observation. There is probably no comprehensive structure of knowledge about society accessible to the intellect, since the shaping elements of society change in nature, force and relative importance through history. Imagine the state of atomic physics if the atom changed its structure every fifty years. The necessary scientific assumption that basic processes are timeless or change in a manner which permit us to deduce the past is directly opposed to the most probable conclusion from human experience, that describing society is like mapping sand dunes on a storm-prone shore.

However, even if some supreme mechanic were to provide us with a description of society as intimate as Ford's manual of engine repair, the huddled tinkerers would soon be chanting incantations. The moment scientific reason is applied to society it necessarily transgresses the self-imposed limitation which made science possible. The ancients constructed cosmologies—astronomical systems— in which the orbit of the planets were circular, because the circle was the most "perfect" or "natural" form. Even the best scientists of the ancient world were enmeshed in the overview that everything, living and inanimate, was part of a universal pattern reflecting the intentions of a Creator or the order of nature. Given this essential unity it was natural for the mathematical achievements of Pythagoras to be the basis of a philosophical or religious sect. Physics and ethics partook in the same ruling principles. Aristotle's belief that all physical objects tended to their proper or innate place corresponded to the Greek notion of justice among men, everyone to his proper station and rewards. So too, an omnipotent Creator would only initiate perfect, i.e., circular, motion. Galileo himself rejected or ignored Kepler's arguments for elliptical orbits. Kepler's admitted brilliance, Galileo pointed out, was flawed by his attraction to such madly mystical notions as a belief that the moon had something to do with ocean tides. "Despite his open and acute mind," Galileo wrote, "he has nevertheless lent his ear and his assent to the moon's dominion over the waters, and to occult properties, and to such peculiarities," ignoring to state that if Kepler was right about the tides it would destroy Galileo's only experimental proof of the earth's motion—the demonstration that ocean waters could only slosh back and forth, thus creating tides, in a sea basin which was moving. (Galileo's revolutionary work, *Dialogue on the Great World Systems*, was first called *On the Flux and Reflux of the Sea*, a title which was dropped at the insistence of

Pope Urban VIII who did not want the work organized around such a "necessitating" proof.)

Modern science began not when Copernicus and his successors disproved the old astronomy, but when a changing human consciousness led men to construct a system of thought to which the statement "a circle is the most perfect form" was irrelevant. True or untrue, the relation between a circle and perfection was a problem for aesthetics, morals or theology—not for science. From the Renaissance onward, science gradually slipped its ties to issues of values, moral order and the nature of Divinity. Henceforth, faith could be maintained only by continually adapting the Creator to our changing understanding of His creation. This was an upheaval in human thought far more important than the particular discoveries and theories of Galileo and Newton. "In our search for the direct road toward truth," wrote Descartes, "we should busy ourselves with no object about which we cannot attain a certitude equal to that of the demonstrations of arithmetic and geometry." (And then proceeded to base a philosophical system on an arbitrary and mystical base.) The telescope which inaugurated this new scientific age becomes its perfect metaphor. No longer would men gaze at the night sky to receive wonder or faith, humility or exultation. They focused an instrument on a planet, star, a patch of sky; carving a narrow tunnel into universal depths; a pathway for the rational mind, leaping from sight to speculation to discovery.

Aristotle wrote that earth could not move because "motion . . . being enforced and unnatural, could not be eternal, but the order of the world is eternal." The scientist responds: "The earth moves around the sun, and, in fact, since Copernicus we have concluded that motion and rest are different aspects of the same thing, or they *are* the same thing differently observed. This is "natural" because it is. Ultimately the earth must perish. The idea of the "eternal" must remain a hypothesis until we determine whether time is finite or infinite. If, in a few billion years, the earth receives a measurable, external shove or new energy is bestowed upon the sun, we will naturally revise our theories and take another look at Aristotle."

The issue here is not merely scientific. It is a difference in world views, which are always nothing more than the titanic projection of individual human consciousness, awareness of experience, at a particular time in history. The ordered universe of Newton, a system of causal forces and obedient objects, was in harmony with the emerging age of reason, industry and a growing confidence in man's capacity to organize his society. Our own time has shattered the social foundations of Newtonian thought. Like all elements of modern culture, the new science—the universe of quanta and space-time, of relativity and uncertainty—has come to mirror the temper and conditions of the age; not because reason led, but because history commanded.

Even though modern science has cleansed itself of moral and theological considerations, aesthetics still seem inescapable. A felt though incalculable beauty, often concealed beneath "principles" of symmetry or simplicity, is necessary to the acceptance of any basic scientific theory. The greatest scientists have testified to the importance such a revelation had in persuading them the truth was at hand. The equations which demonstrate disorder, discontinuity and uncertainty are themselves orderly and categorical. Some kind of aesthetic preconception is probably essential to science. The concepts of order and regularity themselves are the constructs of an aesthetic imagination. Occam's razor was made by men, for men.

The concerns which science shed in order to become "science" are basic to any description or understanding of society. Ask a physicist if it is a good idea to know the internal structure of the atom and he cannot answer the question "scientifically." He must compare values on the practical level, e.g., nuclear power v. the atom bomb, or on the metaphysical level, e.g., the liberating quality of intellectual work versus the consequent diversion of energy from problems of salvation. He may even invoke man's boundless curiosity and lust for knowledge, an exercise in the purest kind of mysticism since it contradicts all observable data. All the most important social issues depend upon just such values, which cannot be proven, which are, by definition, beyond the reach of scientific reason. So whenever scientific reason is systematically applied to society it must either pretend to be proving the unprovable (a circle is the most perfect form) or simply assume a structure of values. Ordinarily, such a rational superstructure implicitly justifies the most widely accepted and dominant beliefs and values. But not always. Some proponents of a "counterculture," for example, argue that the "nuclear" family or sexual fidelity is irrational and so, they claim, are work, the desire for material goods and the "system." The values and institutions of our society may be obsolete or oppressive, but they cannot be impeached by logic alone. The invocation of a systematic logic in support of values is an important instrument of the totalitarian mind, since it denies that latitude which is a crucial guarantor of freedom. It assumes the content of that freedom which it purports to define and elaborate.

Even within its own proper limits scientific reason cannot surmount the inability of the human intellect to transcend itself. "That . . . which is not a circle cannot be the measure of a circle," wrote Nicholas of Cusa at the beginning of the fifteenth century, "similarly our intellect, which is not the truth, can never grasp the truth with . . . precision." Such reasonable humility obstructed the search for truth through science. It limited men to uncertain and subordinate talents. It was therefore rejected by the new age of limitless ambition. Two centuries later, Galileo argued that since God had given us senses, reason and intellect, "He would not require us to deny sense and reason in physical matters which are set before our eyes and minds by direct experience or necessary [i.e., mathematical] demonstrations." This was not an exhortation to believe in the senses, but an assertion that the conclusions of scientific reason were the truth—final and precise. "This grand book," the universe, "is written in the language of mathematics." The entire history of scientific inquiry, from the Renaissance until today, has rested on this assumption. As expressed by a twentieth-century physicist, "nature . . . is made to be understood, or, rather, our thought is made to understand nature . . . the same organizing forces that have shaped nature in all her forms are also responsible for the structure of our minds."

Of these three statements, all unprovable, only that of Nicholas of Cusa rests on its inherent appeal to reasonable men. The scientists invoke higher powers: God first and nature now. Notice how four centuries of experience have constructed a language which permits mysticism to resonate of pure reason. Not God, but "the . . . organizing forces that have shaped nature." Who are they, these organizing forces? We can't be sure, but must surely be grateful to the Great Scientist in the Sky for shaping the entire natural world to conform to human mathematics and logic. It is a tautological truism to say those "forces" shaped us and nature. But why the same, when every snowflake is different? And why to conform with reason instead of revelation, madness, poetry, desire or dreams; all natural, all human. The statements by both scientists are mystical, but Galileo's is the less magical.

We must concede the possibility that the universe could be organized in an infinite number of ways (or its existence might be fashioned so that the concepts "infinite" and "organize" are themselves irrelevant). The discovery that the "truths" of the material universe are precisely adapted to the rational faculties of humanity is so remarkable that it almost seems to require the intervention of some higher power. The belief which created scientific reason is itself an assertion of hopeful faith—a mystical premise. True or not, it has been useful for our purposes. That is, it works. It has given us theories that make it possible to fit a great number of observed events into a few categories and, most of all, it has yielded an extraordinary technology. It is the discovery which launched eight million automobiles and burned the topmost towers of the Orient. The utility of science has obscured its mystical foundation. Once the screen of tangible achievement is removed, that is, when scientific reason is applied to human affairs, its mystic origins are revealed. Finally it is results, consequences, that distinguish scientific reason from mysticism, that keep it, indeed, from being just another form of mysticism. Which is what it is, and must be, when it is applied to society; transgressing limits which are not only historic but necessary.

> How be it they are not to be excused; for if their understanding was so great that they could discern the world and the creatures, why did they not rather find out the Lord thereof.
>
> Solomon, the King

CHAPTER 3

A visit, long ago, to Persepolis, city of the Persian emperors brought
to mind Shelley's well-worn line, "Look on my works, ye Mighty,
and despair." But from my present vantage the Persian ruins appear a testament to the discordant capacities of the human hand:
Artists' hands which shaped stone reliefs to the majesty of Darius;
Macedonian hands which burned the city along the path of conquest; Arab hands which obliterated the human faces in obedience
to the command of Allah that idolatry be obliterated. Hands
that create, burn, scar. Hands moved by fear, art, worship, conquest, the desire for a common humanity. Each in its own time.

The Greeks had iron and water, knew the uses of heat and logic,
but they did not build steam engines. In the last century or two we
have learned that the human mind, for all its suppleness, is confined
not only by its structure, but by its time. The examination of the
ways in which we think and of the objects of our perception is not
just intellectual history, but a glimpse at the nature of society.
Dominant ways of thought such as mysticism and scientific reason
are part of the social reality which they serve. Our consciousness
as displayed in culture tells us of the material world which sustains
it.

By the nineteenth century, the productive forces and technological vision had entered a new and more formidable dimension. Business and industry were ready to complete their conquest of landed
property and, finally, of the entire social process. The companion

ideologies of scientific reason and mysticism increased their ascendancy. The domination of individualism was hugely accelerated. Soon men would begin to talk about "mass man," "the public," "the mob." It was, also, and consistently, a period of growing political and civil liberty, the fact that social relationships or values are conformed to the needs of material structure is not, of itself, a condemnation. We can believe in the goodness of St. Francis whatever our view of the medieval structure which produced him. Moreover, the productive forces of the nineteenth century were also to make a huge contribution to the possibilities of freedom by reducing the barrier of material necessity.

The consequences of individualism were increasingly perceived, not as liberation, but as a source of fragmenting decay in the possibilities of human existence. Around the middle of the century Kierkegaard wrote, "The individual no longer belongs to God, to himself, his beloved, to his art or his science . . ." The "Age of Reason" had ended.

This historical condition is also expressed by thinkers and artists —men such as Kant and Tolstoy—who sought to affirm some form of shared existence as a support for moral authority. Discussing Hindu mysticism, Schopenhauer writes that the good man "perceives that the distinction between himself and others . . . belongs only to a fleeting, deceptive phenomenon. He recognizes immediately, and *without reasons or arguments* [ital. mine] that the in-itself of his own phenomenon is also that of others . . . in fact, he recognizes that this extends even to the animals and to the whole of nature; he will therefore not cause suffering even to an animal." The modern response is that of Saul Bellow's seventy-year-old protagonist in *Mr. Sammler's Planet* who relates that "Tolstoy says you don't kill another human being with whom you have exchanged [a human] look." He is asked by his listener if he agrees with Tolstoy. "I sympathize deeply," he answers, "I sympathize sadly. When men of genius think about humankind, they are almost forced to believe in this form of psychic unity. I wish it were so."

Like other nineteenth-century thinkers, Karl Marx saw that the establishment of a fulfilling existence—his realm of freedom—was only possible within a community. The community which was the goal of communism could only be established by destroying those "relations of production" which were the source of oppression.

That destruction required a revolutionary class, but it also depended upon the assumption that the productive forces of industrialism were approaching or, in some countries, had reached the limits of their potential growth. At that point internal decay would begin, weakening the ruling structures and making successful revolution possible. Marx wrote that "as soon as it [capital] begins to be aware that it is itself an obstacle to development, it takes refuge in forms that, although they appear to complete the mastery of capital, are, at the same time, by curbing free competition, the heralds of its dissolution, and of the means of production which are based on it."

Marx's complicated analysis of capitalist weakness has been among the most controversial and widely debated aspects of his work. That exegesis is now largely of historical interest. For the capitalism of the nineteenth century which Marx described has been supplanted by new relations of production. Indeed, historic capitalism did decline, and in many respects, as he expected, through, for example, "curbing free competition." It is also true, although these are not terms Marx would have used, that whenever any important social process loses its dynamic qualities—is not growing or adapting to changed realities—its power is in danger. In retrospect, however, it can be seen that he underestimated the potential productive powers contained by the industrial relationships of his time. German economic development, for example, moved ahead swiftly after 1860; and the Junker ruling class came to govern in the interests of the industrial and business bourgeois. The United States was just on the edge of its own industrial development. It was not until the aftermath of World War I that capitalist decline and collapse began to be manifest. By that time the process of social dissolution was so advanced that the cohesion, the sense of shared purpose which might have led to the creation of a revolutionary class, was unable to form. The isolation of the individual had stripped him of much of his power over social existence.*

---

* In fact, in the century since Marx the consciousness of social existence has been so nearly obliterated that the ancient tradition of utopian construction has disappeared, and the word "utopia" has come to connote some hopelessly fanciful and millennial imaginings rather than an inquiry into the most worthy goals of human striving. If, for example, we perceive Plato's ideal state as an authoritarian monstrosity, it is not because our understanding has been enlarged but because our consciousness has been diminished.

The collapse of the sources of alienation, in this case the economic relationships of capitalism, did not, by itself, liberate the individual from alienation.

The growth of capitalist productive forces had destroyed the conditions for the establishment of communist society. (Marxism, as a historical reality, has been successful only in countries where those productive forces have not fully developed.) In many countries the choice appeared to be between chaos and order, rather than between forms and goals of order. Where this was the case the frequent consequence was the establishment of totalitarian rule. In the United States, however, new forms of social authority were constructed with a minimum of internal turmoil and within the framework of democratic government. We had the advantage of a unique historical context and different political and cultural traditions. (Marx has affirmed that the character of British life made possible the peaceful overthrow of capitalism in that country.) We had also entered the industrial period later than the nations of central Europe and without the hampering vestiges of feudal existence. The productive forces retained more of their dynamic qualities, and we were better prepared to reshape economic relationships. (Similarly, Japan and Germany can adapt to more recent changes because their defeat destroyed the power of obsolete structure.) World War II was to resolve the clash between these two forms of response.

CHAPTER 4

A friend reported that when Karl Marx saw an electric locomotive on exhibit in mid-nineteenth-century London, he exclaimed: "Now the problem is solved—the consequences are indefinable. In the wake of the economic revolution the political must necessarily follow . . ." In 1867, two years after the Civil War which marked the transition to industrial America, he wrote: "Centralization of the means of production and socialization of labor at last reach a point where they become incompatible with their capitalist integument. The knell of capitalist private property sounds."

When capitalism came to an end, the consequence was not that communism which would bring "the positive abolition of private property, of human self-alienation, and thus, the real appropriation of human nature, through and for man . . . the definitive resolution of the antagonism between man and Nature, and between man and man." For Marx was also right about the locomotive. It signaled and symbolized an economic revolution; the birth of a technology so dislocating that it sundered labor into unforeseen divisions, creating new economic relations, classes and interests.

Marx always contended that technology, man's tools, was at the foundation of economic structure.* It was the new technology which kept the increasingly centralized means of production from

* There is some debate whether Marx thought that technology was the foundation or one of its elements. The issue itself no longer arises in that form.

collapsing; that permitted socialized labor to assert an interest distinct from the general welfare; that disjoined private power from general ownership; and which, in creating the modern bureaucratic economy, intensified human alienation.

The engines of postwar growth were technological development companioned with mass consumption. This technology thrust aside or bypassed traditional limitations upon resources and productive capacity and extended the reach and speed of economic transaction. These technological advances were stimulated and made economic by massive consumption. One does not computerize the production of goods for a handful of the wealthy, or establish a nationwide television network for only 5 per cent of the population. It is now widely recognized that consumption is the foundation of prosperity, or at least of higher numbers for GNP, income, taxes and, more ambiguously, for employment.

However, the prodigious bureaucracies which dominate our present economy did not create these new productive forces. They were consequence more than cause, the beneficiaries of postwar growth. Probably inevitable, they were not essential. No reasons of abstract economic efficiency dictate that the needs and demands of an expanding national market can be met most productively by three automobile companies, one computer company, a single telephone corporation and a handful of jumbo enterprises crowding the other precincts. The modern transaction economy can only be served by sizable organizations. But the extent of consolidation exorbitantly exceeds these needs. The once fashionable argument about economies of scale is so obviously unreasonable that it is rarely voiced. Indeed, some of the largest companies have found it necessary to decentralize and divide their own operations in order to retain some degree of management efficiency and control.

Although consolidation was not the catalyst of postwar plenty, it had similar origins in the mature and weakening capitalist structure. The inclination, the almost irresistible impulse, toward concentrations of capital has been admitted, observed and debated since the early industrial age. Adam Smith, Karl Marx and Lord Keynes analyzed it from their own platforms, while Lenin and Roosevelt tried different solutions. The new mass consumption economy fueled this inherited process with an ever-waxing flow of capital and made possible concentrations on an unprecedented scale. New technology made it feasible to organize, manage and hold together institutions of unprecedented size and reach.

Marx thought that increasing concentration would create unmanageable and unprofitable capital structures which would collapse of their own weight. Instead, the regenerated dinosaur was outfitted with a new brain and more efficient nervous system. As always, growth bred growth. Accumulating capital was able to deter and often eliminate competition. This was accomplished not only, or even mainly, through old-fashioned rough-and-tumble competition, but by generous mergers, by constructing and acquiring a machinery of transaction so large and expensive it could not be duplicated, and by commanding preferential and often exclusive access to the important sources of capital. It proved surer and less costly to preclude competition than to destroy it, and that kind of domination is well sanctuaried from the short arm of the anti-trust laws. And diminishing competition, together with the socialization of labor, energized by the proliferation of demand, shaped the analytical links between concentration and declining profit.

It is now commonplace to acknowledge that man's tools are a significant determinant of economic structure. Segments of prehistory are customarily identified by their implements, and one might usefully divide much of recorded history according to the dominant technology. Since to influence economic process is to partake in the regulation of society, technology has consequences for the entire social process. It is possible for new or "advanced" technology to diminish capacity because of the structures it creates. The cotton gin, for example, made the use of slave labor profitable, at least for upland cultivation. Yet that same profitability helped to barricade the South against the much larger economic benefits of the new industrialism and relegated it to an economic backwater from which it has not yet fully emerged. New technology empowered an agrarian oligarchy to resist changes which would have been to the economic benefit of the society.

Much technology of the postwar period is the technology of organization. The devastation of our environment, community and way of life comes most directly, not from new inventions, but from the products and techniques of the old industrialism—cars, oil, construction, roads, industrial waste—endowed with sudden, unrestrained, and almost limitless energy and reach by the new technology of organization. In this way the potential power of new knowledge to improve the human condition has been diverted to the perpetuation of old, and increasingly oppressive, techniques and forms, interests and repositories of power. The technology which has fastened economic bureaucracy upon society has become a source of waste and economic inefficiency as a consequence of the forms, the reach and arrangement of wealth and power, which modern technology has evoked. Bureaucracy is the logic of technology.

Much of this book analyzes the economic relationships, the social process, encompassed in the term "bureaucracy." Bureaucracy has extended the power of external authority over our lives and intensified the assault on the forms of shared existence and upon our awareness of our social nature. We have tried to imagine the time before the bonds of medieval hierarchy began to loosen, when men were conscious of their existence, their identity, as constituted in some large measure by relationships with others, a community and a place. To find the consciousness that attends individualism most of us only have to look within.

Some historical societies contained strong elements of both individualism and hierarchy. The incomplete records of Periclean Greece, Renaissance Italy, Elizabethan England and revolutionary America show races conscious both of individual powers and of participation in an organic community.

We citizens of the advanced industrial, postindustrial, space-age West do not inhabit such a time of relative symmetry and compensation. We live under the domination of an individualism whose conquest has been so complete that it has torn the thread of individual life from the fabric of humanity. We have been sundered from the wholes which gave us life. And it is far from certain that the process is at an end. For the ideology of individualism is so powerful that we still look on bonds as restraints; values as opinions or prejudices; customs as impositions. The remaining structures of shared existence, the restraints which make it possible for people to live with, and through, and not merely alongside one another, are assaulted as unjust restraints on liberty, impediments to the free assertion of the self.

The new consciousness through which the Renaissance attacked the injustices, stagnation and material misery of the Middle Ages now, inevitably, suffocates human freedom. Its unparalleled domination frustrates and denies the organic unity of social existence which is essential to freedom and, finally, to life itself.

CHAPTER 5

Today some speak of the community of nations, the community of free men, and even the community of Christian souls (a once lively place now suffering from a severe population decline). At best, such abstractions reflect a vague inclination to believe that a lot of people are in the same boat. So enlarged, the concept of community is destroyed.

What seems to be only a lax use of language is an aspect of a more general destructive force—the drive toward more comprehensive systems of thought and organization whose consequence is the dismemberment of organic wholes. No individual can make personal contact with such immense constructions. One cannot see, touch or explore them. As a result, the effort to create larger unities brings about the atomization of human life. The smaller components become important, not for themselves, but only as a part of some larger whole. Since the larger structure cannot provide substitute connection, individuals are set adrift to become strangers to each other and to themselves.

This is the social counterpart to the method of scientific reason run wild. For science explores knowledge through dissection, by reducing phenomena to their smallest distinct components in order to formulate more general rules. Reason must dissect in order to generalize. If we break a piece of wood into its constituent elements in order to find a chemical formula which will describe the essence of wood, we may well discover numbers and symbols which are valid for all wood. They will not, however, re-create the experience of contact with a particular piece of wood, how it feels or the patterns it reflects. The formulas are not wood. If someday we can describe every chemical and physical reaction of the human body; if we can trace every circuit in the brain and unwind every mystery of the genetic code, we will not have described a single individual.

Aristotle tells us that the ideal state is one whose entire territory can be surveyed from a hilltop. Even during the great world empires —Macedonian, Roman and British—most of life was centered in a small community. From the remote centers of the world came armies to devastate or protect, new governors and despoiling collectors of revenues. An ultimate power might reside in Rome or London, yet most aspects of everyday life were regulated by the community. Men ordered their affairs according to local customs and law. Among neighbors and a familiar landscape men developed the identity which sustained them, found satisfaction in the knowledge that their acts and labors had human consequences. No empire of the past conceived of exercising central authority as blanketing and diverse as that which flows daily from Washington and Moscow or from the massive institutions of the modern economy.

"I am Paul of Tarsus, no mean city," said St. Paul in Jerusalem. Shakespeare was the Bard of Avon, not of England. And the word "city"—not state or nation—was, until yesterday, the metaphor for human society; from St. Augustine's City of God to William Bradford's America, a "city upon a hill."

The community essential to freedom is small and tangible. It must exist within an area that can be comprehended by the senses —a place whose roads and shops, landmarks and physical hazards can be known to each inhabitant. It can be part of a much larger whole, as were older city neighborhoods, but it must also be distinguishable to its inhabitants. All the immaterial benefits of a community derive from this physical base. This is why Greek philosophers were concerned to establish the size and population of the ideal community—a concern that has now been transformed from a problem of philosophy to one of engineering.

Compare this contemporary account of life in Renaissance Florence to the end of the rush hour in New York, Chicago or Los Angeles: "Now at Florence, when the air is red with the summer sunset and the companiles begin to sound vespers and the day's work is done, everyone collects in the plazas. The steps of Santa Maria del Fiore swarm with men of every rank and every class; artisans, merchants, teachers, artists, doctors, technicians, poets, scholars. A thousand minds, a thousand arguments; a lively inter-mingling of questions, problems, news of the latest happenings, of jokes; an inexhaustible play of language and thought, a vibrant curiosity; the changeable temper of a thousand spirits by whom every object of discussion is broken into an infinity of senses and significations—all these spring into being, and then are spent. And this is the pleasure of the Florentine public." Florence, of course, was not a democracy.

Community is a corner of society where the individual can feel some confidence of acceptance on fairly honest terms and can maintain continuing association with others whose familiarity is comforting. Community provides a mooring for the spirit. For community is a restraint that liberates. It relieves us of the necessity to continually prove our worth or to seek reassurance of that worth. It diminishes the destructive social process of judging and being judged which cripples our capacity to think and act freely and with honesty. Members of a community may not be friends, but they are not strangers. Even though interests and careers have diverged, many people retain a special affection for the companions of youth. They are the relics of that classroom community which is the last many have known.

An extravagant parody of social existence without community can be found in the upper echelons of political Washington. There when "friends" gather for a party no conversation is sufficiently absorbing and no woman beautiful enough to prevent every eye from shifting when a high-ranking official enters the room. No one talks to anyone very long for fear of not having a chance to talk with someone else. These at the top of the ladder need only wait for the others to move past. Underneath this frenzy there must be a desire to impress or at least to be noticed. Such practical motives would be reasonable. But the fact is almost everyone knows it makes no difference, that the decisive appraisals leading to advance or decline are not made here. Yet the ritual dance continues. Of course, political Washington is a caricature of society, a fabricated city inhabited by strangers whose simulated camaraderie is both facade and necessary lubricant for unceasing competition. But many of its characteristics can be found in any modern city.

The relationships of community also provide that sense of shared purpose and concerns which is elemental to the concept of society itself. All the rest—culture, language, ideology, economic process and political structure—have crystallized around this nucleus. In an agricultural community, for example, most people have a stake in the size of the harvest. And those whose income is independent of the crops tend to share the common concern. Here, in Kingfield, Maine, skiing is the most important business, and everyone discusses the prospects for snow; even those who may be inwardly indifferent feel obliged to express concern. The residents of a city neighborhood may be dissatisfied with transportation or police protection or with the kind of education their children are getting. What characterizes a community is not that many individuals are dissatisfied, but that they share dissatisfaction, can discuss it and may at least contemplate shared protest or action. Within a community there is room for common aspirations and achievement, for better schools or a new sewage system.

This can only take place on a human scale. For as the source of discontent and the possibility of constructive action become more distant, community cohesion dissolves. If the trees are cut by order of the Department of Highways, if the river is polluted a hundred miles away, if the new school awaits a decision in Washington or an equally remote city hall, then community is not possible. Individuals can only be said to share worries and desires when they also share in responsibility and power.

Community is the form of social life, and ours is increasingly a life of motion without form. More than thirty-five million Americans move each year. The physical world itself is on the move. Recently I drove through Harvard Square where I had gone to school ten years before. There were new buildings and roads. The familiar place of law school days did not exist. The experience is familiar to many who have sought the past only to find that its precincts had been changed. Yet man has nearly always anchored his sense of reality, his sense of himself, to a fixed place amid familiar landmarks. Our world itself has become nomadic as the scenery of our life is constantly shifted.

The modern world deprives most Americans of community. The suburb or city block is merely a base from which the individual reaches out to the scattered components of social existence. A man works in one place, sleeps in another, shops somewhere else, finds pleasure or companionship where he can and cares about none of these places. His streets are sterilized of the living reminders of common human responsibility: The aged and decrepit, the senile and retarded are incarcerated in institutions or hospitals or in housing projects for the elderly. While college campuses and city "pads" are filled with young people passionately asserting the value of love, meaning love among the young and healthy, the love that involves little burden or commitment without pleasure.

Within many of our growing suburbs there is often virtually no place where neighbors can anticipate unplanned meetings—no pub or corner store or park. This lack is especially disastrous for those women who are compelled to spend much of their lives at home. Only small towns and lower income housing projects have a common playground or community laundromat—some physical setting where women can meet with some regularity. It is true that there are thousands of clubs and associations, citizens' groups and leagues for recreation. But they are not a substitute for the regular contact of people who share a common environment and its concerns.

The description of community does not merely express a preference for a different way of life. Community is the form of social existence, the elemental unit through which the individual can express and create the social existence which is essential to freedom. It is the institutional embodiment of shared human purpose, the reconciliation between individual desires and the general well-being. It is also, as an institution, the only means through which individuals can regulate and restrain the productive forces of society. It is, therefore, the means to power over the conditions of daily existence—over environment, work, the material content of leisure, the prospects for fulfillment. A single community cannot, of course, regulate institutions and forces whose function is national in scope. One of the causes of decreased community power is the necessity to liberate such institutions from hampering local-isms (which is why responsibility for "protection" of the environ-ment is increasingly centered in Washington). However, the bonds of community are the nucleus from which larger shared social pur-pose can be formed. The weakening of social bonds at the level of community destroys the possibility of a more general social pur-pose. And if the productive forces are grown too large and powerful for such regulation then their existence operates to prevent the re-establishment of the community existence necessary to freedom.*

The dissolution of the ties of community is a consequence of modern economic organization and ideology. It has, however, been hastened by the convergence of a new society with that rest-lessness of the American character which has pursued our history. "Americans are always moving on/It's an old Spanish custom gone astray/A sort of English fever . . ." Ours is a culture of restless-ness, of change and movement in response to an insatiate hunger for experience and a fear of commitment. The heroes of the film *Easy Rider* seem the incarnation of modern youth as their motor-cycles cruise on an aimless search. Yet it is a conventional Ameri-can story.

> You but hardly arrive at the city to which you were
>   destined,
>   you hardly settle yourself to satisfaction, before
>   you are call'd by an irresistible call to
>   depart,
>
> You shall not allow the hold of those who spread their
>   reach'd hands toward you.
>
>   Whitman—"Song of the Open Road"

The Founding Fathers, with their penetrating eye for contra-diction, foresaw the danger to American community. As eight-eenth-century theorists they sought to avert disruption through political structure: Madison denied that the new union would be too large, pointing out, *inter alia*, that substantial powers were reserved to local government. The founders knew, however, that the debate involved more than the capacity to administer authority

---

* The relationships between freedom and shared social existence are elaborated in Parts III and VI.

over a large territory. Only the emotional call of community can explain the uncharacteristic passion of the fourteenth *Federalist* paper: "Hearken not to the unnatural voice which tells you that the people of America, knit together as they are by so many chords of affection, can no longer live together as members of the same family; can no longer continue the mutual guardians of their mutual happiness; . . . Shut your hearts against the poison which it conveys; the kindred blood which flows in the veins of American citizens, the mingled blood which they have shed in defence of their sacred rights, consecrate their Union, and excite horror at the idea of their becoming aliens, rivals, enemies." Although "blood" is a concrete word, it is an abstract concept, not easily assimilable to shared experience.

There is a heroic strain to American restlessness. It is an authentic response to the world as process; a temperament congenial to modern consciousness. Yet when this disposition is fused with the modern society it helped construct, the result is to fray the bonds between men which also link us to the possibilities of freedom. This does not mean that others can escape, for the forces which dominate advanced societies are also able to nullify less congenial cultures and traditions. Indeed, the necessary constituents of the modern world include the summons to restlessness, which is the inseparable companion of the conquering American culture. If the computer and the jet plane, the private car and the modern army are at the center of cultural purpose, the values which created them cannot be escaped. Go to any of the advanced and wealthy nations, watch the businessmen moving through the airport, listen to music and visit the art galleries, or attend a meeting of the bureaucrats and try to decide, from the nature of their concerns alone, whether they are running the U. S. State Department, Sony Corporation, Renault or the machine-tool industry of the people of the Soviet Union. You will find evidence of the most successful cultural imperialism since the decline of Rome. And everywhere it is being welcomed with the same disregard for consequences.

We can guess at the power of our example when influential Europeans believe the "American challenge" consists of superior business organization and technology, as if it mattered where capital came from. The real American challenge is to protect human freedom from these very forces. In this, we cannot expect guidance from a Europe which has persistently torn itself apart in a twentieth-century version of the Peloponnesian wars. If there is to be salvation, we will have to find it here, and among ourselves.

A local paper printed an innocent letter in which a young girl proclaimed the virtues of "her generation." "They" would no longer "accept" hypocrisy and cant, war or aggressive greed. The girl's writing was informed by an almost religious conviction. Although the description of the younger generation is wrong, the letter exemplifies one contemporary effort to build a substitute community—a community of youth—not just being young, but being different because one is young, and sharing those differences with contemporaries. Membership in a generation has many attributes of community—common attitudes, ready acceptance of others with similar qualities and a clear, though somewhat fluid, exclusion of the outsider. Even the pressures to conform can resemble those of a small town. From the self-congratulatory harmony of the Woodstock "nation" to the clenched fist and the upraised V, many of the young seek to establish bonds which can enhance self-mastery. The same desire to re-create community is manifest in the Black Panthers and in the assertion that there is a black community. It can be found among some of the members of Women's Liberation and associates of the John Birch Society. It is evidenced by increasing reference to an "academic community," implying shared values, social standing and responsibility. For those not eligible to any of these groups, President Nixon offered membership in the "silent majority," a coded category for those who are not necessarily silent or in the majority, but who have similar outlooks and hostilities.

We have had such associations before, e.g., within the early labor movement. "You can't scare me, I'm sticking to the union." "For the union makes us strong." But never have so many and diverse groups asserted their connections with such militant intensity. And there is little precedent for the widespread insistence that members of groups adhere to common values and attitudes, even to life styles, which extend far beyond any particular set of goals or grievances. Indeed, the terminology of community and identity is often explicit. This can only mean that individuals are not only banding together for a particular purpose, but in an effort to define the social person.

However worthy their objectives, such groups will prove inadequate as substitute communities. They are both historical and voluntary: historical because they are usually constructed around problems and fears which will change. In a generation or two, for example, the causes of black militancy will have been eliminated or we will be the scene of a social failure so immense that its consequences will have transformed the nature of American life, destroying the assumptions which sustain black militancy in its present form. In varying degrees the same is true of all groups crystallized around social grievances. And although there will always be a younger generation, no individual can be a member for very long. Not only historical, these substitute communities are also voluntary. This means they are not a place where one spends a lifetime, nor can they provide a sense of continuity between past and future. One enters by choice and not by birth, and can easily leave. Such ease of passage is a constant temptation to rupture and a near guarantee of eventual parting. At their best, such groups provide the comradeship of the barracks. But the war will end, and the next one will be different. Still, they are better than nothing, and nothing is the only alternative for many.

Communities originated as enclaves of the natural world. Since the connection with nature was established through the senses rather than by ideology or authority, the individual's perception of himself was strengthened—but within the framework of a shared experience, which helped to sustain the bonds of community. We have seen that a renewed perception of man's relationship to nature signaled the liberations of the Renaissance.

Regular contact with the natural world has virtually disappeared from the life of the largely urban populations of advanced societies. The destruction of that relationship constricts the quality of common existence and diminishes the reach of our humanity. Earth and its sustaining growth are no longer parts of the environment. The natural elements, which were once the source and adversary of community well-being, now intrude on our consciousness only when we decide what to wear, while the rhythm of the seasons, which once ruled all of life, is simply a convenient, if somewhat archaic, way of scheduling activities: Fall is when the kids go back to school, early winter is the time to shop for Christmas presents, spring is not too early to begin vacation plans.

This devastation was latent in the fusion of Americans with their continent beside whose barbarous splendor the lands of Europe seemed like household gardens. We tore wealth from the land with heedless greed and did not hesitate to obliterate those aspects of nature which were of no immediate use or which obstructed expansion. Yet the incitements to conquest were not only economic. We were the only modern people to build a new nation in a wilderness, and that wilderness was not a benign cornucopia, but enemy to our hopes and even our survival. In his *History of Plymouth Plantation,* William Bradford writes, "And for the season, it was winter, and they that know the winters of that country know them to be sharp and violent and subject to cruel and fierce storms, dangerous to travel to known places, much more to seek an unknown coast. Besides, what could they see but a hideous and desolate wilderness full of wild beasts and wild men." Examining the Leatherstocking novels of Fenimore Cooper, D. H. Lawrence thought the essential American character was expressed by the relationship between Deerslayer and the natural world: "He (Deerslayer) says: 'Hurt nothing unless you're forced to.' . . . And yet he lives by death, by killing the wild things of the air and earth . . . All the other stuff, the love, the democracy, the floundering into lust, is a sort of by-play. The essential American soul is hard, isolate, stoic, and a killer. It has never yet melted." The great American novel *Moby Dick* is impelled by the enmity between man and natural force which was to Americans, what defiance of the gods was to Prometheus. This feeling was expectable, and could become heroic when the contest was truly mortal.

The necessities of conquest must always arouse the desire, not merely to subdue, but to destroy. Long after the danger has passed the destruction continues. And although our inherited attitudes are not the cause of this destruction, they do help lower resistance to the imperatives shaped by an early industrialism which was based on the transformation of natural resources into created wealth. This principle—derived from an exchange which initially enhanced life—now directs us to exchange air and water, the natural world itself, for the manufactured apparatus of society in order to sustain the process of production which rests on that principle.

The destruction of our relationship with nature has already limited our freedom. Denied this historic stimulus to expansion, the isolated individual is further turned on himself. The result is a perceptible increase in tension which lowers thresholds of tolerance and increases vulnerability to anger, anxiety and envy. Recently scientists have conducted experiments with individuals who were temporarily confined to blackened rooms where they could not see, hear, smell or touch. Such sensory deprivation has produced emotional turbulences similar to those of severe neurosis. The elimination of nature from our daily life is a sensory deprivation less complete but far more pervasive and enduring. It loosens the ties of community through its effect on our emotional capacities and by removing a traditional bond of shared experience.

CHAPTER 6

O helpless few in my country,
O remnant enslaved

· · · · · · · · · · · · · · · · ·

You of the finer sense,
Broken against false knowledge

· · · · · · · · · · · · · · · · ·

Take thought:
I have weathered the storm,
I have beaten out my exile.

Ezra Pound, 1926

The experience of being an American is more abstract than membership in a community or family. It is not sensible, i.e., it is not something we can see and walk through. It is not organically linked to our daily life, although it has some effect; as the fish which spends its life within a familiar tidal inlet also lives in the ocean and is influenced by the tides. Yet unlike the substitute communities, America is a place. Most of its inhabitants are born there, or have come to stay, and expect their children to be Americans. It is neither voluntary nor historically transient except to those whose detachment grants them a sensibility which can span centuries or anticipate the passage of geological time. (A perspective on contemporary affairs which includes the grand sweep of history, the rise and fall of empires, is an intellectual expression of sentiment rather than feeling; and anyone who worries about the sun burning out has an identity problem of awesome dimensions.)

The nation-state is the characteristic form of modern social organization. Accompanying the rise of modern consciousness, the nation—like its companion, the Reformation—denied the idea of a universal human authority. It could not assume its modern form until economic and technological changes made it possible effectively to organize and govern a territory larger than the semi-sovereign provinces whose size made them vulnerable to an imperial rule. In the last century and a half national structure has been adopted in every continent. Loosely linked fragments have been fused (as in Italy, Germany and Russia), colonies have broken away, and central authority has been extended over territories that were countries in name only (as in much of South America).

Nationalism has been a response to economic forces: the breakup of feudal and hence of imperial authority, the necessity of internal markets large enough to support industrial development, the urgency of uniform commercial regulation, the fact that colonies came to cost more than they produced, etc. Yet such forces do not explain any particular country. In general, national cohesion has been possible only among people with some kind of shared heritage —of language, history or geographical isolation. Authority which transcends such limits must be imposed by force, just as force is usually required to separate people who feel united by shared historical experience. The impulse of the modern state to define itself in terms of traditional concepts—of a "people," a "culture" or a "territory"—is so intense that it has helped to provoke every major armed conflict of the postwar period: Korea, Vietnam, Berlin, East Pakistan and, more ambiguously, the Middle East. That same impulse has also precipitated interventions by the Soviet Union in Eastern Europe and by the United States in South America. How powerful is a drive which can persuade nations and governments to risk loss of power and even total destruction in causes of little economic consequence?

It has been argued that modern technology and new economic forces have made the nation-state an anachronism. Yet even the smallest and least efficient countries are strenuously resistant to the economic logic of merger. Every postwar effort to move toward supranational social organization has been a failure; although some forms of economic collaboration have been institutionalized.*

The cohesion of the nation-state is the process of self-determination which molds community and other social associations. The impulse to define oneself is also a desire for self-mastery, which cannot be fulfilled unless it incorporates qualities which are already part of individual nature. Common language, customs and tradition impinge on us from the moment of birth and rapidly fuse with the inborn elements of our nature. I am a Frenchman because I speak French, was born on French soil, have absorbed French customs, traditions and ways of thought. These elements of being French have enveloped me since memory began. To say "I am a European" also connotes some common tradition, but one which lacks any deep resonance in personal history. (Just as "being Greek" proved weaker and less fulfilling than being Spartan or Athenian; or being Catholic became less important than being Italian or English.)

The nation is not just a convenient form of social organization, but an aspect of individual existence which fulfills irrevocable human needs. If alternative sources of identity, of power and self-mastery, continue to crumble, we can expect national feelings to intensify.

Although the nation, as a form of social organization, continues to extend its authority, the bonds which link the individual to national society are becoming weaker. It is the *idea* of the nation which enhances self-mastery, and that idea can deteriorate even though national authority and wealth increase.

Even though citizens of all countries are involved with their national idea, the idea of each country is different. Witness a few examples of popular patriotic inspiration: France has often appealed

* The economic spread and collaboration of large economic institutions and capital sources are leading toward supranational forms of economic relationships, defying the resistance of governments to a formal merger which may, if current trends continue, become unnecessary and even irrelevant.

to glory. The first line of the "Marseillaise" is "Ye sons of freedom awake to glory," while a song of the French Revolution proclaims:

> Fearing neither sword nor fire,
> France will keep her glory light.

Almost two centuries later, De Gaulle found a response to this same appeal. But few have sought to stimulate Americans to the pursuit of glory. It is too intangible, tied to the idea of the hero, and dominated by the sense of a past which is to be recaptured or emulated.

There seem to be two major themes to Russian patriotism: the motherland and resistance against repression. A hymn of the Soviet Union exhorts:

> Long may she live, our motherland,
> Long may our flag be over us.

Without making too much of a few verses we can note that our own counterpart—"The Star-Spangled Banner"—hopes our flag will continually fly over "the land of the free and the home of the brave." The qualities of the place and not the place itself are important. Long before communism Pushkin wrote:

> The heavy hanging walls will fall,
> The walls will crumble at a word;
> And freedom greet you in the light,
> And brother give you back the sword.

Americans have sung of maintaining the liberty of society, but not of being imprisoned within it.

Conscious of a brilliant past, the English have often been moved by exhortations that they ensure their place in history. In 1852, Tennyson wrote:

> . . . we must speak
> That if tonight our greatness were struck dead,
> There might be left some record of the things we said.

And Churchill's most memorable declaration was to ask his fellow citizens to act so that if Britain lasted for a thousand years, men would say "this was their finest hour." Americans can more easily be moved to action by immediate goals than by the prospect of an honored place in the history books.

This does not mean that the American idea is a practical idea. In many respects it has been the most romantic of all, verging on the religious. Much of our idea of ourselves can be found in phrases drafted more than two thousand years before Columbus: "Now the Lord had said unto Abram, Get thee out of thy country, and from thy kindred, and from thy father's house, unto a land that I will shew thee: And I will make of thee a great nation. . . . Arise, walk through the land in the length of it and in the breadth of it; for I will give it unto thee."

American purpose and institutions were shaped during the brief intellectual ascendancy of the European enlightenment—the time of Voltaire, Montesquieu, Hume and Rousseau—which was the source of that enlightened liberalism which guided the nation's early leadership. Washington admonished his fellow citizens that the fate of liberty and democracy were "deeply . . . finally staked on the experiment intrusted to the hands of the American people." Jefferson hoped we would point the way to other nations seeking to emerge from tyranny. Almost a century later Lincoln spoke of the Civil War as a proving ground, a test whether a nation "conceived in liberty and dedicated to the proposition that all men are created equal can long endure." It was a war to preserve the union, to make the experiment succeed, and not to protect the sacred soil of the motherland or, in the modern fashion, to maintain our territorial integrity.

The idea of America as a great experiment was also accepted by many of Europe's leading intellectuals. In 1778, the French philosopher Turgot wrote that the American people were "the hope of the human race; they may well become its model." Diderot warned Americans to guard their freedom and prayed: "May they defer, at least for a few centuries, the decree . . . that has condemned them to have their birth, their time of vigor, their decrepitude, and their end: May the earth swallow up those of their provinces powerful enough, and mad enough, one day to seek the means of subjugating the others." In his dying days, Voltaire arranged a public display in which he embraced Benjamin Franklin and blessed Franklin's godson with the words "God and liberty." A century and a third later the sentiments of this European elite had their popular counterpart in the hopeful crowds that welcomed Woodrow Wilson when he arrived from the New World as the self-designated savior of the old.

In our first and last great work of political thought—*The Federalist* papers—Madison summed up the American difference: "Is it not the glory of the people of America, that whilst they have paid a decent regard to the opinions of former times and other nations, they have not suffered a blind veneration for antiquity, for custom, or for names, to overrule the suggestions of their own good sense, the knowledge of their own situation, and the lessons of their own experience? To this manly spirit, posterity will be indebted for the possession, and the world for the example of the numerous innovations displayed on the American theater, in favor of private rights and public happiness."

Those dawn days were filled with a sense of enormous possibilities. We had staged the first successful colonial revolt and established the first national democracy on earth since the Renaissance republics. Our models existed centuries in the past, or as the theoretical constructs of eighteenth-century thinkers, themselves writing in a Europe where absolutism was tightening its grip. We had an ocean to protect us and a rich continent to nourish the future. Poets as well as political leaders felt the excitement of our prospects, and expressed that excitement with even greater intensity.

William Blake detested liberal thinkers. He attacked Voltaire, Rousseau and Locke, men who contributed to the thought of the founders. Blake saw rationalism and atheism as threats to the human spirit, and after two centuries, his intuitions have become the sternest of realities. Yet despite his ideology Blake also sensed in America a new hope for the liberation of the human spirit:

> Washington, Franklin, Paine & Warren, Gates, Hancock
> & Green
> Met on the coast glowing with blood from Albion's
> fiery Prince.
> Stiff shudderings shook the heavenly thrones, France,
> Spain and Italy.

They slow advance to shut the dive gates of their
        law-built heaven,
Filled with blasting fancies and with mildews of despair,
With fierce disease and lust . . .
But the dive gates were consumed, & their bolds and
        hinges melted;
And the fierce flames burnt round the heavens & round
        the abodes of men.

The special nature of our society and its purpose—even its moral mission—have dominated the idea of America far more than have tradition, cultural heritage, common language or territory. To be French or British, Chinese or Egyptian is to be part of a cluster of events and beliefs transmitted across centuries. The American idea could not be formed from such continuity. The wilderness had sheltered no Roman legions, no Peter and Constantine, no Renaissance or Elizabethan Age. We could not reflect on that interminable procession of rulers and artists which provides a Frenchman with his proudest moments. The two basic constituents of nationhood—population and territory—constantly grew, and changed in composition. We could only form a stabilizing association with an idea derived from national character and direction. We were the land of opportunity and freedom. We were also William Bradford's "city on a hill," Jefferson's "chosen country," Lincoln's "favored land," and from there, in a direct line, to Wilson's Fourteen Points and Roosevelt's Four Freedoms. This national idea differed from that of other nations in a crucial quality: It had to be constantly renewed, always contemporary. It could not be sustained by saying we had been a land of opportunity or that once upon a time we had a great purpose; as other countries could support their present with the experiences of the past. Even when we invoke tradition or recall the words of past leaders, it is as a guide to the future and critique of the present more than a celebration of the past.

These themes have defined the American idea with remarkable consistency, although the early assertions gave way to apprehensions about our capacity to withstand the corruptions of growing wealth and power. In 1854, William Cullen Bryant rhapsodized:

Deep in the brightness of the skies
The thronging years in glory arise,
      And, as they fleet
Drop strength and riches at thy feet.

In the same decade Herman Melville made a darker and more
ambiguous suggestion:

Power unanointed may come—
Dominion (Unsought by the free)
      And the Iron Dome
Stronger for stress and strain,
Fling her huge shadow athwart the main;
But the Founders' dream shall flee.

Even Melville, as he echoes Diderot's warning that power is cor-
rosive, also affirms, and not cynically, the "Founders' dream," just
as Whitman in the same period saw a:

Beautiful world of new, superior birth, that rises
                to my eyes.
I feel thy ominous greatness, evil as well as good;
I watch thee, advancing, absorbing the present,
                transcending the past;
But I do not undertake to define thee—hardly to
                comprehend thee
I but thee name—thee prophesy—as now:

The basic themes of the American idea run through two centuries of patriotic and political literature, from Washington to John
Kennedy's "the same revolutionary beliefs for which our forebears
fought are still at issue around the globe. . . . We dare not forget
today that we are the heirs of that first revolution."

The accumulation of wealth and power is also part of the national idea. The land of opportunity is also the land of abundance.
Still, the American idea has not celebrated the national wealth for
its own sake but as opportunity for the individual to achieve a rising income. Abundance is linked to the idea of just distribution.
The conception that individual well-being is connected to the crea-

tion of social wealth is so natural to Americans that it is easy to forget how often the policy and goals of other nations have focused on making the country richer, with the individual—except for the privileged and powerful—but a subordinate beneficiary.†

Although we have been committed to continental expansion, military power for its own sake has, until very recently, rarely been an American goal. Except for extending our own borders, we have been fairly isolationist for most of our history. We made no peacetime effort to maintain a military establishment which could compete with other powers. Until the post-Korean period, we downgraded, cut back and almost eliminated our armed forces after each of our wars, including World War II. Our pride in military exploits outside the continent has centered on the idea of winning—of victory and success—rather than our capacity to occupy, subdue and rule.

Even a revisionist explanation of American history as one of aggressive imperialism does not refute the assertion that citizens have believed our acts to be consistent with the American idea. Before Vietnam our two least explicable wars—the War of 1812 and the Spanish-American War—were, at the time, justified in traditional terms. In 1812, even though the group which wanted to annex Canada was probably decisive, the British depredations on our ships and our frontier were an unjustified use of force against a smaller nation. And even with this provocation, the war was so unpopular that the New England states refused co-operation with the federal government and came to the edge of secession. The Spanish-American War derived much of its popular support from our announced intention to liberate the oppressed Caribbean colonies and secure Cuban independence. Those who had colonial expansion in mind at its inception were few and secretive.

The conquest of the continent, which included the Mexican War, is of a different dimension. Americans simply moved west, occupying and settling the land. The only realistic choice was

† This conception is, of course, a distortion of the reality. All do not share, or share equally, in rising wealth. Nevertheless, the idea remains a social reality. Americans have celebrated the announcement of a higher GNP as if they had received a raise in pay; the rate of national growth has even been, as in 1960, a "gut" or "bread and butter" political issue—All this despite the continuing maldistribution of rising income. Similar increases in some other countries are paraded as a national achievement, a step toward increased status among the social sovereigns.

whether the new lands would become part of the union or form independent nations. The rights of the Indians were betrayed. But one must remember that the pioneers were not affluent, middle-class Americans. Millions of people, fleeing the poverty of Europe, came to the margin of rich lands which were virtually empty and unexploited. Great wrongs were done, but the clash was unavoidable, and the moral questions often ambiguous. It is true that the nation has been materialistic and, at times, militaristic. But in discussing the idea of America—the inner sense of association—we must recognize that those descriptions have never been used as worlds of flattery, praise or braggadocio.

We are not here trying to evaluate the validity of the American idea, i.e., its relationship to American reality or even its moral value. Behavior has often contradicted faith—professed and believed. The important thing is that the idea has provided us with a sense of shared social worth and social purpose. Most citizens associated themselves with the American idea even when our actions and policies seemed in conflict. We may have had warlike majorities, destructive majorities or greedy majorities, but we have never had a majority of cynics.

The American idea has usually served as a reference point for attacks on national policies thought to be immoral or destructive. The conquest of the Philippines was to its opponents, the American Anti-Imperialist League, not merely wrong but "open disloyalty to the distinctive principles of our government"; the "great aberration," a leading historian called it. Our fiercest critics from within have usually framed their opposition as an attempt to vindicate the American idea, not to deny it.

At the moment he took command of the most nearly successful effort to dissolve the territorial union, Jefferson Davis, in his inaugural, said that "through this instrumentality [the Confederacy] we hope to perpetuate the principles of our Revolutionary fathers." Nor is there reason to doubt Davis was unquestionably sincere. Throughout our history it had been maintained by many of our leaders and theorists, including Thomas Jefferson, that a state had the right to resist the central government, a right whose logical conclusion was secession.

Of all our modern poets, Robinson Jeffers was unequaled in the bitter intensity of his hostility to the course of modern America. Yet he also spoke out of a sense of betrayal. In 1925, before he moved toward a denial of humanity itself, Jeffers instructed the Republic:

> But in one noble passion we are one; and Washington,
> Luther, Tacitus, Aeschylus, one kind of man.
> And you America, that passion made you . . . You were
> not born to prosperity, you were born to love
>   freedom.
>
> The states of the next age will no doubt remember
> you, and edge their love of freedom with contempt
>   of luxury.

To observe that most individuals "believe" the American idea comprises two different statements. The first is that their concept of America contained and was shaped by the idea. However objectionable the moment, an essential national spirit, a standard, urged us toward correction. As with the Platonic virtues, experience and behavior were a distortion of the idea as guiding reality.‡ The second aspect of belief is the incorporation of the idea by the individual as part of the process of self-definition. As a result, any weakening of association with the nation must needs diminish the power of the individual by striking at the sources of self-mastery.

The American idea is more vulnerable than most to the fragmenting and coercive forces of modern society. To the extent a national idea is composed of historical and cultural traditions, or the rooted possession of territory, common ethnic origins and language, it is fortified against temporary misfortune or aberrations. It requires a sustained and prolonged assault for the present to destroy the past. But the idea of America is always in the present. "Justice," "freedom," "opportunity," "model and exemplar to the world" are either present realities or the idea is dead.

The concept of discontinuity, freedom from ties with the past, was formulated as a principle of moral politics by men like Jefferson, who said no generation could bind the next, and that re-

‡ Today many have turned virtue upside down, holding that the ideal is the goal of the idealist who is therefore unrealistic; whereas the most grotesque distortions which we perceive are the only proper subject for practical men who are thus realistic.

current revolution was essential to liberty. The same tradition of the untraditional informed Lincoln's statement that "the dogmas of the quiet past are inadequate to the stormy present." Such an approach to social change is not possible in any literal sense, but it expresses that quality in the American idea which requires each generation to measure its elements against sensed conditions. This has been a great source of strength, enabling us to undergo important social change with a minimum of violence or ideological strife, and without dissolving the political forms. (Although the nature and distribution of authority within those forms have, necessarily, been conformed to social change.) Since the idea contained the present, was the present, the social struggle has been framed as an effort to conform the conditions of life to that idea. Jefferson's revolutionary principle has been profoundly conservative in a most important aspect. And although we have had many who favored change for the sake of change, little energy or eloquence has been expended in defense of standing still. There has been no American Edmund Burke. Those who have defended the status quo, whether from interest or conviction, have tended to argue its utility rather than its sanctity. An idea with so contemporary a character can be sustained through a great deal of hypocrisy and contradiction, provided its major elements are felt to possess vitality. But when national behavior or conditions do not conform to basic values over any prolonged period, the idea must lose its hold on individuals. The idea which contains the present demands present nourishment for its existence.

In St. Louis, on June 26, 1970, President Nixon proclaimed that it was time to "stand up and speak about what is right in America." It is an incitement that would not have occurred to previous American leaders. Surely, among those who cheered the statement were many who did so because they sensed the need for reassurance. In the past it seemed more relevant to caution Americans against braggadocio and righteousness rather than excessive self-criticism. De Tocqueville explained to his European contemporaries: "Much . . . of the self-importance which the American assumes, particularly abroad, is less traceable to his mere citizenship than to his conscious identification with the success of democracy . . . the source of his pride is a legitimate and a noble one. It involves not only his own position, but also the hopes and expectations of humanity." More than a century later another friend of America—a high official of Canada—offered a poignant counterpoint. We Canadians, he explained, are concerned at the "sudden and tragic disappearance of the American dream. . . . We wonder what did happen to that bright star of hope . . . which as recently as the post World War II period was the cynosure of all eyes, an example for all mankind. . . ."

Loss of faith within America is not limited to those who desire a more liberating society. It infects white racists and black militants, warriors and peaceniks, those who flaunt the flag and those who trample it. It is inescapable. One may believe that blacks should be suppressed, but one cannot justify such beliefs in terms of the American idea. It is possible to argue against helping the poor, but few will be heard to say that the poor should be ignored so that we may increase individual opportunity, enhance justice or expand the pursuit of happiness. One can submit that the pragmatic realities of the world require us to support repressive dictatorships, impose our will on small countries and oppose the forces of popular desire because they are led by communists; but disbelief or scorn is required in response to any assertion that such acts are in fulfillment of a historic American mission to point the way toward liberty and increased well-being for all peoples. Such convictions can be supported by argument—e.g., the necessities of defense or of economic stability—but only by arguments which distance themselves from formerly expressed conceptions of the country. To make such arguments and to believe them itself manifests a profound loss of faith.

A nation cannot exchange its national idea for a newer model any more than it can exchange its territories or population. The idea is the nation. It came on the *Mayflower*. It was alive before the first settlers crossed the Alleghenies. It has been bred into every generation. To change it, however compelling the reasons may seem, is to lose it; and to lose it is to lose the nation. If the American idea dissolves altogether there may still be an organized society occupying the North American continent, but it will not be America, whatever it is called. Since the American idea is of continual movement toward a significant and worthy future purpose, it cannot be contained in policies of defense and self-protection any more than in the denial of justice and narrowing of opportunity.

> We're going West tomorrow, where the promises can't fail
> O'er the dills in legions, boys, and crowd the dusty trail.
> We shall starve and freeze and suffer. We shall die and
>   tame the lands.
> But we're going West tomorrow, with our fortunes in
>   our hands.

The American idea is one of the elements from which the individual constructs himself. It enters into that personal framework which transforms an amorphous social impulse into a particular social person, one who exists in a particular place at a certain moment in the historical flow. When the idea weakens or starts to yield, the framework which sustains individual power is menaced. When construction workers attack young protesters amid the predatory towers of Wall Street, more is at stake than the wisdom of American foreign policy. Each side is defending the self. Each is demanding confirmation: one by disassociation from the realities which have hollowed out the values; the other through a fierce, violent and ultimately futile reassertion of a treasured and necessary association.** We have had witch hunts and loyalty scares before, but today the issue of "Americanism" swarms about a host of issues—from drugs to foreign policy—which, in other periods, could more easily be debated without provoking challenges to the nature and morality of American society.

The need for community and family is more deeply rooted than the bonds of nation; their loss is far more devastating to the possibilities of individual freedom. But for modern society as a whole the loss of faith in the national idea, the growth of sensed disbelief, can have more tragic consequences. For the physical nation entraps us. Our lives are directed and confined by its economic structures and political institutions. It has pervaded our experience since early youth and been imprinted on habits of thought and behavior. There is no "substitute community" for the nation because all other associations are contained within it. Some may

** The individual self-mastery which sustains freedom can only derive from social institutions whose authority is not perceived as external to the individual's life.

depart the frontiers to become strangers in another country, but few are endowed with the inner resources to renew their power in emigration and exile; and should one flee to another advanced nation, the afflictions of modern life are not far behind.

The idea of America is menaced not simply by the presence of contradiction, but by our awareness of that contradiction. Thus one could identify with the American idea in the presence of slavery until historical change made men aware of slavery as an avoidable evil. Similarly, through the early postwar boom there was a great deal of poverty and racism in America. Yet it was not until the late 1950s that the public began to become aware that these conditions existed and that they were inconsistent with our view of the nation. The idea is threatened when we become aware of the condition, aware that it is a contradiction, aware that it is remediable and aware that we are failing to remedy it.

The dissolution of shared social purpose, like that of community, is contained by the modern social process. Often appearing as liberation of the individual from formal creed or ideological illusion, the weakening of the American idea slackens the bonds of civil society, swelling the power of authority which is made external to the citizens it rules. Leaders and citizens are equally caught up in the remorseless progress of human fragmentation and alienation. Finally, of course, the contradiction will be resolved. For if the reality is not changed, the idea will be transformed to suit the new reality.

CHAPTER 7

> . . . it is impossible for a republic to remain long in the quiet enjoyment of her freedom . . . even if she has no foreign foes, she will find domestic enemies amongst her own citizens, for such seem to be the inevitable fate of all large cities.
>
> Machiavelli, *The Discourses*

> I will make [you] a new covenant . . . I will put my law in their inward parts . . . and they shall teach no more every man his neighbour, and every man his brother, saying, Know the Lord: for they shall all know me . . . If these ordinances depart from before me, saith the Lord, then the seed of Israel also shall cease from being a nation.
>
> Jeremiah

> Love is not an organizing principle.

Although the exclusion of blacks from the American community is as old as the nation, the present form of that exclusion—its consequences for the country and the obstacles to its termination—is determined by the particular circumstances of modern America. Yet, black existence and the state of poverty for blacks are also distinctive, incorporating a more absolute exclusion from the society than that which is implied by material deprivation alone.

Black poverty is not exclusion so much as it is one of the consequences of exclusion.

For most of the period between the end of Reconstruction and World War II the black condition was not generally perceived either as exclusion or as a contradiction to the American idea. To most Americans, blacks existed beyond the society, outside the general awareness of what constituted the possibilities and values of the nation. It is difficult for us to re-create that sense of black exclusion as an aspect of the natural order of things. Moral feelings and values are bounded by perception, and we can no more re-create the perceptions of the past than earlier generations could have prophetically experienced our own awareness. However, history contains enough parallels to permit us at least to admit the possibility that sincere moral convictions and libertarian social ideals can coexist with what are now seen as great wrongs. The most eloquent defenders of ancient Greek democracy accepted, almost without notice, the slaves whose labor made that democracy possible. For generations, the British nation struggled to form the principles of democratic equality which still dominate our present ideology, while conducting what is now judged as a ruthless devastation and exploitation of foreign colonies. There is little doubt that the future will also judge us harshly for conduct which appears to be appropriate and wise, perhaps even for the struggle to increase the individuals right to pursue his own desires and gratification which we regard as an enlargement of freedom.

One of the factors which links the exclusion of Greek Helots, British colonials and American blacks is that the presence of a large under class served an economic purpose: it was an aspect of the dominant economic relations which limit social consciousness. Moreover, the productive forces of the time were not adequate to eliminate the economic circumstances which bound large masses to relative poverty. And that for which no satisfactory solution exists is not perceived as a problem.

In 1896, when the Supreme Court gave constitutional sanction to segregation, counsel for the blacks made an argument which demonstrated an awareness of the economic foundation of black exclusion. He seems to have asserted that segregation established whites as a dominant class; that membership in a dominant class was property; and that blacks, therefore, were being deprived of property in violation of the Fourteenth Amendment. This argument, and the analysis which must have supported it, is decisive and was affirmed by the subsequent economic history of black Americans. However, the argument is not one which an American court could review, even as late as 1954 when the earlier decision was overturned. The 1896 Court disposed of the point by stating that a black "is not lawfully entitled to the reputation of being a white man," i.e., black is not white.

After the brief upsurge of hope, which followed the Civil War, had been suppressed, blacks entered their southern period, which lasted until the New Deal, war and the advent of a new economy had prepared the ground for a second black insurgency. During this southern period the black man did not endure poverty amid abundance. He was just the poorest of the poor. The entire South, and especially the rural South, was an underdeveloped country. Toward the beginning of the New Deal, President Roosevelt asserted that the South was "the nation's number one economic problem," and the supporting statistics sound like a litany recited by the World Bank to prove the need for foreign aid. With a third of the people, the South received less than a fifth of the country's income. On the eve of World War II (1938), a presidential investigation reported that two million Southerners were infected with malaria each year, cutting industrial production by a third; that pellagra was a southern endemic; and that 60–80 per cent of all low-income families, i.e., most families, black and white, could not buy enough to eat. Death rates and infant mortality were as high as those in many of today's underdeveloped countries.

In the decades before the war it seemed that the general poverty of the South might bring an improvement in the black condition. A handful of populists and even an occasional radical began to thrive on the growing regional consciousness of injustice. (Huey Long wanted to "share the wealth," and Hugo Black, acting later, voted to strike down segregation.) It looked as if people might believe their poverty more important than their whiteness. For many reasons that phenomenon faded, although the reality of common economic interest among lower income whites and blacks remains.

For the most part, however, southern poverty strengthened the repression of blacks. It provided an economic motive for maintaining cheap black labor and, since resources were severely limited, the exclusion of the blacks meant a larger share for whites—at least some of the whites. It was economically convenient to have a colony within southern boundaries. The environment of poverty combined with legalized terror to deter any consciousness of a gap between the black condition and the possibilities of the society. That consciousness is the foundation of revolutionary awareness. There can be no will to revolt unless liberating change appears to be a physical possibility. This lack of awareness must have been especially marked in the rural South where a man's world was bounded by a few familiar landmarks, where the rest of the country must have seemed little more than a rumor. I once talked with some workers in an Andean field who were cutting crops with a scythe for about thirty cents a day. They did not know the name of Peru's president, none of them had seen a town of more than five hundred people, the large city only seventy miles away was in a different universe—they were not revolutionaries. A similar kind of geographical isolation inhibited the growth of revolutionary awareness among American blacks. Nor in such a society could any but the most defiant escape suspicion that there might be some substance to the white man's claim of superiority. It was part of a higher rationality, an effort to escape from the pain of knowing that hopelessness is also totally unfair.

World War II marked the beginning of the end of the southern period. The war and postwar growth not only improved the black condition, but reduced the barriers to awareness, making black resistance possible and, ultimately, inevitable. An increasing movement to urban areas, first for defense work and then for escape and opportunity, together with the spread of modern communication and transport, made it possible for the black man to measure his lot against the standards of the entire society. The black no longer felt himself the poorest of the poor, but the oppressed among the rich.

In the two decades since 1950, America's black urban population increased by more than seven million, more than the total immigration by any one ethnic or national group in American history. (From 1820–1967, about 6.9 million Germans came to America, while in the same period there arrived about 5 million Italians, 4.7 million Irish and an equal number of English.) Although southern cities have absorbed some of this immigration, more has gone North. In 1940, almost 80 per cent of all blacks lived in the South; today, little more than half.*

The postwar period which heightened black awareness also increased white perception of the conflict between racial oppression and the American idea. The disabilities of the blacks became a threat to shared social purpose and thus to the identity, the self-conception of the white citizen. The changed relationship between white consciousness and the black condition was not caused by the urban migrations themselves, but the evolving economic structure which propelled these migrations. The economic framework of black exclusion was dismantled by the evolution of productive forces which did not depend upon a large under class and which has acquired the still unutilized capacity to eliminate the historic forms of poverty which characterized black society.

These changes have led to an improvement in black economic possibilities—not simply because we can produce more wealth, but because of the forms in which that wealth is produced, because of new relations of production. An economic process based upon mass consumption depends on increasing the numbers of those who possess purchasing power beyond necessity. Such an increase has been the foundation of postwar growth, just as the current stagnation in that process, the inability to end remaining poverty, is among the most serious weaknesses and portents of vulnerability in the bureaucratic economy. Because that economy is bureaucratic it is also impersonal, depending upon standards and criteria of judgment rather than individual evaluation or belief. Since race is largely irrelevant to the functioning necessities of bureaucratic structures, historic enmities and non-rational racial feelings—although possessed by individuals—are less likely to obstruct opportunity within the structure. This is especially so when the use of racial criteria causes disturbances—opposition, protest or condemnation—which may hamper the tranquil operation and expansion of governing economic institutions. (This factor only operates, however, as long as the disturbance caused by racial discrimination

* Similar large-scale internal migrations have taken place in many societies during the last quarter century. The result has been a heightened revolutionary awareness and, in some countries, a transfer of power to populist leaders, as in Peru. However, in such countries the poor were a majority and the dominant economic institutions were obsolete.

exceeds that which is produced by the elimination of that discrimination.) Nor can structures whose growth has extended their reach to the entire nation defer to regional feelings. It is regional values which must yield, as is now happening in much of the South, the change being proportional to the pace of economic growth.

Despite recent economic gains and the institutional compulsions of the modern economy, blacks are still excluded from the American community. Indeed, in recent years, the barriers have hardened. Some of the reasons for this are historic, but most important is the process of social fragmentation, which is continually fortified by the same economic process which has also increased black opportunity. In a sense blacks are knocking on a door to an illusion. They seek to establish themselves within a community and a national conception which is itself disintegrating. The weakening of human connections within society also weakens the capacity and will of white Americans to forge new relationships. The entire momentum of the social process is in the opposite direction. As the idea of America weakens, it loses its persuasive force. While the black condition can now be perceived as injustice, as contrary to American standards, that awareness has lost much of its corrective power. The weakening of civic obligation infects and distorts the will of every citizen.

Social fragmentation deprives the individual of power over social existence. The response to impotence is not resignation, nor is it merely a desire for self-protection. The inner reality of social existence cannot be denied. If it is not expressed through "bonds of unity," it is corrupted into fear, hostility and even violence. Black Americans are a natural object for these emanations of a sensed impotence which, if it continues to deepen, will continue to intensify racial feelings.†

The personal experience of almost every white, the continual reminders of social intercourse, contain evidence of a nearly universal prejudice which, since its objects are black, is known as "racism." Many who share this feeling would not deny economic equality to blacks. Justice does not rest on affection, or there would be very little of it. However, racial feeling loses its mildness when this majority ideology is acted upon by the poor and uneducated.

---

† These aspects of alienation, and the consequences of the impotence intrinsic to alienated existence, are elaborated in Part III.

There is a direct line between an exclusive all-white New York club and a street fight on the edge of Bedford-Stuyvesant; between the expensive resort at Bar Harbor and the local construction union that refuses to admit black workers. In the context of the black historical experience, exclusion from any aspect of society implies an assertion of black inferiority. This may not, in fact, be the motive for exclusion. But the meaning of a social act is determined not by subjective intentions but by the history and present conditions of society. Individuals who exclude blacks in the exercise of their liberty to select associates are acting to sustain values which may not be involved in either the particular issue or in conscious motives. The only beliefs that exist for social man are those contained in behavior. One can hold an inner conviction of equality and abandon that conviction through failure to respond to the denial of equality; just as the most peaceful of men can be an accomplice in violence. Although such values often can be maintained in a relatively civil and innocuous fashion at the upper levels of the social structure, they are translated into a more violent response at lower levels. For at those levels people do not have the resources to escape the problem, and the associations which are important to them—unions, housing projects, schools—are also essential to black opportunity.

The varied manifestations of black separatism—social and aesthetic—are a psychically necessary response to racial division. Individuals must evolve some form of association with others who share the common life. They must find a place within a society. If blacks are rejected by the larger American society they have no choice consistent with freedom other than to form their own.

Although the capacity to end poverty exists, we cannot be so confident of society's ability to eliminate racism. Draw a circle on a piece of paper. There are two ways to define what is inside the circle: by describing the interior or by eliminating all that is outside. We all live in the midst of concentric and overlapping circles— nation, religion, race, community, family, etc., within which we confirm and define our existence. It seems that man is so fragile that he can often attain to a belief in his own worth only by contrast, by degrading all that lies without. It is history's chasm between the social being and the human being. Racism, then, is terror

—not of the black, the other, but of one's own existence. It can only be overcome by widening the community, something which is possible only in a society which is enlarging the possibilities of all its members. That itself cannot be accomplished through an effort of will or an increase in production. It requires far-reaching changes in the material structures and relationships which dominate modern life. Black freedom is tied to the freedom of all the rest.

CHAPTER 8

MR. DEASY: All history moves toward a great goal, the manifestation of God.
STEPHEN DEDALUS: God is a shout in the street.

James Joyce

The natural sciences . . . will become the basis of a human
science.

Marx, the utopian

The only object of theoretical physics is to calculate results
that can be compared with experiment and it is quite unnecessary that any satisfying description of the whole course of the
phenomena should be given.

Dirac, the physicist

The end of the moral interpretation of the world, which no
longer has any sanction after it has tried to escape into some
beyond, leads to nihilism. . . .

Nietzsche

Our analysis began by positing freedom as a value or end by
which to appraise society. No society exists without values, whether
they are based upon belief, force or material relationships; whether
they can be coherently expressed or are masked as forms of neces-

sity or function. They prescribe what is to be valued, what constitutes the "good life" or the pursuit of happiness, and they govern attitudes—individual and social—toward artistic creation, the accumulation of wealth, leisure, work, etc. Since all societies have purposes, even though they are only revealed in behavior, the concept of society includes systems of values. Values are always accompanied by a morality of right conduct, a regulation of social behavior whose mandates can be values in themselves as well as ways to maintain the social order within which values can be expressed and pursued. Through most of Western history a shared morality has required authority superior to the individual will, a body of supreme legislation, deriving for the most part from secular or divine mythology.

At times, men such as Plato have thought to discover an unassailable authority through reason. But Plato also believed that the Good was an immutable and immanent reality, discoverable through the cumulative power of human thought. "(T)he Greeks," Bertrand Russell explains, "had a theory or feeling about the universe which may be called religious or ethical. According to this theory, every person and every thing has his or its appointed place and appointed function. This does not depend upon the fiat of Zeus, for Zeus himself is subject to the same . . . law . . . but . . . there is a tendency to overstep just bounds; hence arises strife. Some kind of impersonal super-Olympian law punishes hubris, and restores the eternal order. . . ." This, then, was a secular mythology, a belief in an overmastering order of the universe, governing men and gods alike. It was fate and necessity, an aspect of the nature of things. It *was*, and needed no theology to elaborate it, or clergy to serve it. The concept of the natural rights of man—from the Stoics to Jefferson—although often attributed to divine will, descended from confidence in this natural order of things.

> Into that from which things take their rise they pass away once more, as is ordained, for they make reparation and satisfaction to one another for their injustice according to the ordering of time.
>
> Anaximander

In the modern period, what Nietzsche called "the end of the moral interpretation of the world, which no longer has any sanction," has stimulated a search for new ways to legitimate a morality of right conduct. Right conduct is, like community and social purpose, the victim of social fragmentation. Values and moral conduct which are enforced by belief and inner restraint cannot exist without community, for they are manifestations of a society wherein the consciousness of each individual includes his connection to others. That form of consciousness, in its historical appearances, linked the individual not only to contemporaries, but to the human flow. Values and moral standards which were timeless, part of the order of things, could only be conceived as expressions of authority which transcended human existence.

During the eighteenth and nineteenth centuries, the principal attacks on religion came from the liberal thinkers who represented the new commercial classes. Looking back more than a century, it seems clear that religious structure was an obstacle to industrialism; that a materialistic, rational and secular ideology was better suited to the needs of ascending capitalism. Yet this attack on religious faith also eliminated a source of reconciliation, of social order, for which no replacement has been found. It was then thought that religion contained the alienated powers of humanity, that its rejection would liberate men to exercise those powers in their own right. It is another example of the extent to which principles of conservation dominated the thought of the nineteenth century, i.e., men could not give away more power than they had; myth could not exercise greater power over men than men could exercise over themselves. The twentieth century has disclosed the possibility that a dynamic system—whether material or of belief— can be more than this sum of its elements. Even though myths were the creation of human society, it is still true that the mythological structure had power which its creators lacked. It acquired an authority, a persuasive force, which other men or the society of man could not exert. For myth combined its regulation of the social order with the connection to human existence and the natural order. Marx himself wrote that religion was "the soul of soulless conditions," but anticipated its replacement by a science of man.

Nearly all formal structures of belief have served the purposes of the institutions and forces governing society. Nevertheless, to create a system of values and a moral code with authority over human behavior does not, by itself, constitute alienation. The regulation of conduct within the utopias of Plato or Marx, for example, would not be oppressive since those codes would express the shared will and judgment of the community.

The fragmentation of social existence, having destroyed previous forms of authority, also makes inconceivable the establishment of an accepted system of values and right conduct. That which is to be valued inevitably becomes, or seems to become, a matter of opinion —infusing life, work and human relations with enervating confusions, crippling the commitments necessary to the extension of existence; imposing on each individual the enslaving and impossible task of legislating an entire ethic.

The consciousness of individualism has increased the vulnerability of all human relationships, weakening the responsibility, the assumed obligation, which support friendship, love, community and all forms of shared life and endeavor. The relationships between human beings become externalized and to that extent subsist as a form of coercion and not as expression of freedom. What has been termed the "philosophy of the absurd" is the culmination, the logical end of individualism.

There can be no morality of right conduct without community. God is the creation of a collective humanity. Moreover, without an authoritative system of values and moral conduct the community necessary to freedom does not exist and cannot be created. Values and codes of conduct are the form of society. A receding belief must yield to enforcement. Laws, force and the purposes of governing economic institutions take the place of inner restraint. This requires an enormous growth in the coercive apparatus of the society, and that apparatus, given the nature of the state, of bureaucracy and of political man extends beyond its mandates to steadily reduce the power and the freedom of the individual. This is what Henry Adams was predicting in 1905 when he wrote that within a century "law . . . would disappear as theory or a priori principle, and give place to force. Morality would become police."

It was not until 1882 that Nietzsche's madman rushed into the market place to announce God's murder. Angry at the seeming disbelief of the silent bystanders, he throws his lantern to the ground, shouting, "I come too early . . . my time has not come yet. This tremendous event . . . has not yet reached the ears of man." But there was another explanation for the apathy of the citizens—the news may have been equivalent to a proclamation that here had been a flood in China—interesting, sad, and now let's get the groceries and go home. For the madman was no seer but, at best, a dramatic variant of the child who announced the emperor's nakedness. For more than two centuries before this moment in the market place the discoveries of scientific reason had been consuming the intellectual pillars which sustained belief. For more than a century thinkers and writers had been wrestling with the consequences of this destruction. The buoyant expectations of an age free from superstition and dogma were increasingly accompanied by a mounting awareness of a perilous difficulty: where was liberated, rational, disbelieving man to find authority for values and morality; and what sanction, besides force, could persuade men to observance.

It was natural for men to turn first to the ascending ideology of scientific reason. They found their text in the words of Sir Isaac Newton who had been transformed into a secular deity by the eighteenth century. In the conclusion of his treatise on Opticks, Newton prophesied that "if natural philosophy [i.e., science] . . . shall at length be perfected the bounds of moral philosophy will also be enlarged." This simple, non-scientific and erroneous statement presaged a swarm of varied philosophies derived from the expectation that laws of nature and/or the application of scientific method to human affairs would yield a system of rationally ordained values and rules of conduct. Yet no matter how industriously men searched the skies or squinted through microscopes they could not seem to locate the Good, the Just, the Beautiful or the True. In an autobiographical note the physicist George Gamow tells how as a Russian teen-ager he examined, under a microscope, a bread crumb that had been dipped into wine during holy communion and transubstantiated into the body of Christ. He then compared it with a crumb of ordinary bread and with a small piece of his own skin. The microscope revealed that the structure of the wine-dipped crumb was like that of ordinary bread and totally different from skin. This, he reports, was "the experiment which made him a scientist." Of course, he could just as reasonably have rejected science and become a priest. It all depends on the assumptions you start with.

In the nineteenth century, emphasis shifted to the other aspect of Newton's cryptic assurance—the use of reason to create a science of man. Marx promised that "Natural science will one day incorporate the science of man, just as the science of man will incorporate natural science." And again: "The natural sciences will then abandon their abstract materialist, or rather idealist orientation, and will become the basis of a human science . . . one basis for life and another for science is *a priori* falsehood." Marx labored prodigiously but, inevitably, the values of his utopian structure were supported by their persuasive appeal and not by logic. He could not "prove" them by demonstrating their "scientific" inevitability.

A similar intellectual impulse produced bourgeois philosophies such as utilitarianism, social Darwinism and pragmatism. They too rested on a confidence that human or social "laws" which could prescribe values and right conduct. None of these doctrines, however influential, created a persuasive moral force. And by now the expectation that an authoritative moral system can be produced by rational exposition or the application of scientific method has dissolved. Indeed, the once unchallenged presumption that certain understanding of nature's laws was within the grasp of science has itself been toppled.

> What does nihilism mean? That the highest values devaluate themselves. The goal is lacking; the answer is lacking to our "why."
>
> Nietzsche

"I am a sick man . . . I am a spiteful man. I am an unattractive man. I believe my liver is diseased . . . I refuse to consult a doctor from spite . . ." came the voice from the nineteenth-century underground, sounding the theme for Western man's other great effort to elude the consequences of the end of myth. Dostoevsky addresses men of learning, bares their intentions and hurls his passion against them. "You say," he writes, "we have only to discover these laws of nature, and man will no longer have to answer for his actions and life will become exceedingly easy for him. . . . Then—this is what you all say—new economic relations will be established, all ready-made and worked out with mathematical exactitude, so that every possible question will vanish in the twinkling of an eye, simply because every possible answer to it will be provided. Then the 'Palace of Crystal' will be built." But something has been overlooked, Dostoevsky writes: "One's own free unfettered choice, one's own caprice, however wild it may be, one's own fancy worked up at times to frenzy—is that very 'most advantageous advantage' which we have overlooked, which comes under no classification and against which all systems and theories are continually being shattered to atoms." Should science demonstrate all the laws of nature and society with mathematical precision then man "would not become reasonable, but would purposely do something perverse out of simple ingratitude, simply to gain his point. And if he does not find means he will contrive destruction and chaos, will contrive sufferings of all sorts, only to gain his point."

With myth gone and science rejected, what was the underground man's answer to our why? "Perhaps the only goal on earth to which mankind is striving lies in this incessant process of attaining, in other words, in life itself, and not in the thing to be attained which must always be expressed as a formula, as positive as twice two makes four, and such positiveness is not life, gentlemen, but is the beginning of death." *Notes from the Underground* was brilliant, shrill, absurd, a prayer masquerading as spite; but, most of all, it was propelled by a lucid historical logic. If myth had dissolved and science was a threatening illusion, the individual would embrace his isolation as the opportunity to discover and shape his own moral being. The answer to our "why" was "because." And the question was not "why?" but "what?"

The label "existentialism" has been used to yoke the diverse philosophies of striving, systematic and fragmentary, sacred and secular, which diverge from Dostoevsky's intuitions and from the poetic revelations of his contemporary, Kierkegaard. Existentialism does not describe a philosophic school in any traditional sense. It includes Christians as well as atheists, those who deny the term "existentialism," and those who wrote before it was invented. After World War II, propelled by Sartre's literary polemics, the word entered the pop culture, and the so-called "existential act" became virtually anything done by anyone who had heard the word.

The existentialists were not primarily concerned with devising a morality of right conduct; indeed they were almost unanimous in rejecting the concept of shared morality, a moral code. Much of their work concerns itself with the most troubling and traditional problems of philosophy—the nature of existence and knowledge, the constituents of freedom and the question of human purpose. Few are preoccupied with the issue which concerns us here: the values which should inform individual conduct and the source of authority for these values. This question was of greater significance to Kierkegaard and Nietzsche than to more recent thinkers who have tended to concentrate on the metaphysics of the human condition. However, none completely omitted the question of right conduct. Only recently has existentialism descended toward the total moral relativism and the doctrine of absurdity which were implicit as a possibility from the beginning.

The existentialists—the philosophers of striving—are philosophers of protest. Their inner quarrel is with history. They seek to arrest alienation and restore man to himself, or, at least, to illuminate the ways in which the individual can recapture his own existence. To do this, they find it is first necessary to admit without equivocation the conditions of modern life. They shared the rejection of mythology as authority for moral values and spurned the pretension that a logically persuasive moral structure could be constructed through scientific reason. The ascendancy of science itself heralded a world in which man and knowledge would become increasingly abstracted from the non-rational qualities which composed reality; in which, therefore, existence would be destroyed and the individual would become an object. "*In summa*," writes Nietzsche, "science is preparing a sovereign ignorance . . ."

However, one did not admit these realities in order to censure, but to welcome them as providing a historically unprecedented opportunity for each individual to discover and shape his own moral being—to attain freedom. "There is," wrote Nietzsche, "no place, no purpose, no meaning, on which we can shift the responsibility for our being, for our being thus and thus . . . this is a tremendous restorative; this constitutes the innocence of all existence."

Fundamentally, however, existentialism is not a response to the death of God or the power of science. It is a confrontation with the accelerating fragmentation of social life which is at the heart of the modern condition. This confrontation is often not explicit, but it is fundamental to all existentialist thought, it is the historical reason for existentialism. Almost unanimously existentialists condemn "mass man," the "herd" and the "public"—the congeries of individuals coerced into conformity by the authority of institutions and ideologies. By mistaking private liberty for freedom, the individual is condemned to mediocrity of spirit and to enslavement. Kierkegaard writes: "The individual no longer belongs to God, to himself, to his beloved, to his art or to his science, he is conscious of belonging in all things to an abstraction to which he is subjected by reflection, just as a serf belongs to an estate. . . . The levelling process is not the action of an individual but . . . an abstract power . . . a demon called up over whom no individual has any power, and though the very abstraction of levelling gives the individual a momentary selfish kind of enjoyment, he is at the same time signing the warrant for his own doom."

Moreover, Kierkegaard explains, the process is irreversible: "It is quite impossible for the community or the idea of association to save our age. . . . Nowadays the principle of association . . . is not positive but negative . . . the principle of association, by strengthening the individual, enervates him; it strengthens numerically, but ethically that is a weakening. It is only after the individual has acquired an ethical outlook in face of the whole world, that there can be any suggestion of really joining together."

Existentialists are united in the conviction that the individual cannot recapture his alienated existence through association with his fellows; although many do not participate in Kierkegaard's overtone of regret. All see this "fact" as a sometimes painful, but necessary condition for achievement of the highest freedom. It was even possible to rejoice in isolation as providing the necessary condition for self-realization. Stripped of assistance from religion or society, the discovery, definition and attainment of freedom had become a task for man alone—for The Individual: In all the universe, on that rock only, could belief be founded. "Thus we have neither behind us, nor before us in a luminous realm of values," writes Sartre, "any means of justification or excuse. We are left alone without excuse."

Through the rich diversity of existentialist thought run the key words of individual exertion: "striving," "choice," "overcoming," "will," "commitment." The acts and choices of the individual create the moral drama; each deed another stroke of the sculptor's chisel, altering and defining inward form. The Way can be revealed only through the decision, the commitment, the striving of a free and fearless will. Not the will of rational man, but the whole man— passionate, sensible, aware and anguished by his awareness. "What our age lacks is not reflection but passion," aphorized Kierkegaard. Two World Wars and multitudinous horrors later, we can safely conclude that is not the problem of our own age. But, then, we also lack Kierkegaard's faith that the "inward leap" would terminate in the arms of God.

For many of the existentialists this principle was the path to self-discovery, leading to one's own existence and, through that doorway, to existence itself. Some believed that freedom was not a goal, but consisted in struggle itself, in defiance and negation. We are not here concerned with existentialism as a means of understanding the human condition, but its value as a guide to social action, i.e., those acts of the individual which have consequence for others. Here the latent difficulties of existentialism are obvious. How can one give moral sanction to the unrestrained individual will without also legitimizing the most monstrous evils? And beyond good and evil is the problem of social order without the shared standards which permit, for example, works of existentialist philosophy to be published, distributed and read.

For the most part, the leading figures of existentialist thought are deeply committed to virtue, and some regarded themselves as spiritual leaders. Their resolution of the problem of social action can be grouped into three general forms, although in so doing we must be unjust to the subtleties and intellectual energy of this multiform philosophy. All striving is not "existential"; the individual or existential act or choice is that of one who has liberated himself from external constraints and inner restraints or weaknesses, who has come to terms with suffering and despair, who has learned, in Nietzsche's phrase, to "love fate," however cruel or whimsical it might appear.

In the presence of God, the steadfast pursuit of the inward search leads to a religious existence where the individual would find himself in relation to the Divine. The journey must be solitary, but finite man could not make the transition to his juncture with the infinite without divine assistance. The religious existence would contain its own morality.

Since most existentialists rejected not only mythology but the existence of God, they were forced to seek other forms of resolution; either by erecting the existential process itself into a moral imperative or first principle, or by asserting the reality of some form of psychic unity, i.e., a fixed element of human nature necessarily revealed by the inward search and which would guide the life of those who had become free. It is often difficult to discover which of these choices are being made amid the poetic abstraction which characterizes much of existentialism.

Sartre's essay *Existentialism Is a Humanism* exemplifies the first of these secular possibilities (although it also intimates the second): ". . . once man has seen that values depend upon himself . . . he can will only one thing, and that is freedom as the foundation of all values . . . And in thus willing freedom we discover that it depends entirely upon the freedom of others and that the freedom of others depends on our own." That freedom which is spur and goal of the existential search becomes a moral command.

Those who state that existential existence *must* have certain consequences for the individual's relationship with others are issuing a moral command. Any such necessity is an external value even if it is incorporated into the description of existentialism or the definition of a free existence. Unless, that is, the social acts of the individual are dictated by human nature, by the structure of existence.

Nietzsche's will to power can be interpreted as an example of this second, more biological, form of secular resolution: "A table of virtues hangs over every people. Behold, it is the table of its overcomings; behold, it is the voice of its will to power. Praiseworthy is whatever seems difficult to a people; whatever seems indispensable and difficult is called good; and . . . the rarest, the most difficult—that they call holy." This conclusion is not drawn from an analysis of comparative history. "Only where there is life, there is also will: not will to life but . . . will to power . . . *Thus life taught me.*" (italics mine.) The revaluation of all values rested on a description of human nature, a science of man. This interpretation is fortified by Nietzsche's conviction that it would be necessary to breed a superior race in order to liberate the will to power for its highest expressions.

It is possible not to resolve the problem of right conduct at all—by not regarding it as a problem. One can maintain it is for the individual to strive, choose and commit, regardless of the consequences for others, unless he also freely wills those consequences. Few existentialists are willing to grant such unbridled sanction. But the temper and attitude of most existential writing implies that much of what we have called moral would have to yield to the individual in search of freedom or of "becoming." That implication intrudes itself on even the most abstract and mildly conceived works because it emanates from the premises of the philosophy. It is of the existence of existentialism; contained in the concept of an individual who can end alienation, either in achievement or through struggle, only in isolation, without guidance, authority or help. On this affirmation each of the existentialist teachers has tried to build a superstructure of moral hope. But a morality of right conduct is not possible without some authority whose origin is external to the individual—the religious life, the scientific description of human nature, or a moral imperative. And so, inevitably, the superstructure is shattered by the force of its own first principle.

This failure is not one of intellect or wisdom. For the problem the existentialists set themselves was not one of philosophy. Dostoevsky, Kierkegaard and Nietzsche apprehended the onrushing forces of the modern world with prophetic clarity. The estrangement of individuals from each other and from themselves, complementing the growth of coercive authority, was transforming social man into mass man, a people into the "public," which arises, Kierkegaard says, "when the sense of association in society is no longer strong enough to give life to concrete realities." Amid the splintered remains of common life the defiant individual would end his own alienation. However, the existence to be recaptured is also social existence. Man alone—non-social man—is a mystical abstraction, a fiction of desire. Modern alienation cannot be overcome by even the most heroic exertion of individual will. It is the consequence of social structure and economic process which can only be altered by a common effort. These cannot be thought or willed out of existence.

Since it cannot recapture social existence—mistaking alienation as an inward bond—the freedom existentialism offers is illusion, whose phantasmic qualities are betrayed by the tone of this philosophy. One would expect the liberated will to be expansive, joyful in creation. But with rare exceptions the expressions used to give form and atmosphere to striving are the most cheerless of all philosophy: sickness, dread, anguish, suffering, fear and trembling. These are not the feelings of power and freedom.

We can perceive existentialism as itself an aspect of the fragmenting individualism whose consequences it defies and seeks to overcome; as a secular offspring of that mysticism which has accompanied scientific reason throughout the modern evolution. To say this, however, is only to say that, like all philosophies, it is a historical creation, a fact which does not entitle us to discard its analysis or its message. The existential spirit of resistance, of willed defiance and negation, is necessary to those who wish to change social realities and recapture social existence. And by imposing a personal, existential responsibility for freedom on each individual it states a condition which, in our time, must precede the creation of a common purpose.

Moreover, the affirmations of existentialism reveal the spirit of modern oppression. Dread of choice and the anguish of decision tell of the sickness of the world. The man who is sane and well and strong does not spend his hopes and energies on a search for health. What then of those who "in fear and trembling" require that men should choose and act out of the freedom of their individual will. In former times men did not ask God for what they already possessed.

As the Roman Empire moved toward collapse, Plotinus counseled men to embark on an inward search for "a nobler principle than anything we know as Being; fuller and greater; above reason, mind, and feeling; conferring these powers, not to be confounded with them." "But how is this to be accomplished? Cut away everything." It was not until the city of Rome had been sacked that philosophy built the City of God. Nevertheless, as the "dark ages" came to an end these philosophies of collapse entered into the work of reconstruction.

> Likewise the absurd man, when he contemplates his torment, silences all the idols. . . . The absurd man says yes and his effort will henceforth be unceasing. If there is a personal fate, there is no higher destiny, or at least there is but one which he concludes is inevitable and despicable. . . . At that subtle moment when man glances backward over his life, Sisyphus returning toward his rock, in that slight pivoting he contemplates the series of unrelated actions which becomes his fate, created by him, combined under his memory's eye and soon sealed by his death. Thus, convinced of the wholly human origin of all that is human, a blind man eager to see who knows that the night has no end, he is still on the go. The rock is still rolling.
>
> Camus, *The Myth of Sisyphus*

> The world is not absurd, only incomprehensible.
> Absurdity is the modern term for mystery. But it is also a judgment—men are not what we would have them be. It is helpful, as it adds to understanding or tempers arrogance. It is disastrous, as it persuades us to the reality of present reality. A living Sisyphus is a slave. The absurdity man experiences is but the self-created logic of his circumstances. Only a God creates true absurdity, for it can consist only in relation to divinity.

In the centuries since the Enlightenment the prospect of a rational science of man has been more widely and intensely reflected in theories of social organization than have the philosophies of striving. But we have discovered no "science of man"; few any longer believe we will; and most men of sensibility would now regard the prospect with dread. The "Palace of Crystal" has become a vision of the layrinths of Hell. The alternative philosophies of striving imply that man retains his powers and the possibility of freedom, despite the growth of an enfolding apparatus of coercion, thus diverting awareness and defiance from the external sources of oppression. Marx's dictum that "the ideas of the ruling class are, in every age, the ruling ideas" can be rephrased as: The ideas which protect the ruling institutions and forces are, in this age, the ruling ideas. Indeed, if the evolution of society continues along present lines one can expect the ideology of individualism to be drained of its active principle; finally, to define freedom as being unhindered in one's private life without the obligation to choose, commit or act. Let us not be molested within our cells.

CHAPTER 9

This being an appropriate moment for diversion, I offer the following monograph to caution author and reader alike, and as a reminder that if one looks through the object lens of a telescope (rather than the eyepiece, as is customary) one seems to see to the very origin of things, no matter where the instrument is pointed.

COOKING IS THE CONNECTION

In the days before prehistoric tribalism the human race was one large family innocent of ethnic differences and dynastic rivalries. Bound together in defense against common enemies such as dinosaurs, if men killed each other it was only for the meat. Such a relatively idyllic existence was only possible because men and women alike (obviously there was no need of a division of functions —not yet) ate their food raw. Whenever they found an edible plant or killed an animal they just sat right down, bit in, chewed and swallowed. *Everywhere was their home, not somewhere. Everybody was their neighbor, not somebody.* This exemplifies the racio-genetic-id-type memory behind that passage in the book of Genesis when the Hebrew God tells Adam (the first man), "Of every tree of the garden thou mayest freely eat." Every tree, not just some trees. Clearly "the garden" means the whole earth (no other place is mentioned until, significantly, later), nor is it pure coincidence that the name of the garden was "Eden."

Sometime, we don't know exactly when, in what we might call the blissful prepreparation era, a careless anthropoid dropped a piece of meat into a fire. This man (or woman) who literally held the whole future of the race in his hand took a bite of it, liked it and then, still imbued with the humane spirit of prehistoric (pre-preparatory) camaraderie, generously offered a bite to his companions. The primal act had been consummated. Cooking began, and with it, the descent of man.

What happened next should be obvious, once you grasp the principle. If you wanted to cook you needed fire. One could hardly postpone eating until a lightning bolt struck a nearby tree, and, of course, no one in those days had matches. (The invention of the ignitable stick, or match, was to be a far-reaching consequence of cooking.) The only solution was to keep a fire going at all times. This required a place (to keep the fire) and a person (to tend the fire). Obviously the male, by virtue of his distinctive anatomy, was more likely to be burned if he stuck around a low fire all day. So either from compulsion or out of generosity (the initial stimulus is of trivial historical interest whatever its psychological implications for modern moralists), the female was placed in charge of the cooking fire. In this fashion began, not only the "home" (a variant of "hearth" or "place of fire") but also the family (a variant of "famished"). It was most economical to increase the number of fires and divide the eaters into the smallest possible units: The one who got the food, or man; and the one who cooked it, or woman.

The age of rhapsodic innocence had come to an end. Man who had once looked only outward and onward—what I call dispero-oriented—now became "centro-oriented." Since he could not go too far and still make it back to fire and family, he quickly became range-limited as well as centro-oriented. Clearly, it was easier to stay in one place rather than move the fire. So our range-limited, centro-oriented man settled down, and groups of such families became known as settlements, then villages and finally countries. Freedom was traded for cooking.

Cooking not only created society but forever altered the structure of human thinking, feeling, perception and everything else too—and not, one might add, for the better. It radically mutated man's concept of space and process (which combines things and time, for a process is what happens to things—and people too, as a species of thing—through time). His focus on the largeness of outdoors became refocused on the smallness of indoors which was now both the terminus of his day (time) and the site of his fundamental animal act (eating). Previously, killing and eating had been just animal acts and the only variations were those provided by nature or physical endowment—you killed and ate what you could find depending on luck (nature's bounty) or individual speed and strength (natural and physical faculties). This was still true, of course, but only of killing, not of eating. For cooking was a human (or non-animal) act, and involved "technique," which merely means that different ways of doing things give different satisfactions. From rather rudimentary variations (such as rare or well done) man rapidly evolved an almost infinite variety of "preparations" or foods.

More important in the long run than the changes in cooking (although these must have seemed paramount at the time) was the shift to "technique-mindedness," the application of thought to physical materials in order to produce a desired result. Unfortunately, the only kind of thought that seemed to work with cooking was rational thought. Once people began to reason about food, it stood to reason (or seemed to) that that was the way to think about things of lesser importance. Reason was produced by technology ("technique") and not the other way around. And this new techno-reason tended to be self-fortifying, as dramatically illustrated by the invention of the printing press, a direct consequence of techno-reason, i.e., cooking, which in turn made it possible to spread new recipes to huge areas and thereby strengthen the already dominant orientation toward preparation.

Thus, our centro-oriented, range-limited, technique-minded man sacrificed his random communion with nature and what I call the "other" (meaning men and women) for an inward, cave-dwelling techno-reason. The fatal flaw, of course, was that the intellectual product of cooking was reason, and reason just happened to be the only form of thinking that could be, indeed begged to be, carried to a "logical conclusion." That conclusion is all around us.

Our preparatory man, being centro-oriented, created the family which not only provided the spatial limits which insulated men from their natural environment, but which, more importantly, initiated the division of functions and specializations which was to be the core of future economic, social and techno-rational development. Almost incidentally it also led to the subordination of woman, since the outdoors was still retained as a racio-genetic-id-type-remembered cachet of moral superiority, and outdoors was now the man's place, not hers.

Range-limitation naturally created different places for what had previously only been different people, and the two concepts became assimilated so that a person was (also) where he was. This led to a feeling that people who were somewhere else weren't people, for how could they be, since they weren't here; a sense which the psychiatrists have correctly identified as a limitation of identity or, more precisely, an "exclusive" identity rather than an "inclusive" identity.

As our early preparatory man calmly, even joyously, munched his barbecued predator, the foundations of tribal rivalries, or what I call "inter-human" struggles, and finally of the nation-state itself were being laid by the inexorable bricklayer of history. At the same time his "technique-mindedness" (with its consequent "techno-reason") blazed the inevitable "logically conclusive" trail to the computer, and all that means.

Let me momentarily digress to make the (perhaps self-evident, but you never know what people are thinking) point that the above history definitively disposes of some recently faddish theories of humano-social evol-revol-ution. As a sci-scholar, I am forced to recognize that whether these theories are right or wrong is irrelevant to their intellectual-moral-academic importance. They are, after all, insights; and as such are automatically heuristic, i.e., they teach us a lot even if in error. But as a purely practical matter, they are wrong, irrelevant and grossly misleading. Some, for example, have said that everything is sex. It hardly takes a moment's thought to see that everything *isn't* sex. At least this theory, unlike some others I could and will name, does relate things to a biological fact, i.e., sex. Nevertheless, it puts the cart before the horse, or, to use a less mechanical and more anatomical metaphor (which is more appropriate since we can at least admit that sex came before carts), it put the tail before the front. For although cooking was a derivative of eating, it soon became assimilated to mastication itself. Cooking *was* eating (or the only form of eating that was practiced, which amounts to the same thing). It is possible, indeed common, to eat without sex. But sex without eating is impossible, except for short and historically trivial intervals. Employing the tested "priority-oriented" approach (what comes first often causes what comes second, but what comes second can never cause what comes first), we see that cooking is more seminal than sex.

Many recent popularizers have found it significant that man is the sole creature who kills members of the same species, and not just for food. What has been overlooked is the fact that man is also the only creature who cooks. Using again our indispensable priority-oriented approach, we can see that cooking and eating are more basic than killing. In point of fact, you can't kill if you don't eat. Ipso facto, cooking comes before killing and has to be its cause. Most animals have to kill and eat right away or the food would spoil. This was also true of our prepreparatory man. Once he developed the cooking skill, however, it was no longer necessary, or even desirable, to eat right away. He could kill now and eat later. This meant he no longer had to co-ordinate his killing with periods of hunger, which, as we have seen, led to the possibilities of economic organization, specialization of function and even professional killers who later evolved into farmers.

Unfortunately, the old killing instinct—once so necessary to survival—remained. With clocklike regularity it would surge forward at "bio-instinctive hunger intervals." So men killed even though they no longer needed the meat, and since it seemed absurd to kill animals if you were not going to eat them, they began to kill each other. Naturally, this impulse was greatly reinforced by the new centro-oriented range-limitation—which, sadly, had fused the concepts of "person" and "place"—meaning they no longer thought of each other as each other if they were in different places.

Frankly, I don't think much of using literature to support scientific theories. After all, most literature was, in fact, written by someone: either by a particular person or a group of persons. (In fact, that is not a bad definition of literature, but it is not my field.) And one must always ask oneself of such a person, "What did he know anyway?" Indeed, this question is probably more important in literature than with other kinds of writing. Science naturally has other traditions which, if not quite so delightful, are more rigorous. I must admit, however, there is a body of thought (given impetus by the now discredited sex theorists who were inclined to identify the pen as a pseudophallus. One wonders how they explain the typewriter!) which maintains that even though literary artists don't know anything, once in a while they unconsciously, i.e., accidentally, hit on something that is so. That is also true of everyone else, but the difference, undeniably an important difference, is that they write it down. In later years when a sci-scholar makes a discovery there is usually someone around to point to an old book and say, "Look, he thought of it first, only he wasn't conscious of it." Thus is born the prophetic mystery of art.

Nevertheless, the literature-oriented technique had proved useful to other sci-scholars in eliciting the quite important "veracity response" (belief by ordinary people, or popularity). I determined to try it, and having done so, was not surprised to find the results completely irrefutable. For the simplest exegesis uncovered "preparation" history lucidly embedded, not in the works of a few fashionable or merely modern writers, but in the ultimate fount myths of mankind; the spiritual literature of Judaeo-Christian-German religion, and the rational legends of Greece.

Why is Adam driven from Paradise? For eating. Moreover, he suffers the great fall of man for eating the fruit from only one tree which is, not coincidentally, the only *forbidden* tree in Eden. There are but two kinds of food—cooked and uncooked. In Eden there were two kinds of trees: forbidden (one) and permitted (all the rest). The simplest application of a rudimentary-category correspondence proves that the fruit of the forbidden tree was cooked—the sole distinguishing factor between this and the other, permitted fruits. Now we can understand why, in the legend, Eve (woman) hands Adam the apple; for, as we have seen, fate (or fire) had made woman the cook. And, as if to make sure the point is clear, when driven from Eden, their return is forever barred by a flaming sword—the primal fire and the symbol of the skewer which held the meat. It is as if the legend says to us: "For cooking ye have been forever thrust out, and by cooking shall thy return be barred."

The same motif recurs in the shaping myths of the pagan rationalists: The chief god is Zeus and his weapon to chastise and destroy the disobedient is, as we could have predicted, the lightning bolt, the very bolt which ignited that fateful fire into which the first raw and dripping meat was to fall. The punishment of Zeus indeed! The burden of cooking was too much even for this Olympian master to bear, hence the shifting of blame to Prometheus. Only the mightiest of gods could have set the seminal cooking fires ablaze, yet how could one worship such a god? The answer was Prometheus.

Were this the entire story one could hazard little but despair. For centro-oriented, range-limited, technique-minded man has relentlessly proceeded down the path of techno-reason—following cooking wherever it led—until with the advent of fission and fusion, he has finally developed the ability to cook himself, and on the grand scale indeed. Yet there is some hope after all! For while man's cooking or "preparatory powers" have reached new heights, we can also witness the faint pulse of a new postpreparatory age. Techno-reason, it appears, may contain the seed of its own destruction. The same technique-minded approach that gave us the airplane and the revolver is also making possible frozen and instant foods, television dinners and precooked food in cans. In other words, we are creating a new (and yet prelapsarian) world of eating without cooking. The development, for example, of the TV, or precooked, dinner exerted an irresistible compulsion to fill the now-deserted cooking or preparatory space: and thus television was invented, taking its name from the food which had made it possible. That very postpreparatory television helps even further to break down the old centro-oriented barriers. As we look at a set we can begin again to feel atavistic stirrings. It seems almost to say again: *Everywhere is our home, not somewhere. Everybody is our neighbor, not somebody.*

The astronauts, our supreme technique-minded men, eat food from little plastic tubes; as if man had to go to another world to escape the primal curse of this one. Yet as life becomes more and more frozen, instant, prepackaged, pop-in-and-serve, or unwrap and serve (which is even better, at least for our purposes), men and women alike (for they will be alike in such a dawning new age) will again be free to wander, to re-establish their brotherhood with their fellow eaters. Centro-orientation and range-limitation will give way to disperso-orientation, techno-reason to mystical consumption, and the human species may yet win the race between cooking and survival in a way that no one envisioned—through the elimination of cooking itself. Once it seemed cooking and eating were here forever. Now we can say—eating, yes; cooking, maybe.

PART III

FURTHER INQUIRY INTO THE MEANING
OF FREEDOM—RELATIONSHIPS BETWEEN
HISTORICAL CONSCIOUSNESS, LOSS OF
INDIVIDUAL POWER AND THE MODERN
ECONOMY

Adventure most unto itself
The Soul condemned to be—
Attended by a single Hound
Its own identity.

Emily Dickinson

INCIDENT AT KENNEBUNK

A newspaper account recorded the angered dismay of the citizenry of Kennebunk, Maine, upon arising one morning to find that the town's Centennial Plot—a remnant of the original village green— had been "removed by state highway crews to make way for new traffic islands." Outrage provoked an inquiry which established that the removal was pursuant to a state highway project approved not too long ago by the town citizens themselves. The green was the most important and visible link with the Kennebunk past, having been enjoyed and admired by more than five generations. It was maintained by a special trust fund established in 1920. And in recent years, a display of flowers had been continually renewed by a town museum entrusted with the nostalgic bequest of the late Colonel Harry A. Naples. It was gone before anyone even noticed. However, the paper tells us, the decision of the town selectmen to request "grassed-over islands rather than the hard-topped type" was expected to "ease the situation—if the grass plots are approved by the state Highway Commission."

Who destroyed the Centennial Plot?

Not the highway crew. They only followed instructions. Most of them weren't even from Kennebunk. Not the voters of Kennebunk. They merely approved a recommendation for a new road to ease the obviously congested traffic on its way to other parts of

Maine. Although the engineering plans were on file in the engineer's office at the state capital of Augusta—about eighty miles away—they did not appear on any ballot. Nor could many have understood them if they had. In any event, the subsequent protest clearly proves that the citizens would have rejected the design had they been aware of its consequence.

The state Highway Commission was not responsible. It was only carrying out its assigned task to draw up plans for new roads which, according to conclusive studies, would benefit the entire area. Having submitted recommendations, they thereafter acted as the faithful agent of the expressed popular will. Moreover, since the particular engineer involved was from Bangor—at the other end of the state—he could hardly be expected to know of the passion and nostalgia attached to that one plot of grass, so like a thousand others on his surveys. The construction of this particular highway was stimulated and assisted by federal funds flowing from that vast and visionary federal highway program, initiated by President Eisenhower. Without these funds it would never have been built. Was it then President Eisenhower who destroyed Kennebunk's Centennial Plot? It seems unduly harsh to blame a man who may never even have heard of Kennebunk, and whose program, moreover, was the only logical response to the enormous postwar boom in automotive transportation. (Statistics reveal that, if they want to, the entire American population can fit into the front seats of its automobiles.) Perhaps we are now getting closer. There would have been no highway program without all the cars and thus—as radical theory predicts—the villains must be General Motors, Ford and Chrysler. The managers of these companies, however, would immediately counter any such accusation by pointing out that they built cars only because people wanted to buy them; acting as the admittedly well-paid economic servants of a free people making a free choice. The argument is unanswerable.

Yet common sense tells us that the millions of people who, year after year, drove their new acquisitions from a dealer's lot did not want to destroy the Centennial Plot. Clearly they didn't mean to. Had a poll been taken, and the issue explained, a majority would probably have supported preservation. Yet when they put their signature on a bill of sale, they helped initiate events which ultimately evoked the futile anger of a Maine town. It was that movement of circumstances, known as "the system," which forever erased the fine old Kennebunk Centennial Plot.

CHAPTER 1

We began by characterizing freedom as the use and fulfillment of our humanity to the outer limits fixed by the material conditions and capacity of the time. We saw that freedom requires that the individual regain control over the conditions of his own social existence, that the purposes toward which he expends his vitality and powers not be fixed by an external authority. Nevertheless, freedom is not possible within a society whose members pursue personal desires in conflict with the general well-being. Within such a society, increasingly powerful coercive forces are developed. A reconciliation between the imperatives of freedom—between individual mastery and social purpose—is only possible if the society is not external to the individual, that is, if he contains and is contained by the existence of his fellows.

We have seen that the identity of medieval man was constituted of relationships—with others, with a place, with a way of life and with a divine order. If the medieval artist did not sign his work it was not from excessive humility but because he viewed himself as the agent of a collective humanity. Contemporary Chinese must similarly regard themselves as being composed, in part, of social relations. What we regard as their submission or sacrifice, they view as rational behavior, since from within their own conception of self to defy the social order is to assault one's own existence.

THE AMERICAN CONDITION   141

Plato's belief that the greatest social good was a "bond of unity" found a modern expression in the goals of utopian communism. Even though labor is set by external circumstances, Marx explained, within a true community "the overcoming of such obstacles may itself constitute an exercise in liberty, and . . . these external purposes lose their character of mere rational necessities and are established as purposes which the individual himself fixes. The result is the self-realization and objectification of the subject, therefore real freedom, whose activity is precisely labor."

The unalienated existence which is the first principle of freedom requires a society whose members have recaptured awareness of their social nature. The "bond of unity" is the only vehicle through which man can assert his own power against the power of the institutions he has created. Within that bond the freely established purposes of the individual can be at one with the purposes of his fellows. "There is no truth more thoroughly established," writes Washington, "than that there exists in the economy and course of nature an indissoluble unity between virtue and happiness."

The conditions of our society make it difficult to imagine a reconciliation between individual liberty and social purpose which is not imposed. But our awareness that such a bond of unity is possible, that it has had a historical existence, advances inquiry into the meaning of freedom. The "humanity" we seek to fulfill conceals an ambiguity.

Our awareness of who and what we are, including the nature of our connection to other human beings and to the physical world, may be incomplete or distorted. The self we believe ourselves to be, our conception of our own nature—of the nature of human existence—may exclude important qualities of that existence; which, being excluded from awareness, cannot be expressed in behavior, value or desire. Therefore, the self we perceive may differ from the self whose fulfillment is freedom. That perception of self we will call consciousness. Consciousness is formed and modified by changing social realities, i.e., it is historical. Important elements of individual consciousness are widely shared throughout the society and constitute the consciousness of the age. That consciousness is formed and modified by changing social realities, i.e., it is historical. Important elements of individual consciousness are

widely shared throughout the society and constitute the consciousness of the age.

The definition of "consciousness" as a self-perception which
may not be coextensive with the qualities and attributes of existence contains the assertion that there is a human nature* which
is not totally the creation of historical circumstance as mediated
through personal experience. That nature includes, and is partly
defined by, an undivided union with others. It is both individual
and shared. This description is not asserted as biological fact (although I believe it has a genetic base), but as providing useful
categories to contrast the modern consciousness with the possibilities of human existence.

"Man is a social animal," "man's existence is social existence"
—assertions as old as recorded introspection—do not mean that
individuals prefer to be with others or that, as a matter of historical
record, people have always lived in groups. They express the
sensed reality that existence apart from society is inconceivable.
The conditions for the development of the intellect, for the fac-
ulty of being human evolved not from the clash of the individual
with the environment, but from the common effort of a group to
master that environment. The ability of our evolutionary predecessors to multiply their powers by sharing the problems of survival
was the harbinger of man. Human evolution was itself a social
process. Man was the creation of society. All we know of biology
and evolution instructs us that the essential qualities which lead
from one species to another are inbuilt and not learned. Shared
existence is part of the definition of man.

The social nature of existence is evidenced by the process
through which we establish our individual identity. William
James wrote: "A man's character is discernible in the mental or
moral attitude in which, when it came upon him, he felt himself
most deeply and intensely alive. At such moments there is a voice

---

* Were this not so, then "consciousness" and "self" would be synonyms. In our
present state of knowledge, the existence of a human nature which is not totally
the creation of historical circumstances, i.e., of personal experience, must be assumed to be grounded in our biological heritage. That assumption, however, results
from the current domination of scientific method and reason. We need not accept
it as necessity. Nor do we need such support for our use of the terms "consciousness" and "self," as categories useful to the analysis of social existence.

inside which speaks and says: This is the real me." James's words "active" and "alive" are words of power. Yet this innermost, uniquely individual power can only be developed in association with other human beings and, for nearly everyone, must be renewed through continuing association. Individuality has its genesis in relationships. One becomes aware of one's own existence because others recognize that existence.

If there is an inward, purely physiological or genetic perception of existence it must be very weak. There are case studies of children who were petted and pampered, but as objects, as dolls; not in response to their expressed desires but as an exercise of the mother's will. In other experiments baby monkeys have been raised with wire dummies instead of a mother. As a result they were catatonic, and often developed other forms of psychosis. These tests illustrate the need for warmth and love. But they also show the need for recognition and response, an affirmation that what is felt within has an external reality. The need for affirmation never completely disappears. We may become less vulnerable, more in control of ourselves, but even the strongest identities must be reconfirmed through the recognition of others. Indeed, as our identities ramify through time, the need for recognition becomes more particular and sometimes more intense. We always seek confirmation that we are. But what we are, or what we perceive ourselves to be, takes on the burden of social expectations, historical conditions and our own evolving qualities and fears. One person may seek recognition of skill or of amiability, another of kindness or strength, still another of his capacity to make money or love. This is because certain qualities have come to dominate our conception of ourselves or have even become coextensive with that conception. The process is the only alternative to permanent infancy, while those denied confirmation are capable of the most extreme and murderous revenge.

"The basis of man's life is two-fold," wrote Martin Buber, "and it is one—the wish of every man to be confirmed as what he is, even as what he can become, by men; and the innate capacity in man to confirm his fellow men in this way . . . actual humanity exists only where this capacity unfolds." This is not a neurotic weakness or an unfortunate flaw in nature. It is an attribute of our humanity, implicit in the reality that existence is social existence. William James wrote: "No more fiendish punishment could be devised, even were such a thing physically possible, than that one should be turned loose in society and remain absolutely unnoticed by all the members thereof."

History and shared experience afford additional evidence for the reality of social existence. There are, for example, judgments as to the attributes of human virtue and the satisfying life which recur throughout millennia of social change. The bonds which link such judgments must, in large part, be composed of persistent and enduring features of human nature. These same constancies explain why we can respond to artists who speak to us across thousands of years, even from the cave homes of unfolding humanity. "Surely it is strange," writes Aristotle, "to make the supremely happy man a solitary . . . since man is a political creature and one whose nature is to live with others." Again, "The state is by nature clearly prior to the family and to the individual, since the whole is of necessity prior to the part; . . . if the whole body be destroyed there will be no foot or hand . . . A social instinct is implanted in all men by nature . . ." "He who is unable to live in society . . . must be either a beast or a God."

This social self is part of the definition of the human species, as are, for example, the capacity for speech and the opposition of thumb and fingers. The idea of the self discussed here can perhaps be clarified by a metaphor drawn from our knowledge of animal behavior, i.e., the social role of bees. The bee as liberated and autonomous individual does not exist. Social role and function are as much a part of being a bee as wings or an addiction to honey. They are the essence of bee-ness. (Yet we must be cautious about the analogy. For the most part the behavior of animals is a consequence of instincts—of innate structure—whose influence on activity cannot be eliminated by an exclusion from awareness.)

To Freud, the instinctual foundation of human life was compounded of Eros and the destructive instinct. The aim of the first is "to establish ever greater unities . . . to bind together." The aim of the second "is to undo connections and so to destroy things." We can view both as different aspects of the drive toward fusion which is evoked by social nature, a drive which can lead to union or, in pathological intensity, to the extinction of the self. The internal dialogue, therefore, would not be between life and death, but between the desire to preserve one's identity and the drive to dissolve it in the common existence.

The barrier to fusion is a fact. "The central law of all organic life," wrote D. H. Lawrence, "is that each organism is intrinsically isolate and single in itself. The moment its isolation breaks down, and there comes an actual mingling and confusion, death sets in." We can never be so intimately joined that our experience is the same as that of others. Even at the most primitive level the body will fight to its own death to reject the intrusive transplantations of another's flesh or organs. The merger of sense, experience and intellect is inconceivable.

The urge toward fusion must always collide with this fact of individuality. They are both basic and irreconcilable; their clash forever restraining man from that fulfillment of freedom which we can vaguely sense would be possible to a harmonious soul. The best we can achieve is a transient accommodation. And since we are moved, not by things, but by processes, any balance is precarious, soon overturned and must be renewed. The state of the confrontation between these elements of existence is the foundation of historical consciousness. To the extent either is denied or subordinated our consciousness is incomplete. We perceive ourselves to be something different and less than we are. Yet, however valuable as description, the relationship between consciousness and self does not "cause" the human condition at any moment in history. That relationship is an aspect of the human condition, which is itself a consequence of the social process. The fixed qualities of the self, what it is to be human, can tell us what life ought to be like, or what it could be like, but not why things are as they are or how to change them. If the dominant consciousness excludes elements of existence, if it omits important aspects of human nature, then the completion necessary to freedom is not possible. In such a time to come to terms with realities is to submit to enslavement.

Consciousness is the basis for life and life style in any particular society. It is the link between the individual and the organization and behavior of society. The values and desires we express arise from consciousness. We want what we do because of the way in which we view ourselves, the way in which we experience our own existence.†

Awareness of hunger creates the desire for food; while the universal nature of this awareness creates agriculture. Occasionally, illness will obliterate awareness of the need for nourishment, resulting in malnutrition and even death. Similarly, awareness of self governs social action and belief. We are unlikely to seek nourishment for those attributes of self which are excluded from awareness. Since consciousness, unlike hunger, is the creation of social process, a deficiency in awareness is not an individual aberration but a universal affliction, making the consciousness of the time, however incomplete or distorted, appear to encompass the qualities and wants of existence.

It is, therefore, expectable that all the significant features of American society should display and fortify the modern consciousness—a consciousness dominated by a perception of the self as a wholly autonomous being whose relationships are, or should be, formed by a voluntary exercise of individual will. The disintegration of community, the decline of shared social purpose, the weakening identification between citizen and nation, and the rejection of moral authority superior to individual judgment or opinion are consequences and manifestations of the modern consciousness. If the links between consciousness and the economic process are less obvious, it is because they are more decisive and fundamental. The fragmentation of social existence, by weakening the social power of the citizen, enables the ruling institutions of a bureaucratic economy to direct society's resources toward their own aggrandizement. The means of this control are so extensive they often seem to be part of a natural economic order, as the foundation of production itself, rather than the supporting instruments of inefficient and oppressive economic relationships.

† Consciousness and not "instinct." Should one assume, for example, an inborn "aggressive instinct" it would not tell us why different societies, at different times, are warlike or peaceful, turbulent or stable. We have uncovered no mechanism which links assumed individual "drives" to the behavior of societies. For this reason the significant works of psychohistory are concerned with the study of individual lives. The most valuable of these works, Erikson's investigation of Luther, does not profess to explain the Reformation itself. We learn why Luther acted, but the tools of psychic analysis cannot tell us why the world responded. Indeed, we must assume that Luther as individual acted purposefully, in relationship to sensed possibilities of external response. His behavior was not only defiance, but an expression of the intuition that success might be possible.

Other parts of this book describe these relationships and the process which sustains them, including, for example, a structure of economic demand which limits satisfaction to wants which are individual in nature. Many of the material requisites of human fulfillment can be created only in response to a collective demand, based on shared values and desires. The inability to express such demand, or even to experience the common understanding which might evoke it, prevents us from choosing the conditions of freedom.

One can find examples, tokens, of this consciousness in aspects of life which seem to be far removed from the commanding sources of social power.

Love, the remaining summit of shared existence, is endangered by the growing belief that it can be separated from the commitment which alone can sustain it. Absent commitment, the shifting circumstances and inclinations experienced by every individual make more likely the destruction of the bonds within which feelings can mature into familiarity and a joined life. Every increase in the objects of choice must be paid for.

The consciousness of individualism is infected by a heightened terror of death. Death is no longer compensated for by the survival of generations, family or community. The fear is so great that the thought of personal death is suppressed, turned outward to outrage at the death of the world—animals, pollution, war. For the isolated individual the death of the world, or any part of it, is a metaphor for his own destruction.

Modern society's assault on the forms of life is also reflected in much of modern art. Art which would earlier have been thought outrageous is accepted with little resistance because the content is vitiated by forms which mirror our society. Forms which break with tradition do not dissent from a time at war with the idea of tradition. Formless assertions often bespeak the joys of slavery, identifying our cells as the chambers of freedom. A fashionable, i.e., widely accepted, culture always helps to describe the social realities which support it. This has been true of some of the greatest art. Indeed, it is the nature of art, and especially of literature, to be conservative. But if art is fashionable, however great, we can be sure that its forms do not clash with the forms of the age. At times Shakespeare's *King Richard II* displays aspects of Beckett's characters in *Waiting for Godot*. Futile in the face of doom, King

Richard alternates between foolish optimism, self-pity and tragic resignation. Shakespeare's characterization is crystallized from a living, organic society; Beckett's from that of man alone. Shakespeare says—"This is King Richard." Beckett says—"This is man." Shakespeare's spectator reacted to Richard. Beckett's spectator sees himself. Both dramatists evoked the approval of contemporaries because the form of their art reflects their world. It is Beckett who recalls the aphorism of Nietzsche: "Romantic pessimism, the last great event in the fate of our culture."

The culmination of social fragmentation is complete isolation. The modern truism that the experience of each individual is unique and can be known only to himself is a historical and not a biological fact. It is truer today than it was in the past. Indeed, since we now define experience as individual or internal, to assert that it is unique is either a tautology or a description of biochemistry. It is historical consciousness which determines the barriers between the self and others. Nor does individual isolation exhaust the possibilities of human fragmentation. It seems that an individual can be detached from his own experience—his past, his future, his environment, even his perceptions—to the extent that some portion of his existence is being lived by a stranger. Not long ago these would have been symptoms of insanity. Now we are not so sure. Madness is a form of awareness, and if that awareness— that way of conceiving oneself and the world—spreads throughout the society it becomes the way things are. Either madness becomes sanity, or the world becomes mad.

> . . . What does it advantage us to be familiar with the nature of animals, birds, fishes and reptiles, while we are ignorant of the nature of the race of men to which we belong, and do not know or care whence we come or whither we go.
>
> Petrarch (The Renaissance)

> Man is and must be, at the center of all things . . .
>
> Diderot (The Enlightenment)

> I'm a man.
>
> Prisoner's cry in Attica courtyard

CHAPTER 2

We can begin to trace the links between the modern consciousness and the rise of coercive authority by examining the individual's loss of power over his own social existence.

Today, nearly every significant social controversy contains an explicit demand for power. Most of the aggrieved still prefer to resolve their problem, to win, even if the decision is made by others. And despite all the debate and protest, very little power has been transferred. Yet, the tenacity of the issue intimates the most resistant sources of modern distress. Large issues of power always imply a demand for fundamental social change even if they are not perceived that way by the participants.

If only one man in a village has a productive farm, and if he can defend it, he will be powerful. Such an individual may decide to refuse power. But the more complex and impersonal interests which dominate our society do not have such a choice. Since the relationship between interests constitutes the structure of society, any effort to reallocate power is an attempt either to change these relationships or to ratify changes which have already occurred. When issues of power enter serious political debate, it means that new private relationships are seeking to replace the old. The fact of that contest does not alone tell us if the new interests will succeed or be repressed, but only that the social structure is being challenged.

Power as an explicit social issue not only unmasks the presence of contradiction, but leads us toward its source. The demands for social authority originate in the inward erosion of self-mastery; a sensed impotence which afflicts not merely the militant, but those who resist their demands along with that more numerous population which is indifferent to public issues. In order to demonstrate that this individual loss of self-mastery has external causes, it will help to define what is meant by "power."

Human life is social life, and all power is social power. Our faculties of thought, perception and imagination evolve through contact with an environment, ordered by the shared purpose and rules of society. Even when engaged upon mystic contemplation or extensive psychoanalysis, the individual is trying to modify the relationships to the external world which formed and tempered his consciousness. Human life can be enhanced only by modifying the relationships of society; by changing environment, beliefs, and the opportunities to extend one's capacities. Although social power can be possessed by institutions as well as individuals, the distribution of power—the content and manner of its exercise—can always be changed by living human beings. Anything that cannot be changed is not power at all, but fate. It follows that all social power has been, at some time, created and bestowed by men.

We therefore set aside those elements of our social existence which are irrevocable, for they are not power, even though they may guide and control its exercise. The fact that we must die determines the way we live, but the inevitability of death is not a manifestation of social power. Other fixed elements include our biological and genetic structure and those elements of our personal history whose consequences cannot yet be modified by doctors, plastic surgeons, psychiatrists, drugs or magic charms. We are also confined by the history of society. All present assertions of power are formed by inherited geography, institutions and ideologies.

History, however, is not fixed as biology is fixed. Take a very simple example—a road that now runs where a forest once grew. At one point in time a historian might analyze the road's importance, while the destruction of the forest would not enter his consciousness. At another point, the cutting of the trees would be part of the conquest of a continent. Later, perhaps today, it would be viewed as an exploitative desolation of the environment. Each generation must look at the past from its own time, imposing a new evaluation, its own moral judgment. We remake our past not only because of what we are but also to serve the purposes of the present. Economic history helped to create the age of modern materialism, but materialism also unveiled economic history.

Individuals can exercise social power they do not possess. It was not the power of the slaves that built the pyramids or sent galleys into battle. The man whose actions are dictated or constrained by another will is merely the vessel of power that is not his. The relationship between the power of institutions and ideologies and the men who exercise it is of the same quality.

The manager of a large American corporation must try to expand his activities and make a profit. He has no choice, for that is the nature of such a corporation. When an individual feels compelled to work for money beyond his true needs, then he has subordinated his own will to the economic process of making money and to the values which sustain it. The briefest reflection makes it clear that everyone is constrained and limited by values, social arrangements and the nature of institutions. Since only power can constrain and limit, these components of society possess power.

Although men are the source of all social power, they can bestow it on ideologies and institutions. And they always have. It is also true that values and institutions might be changed in ways which reduce or eliminate their social power. Economic systems can be leveled, religious beliefs can be denied, and leaders can be overthrown. The power once bestowed can be taken back, unless, of course, men have retained so little power that they lack the strength to end their servitude. The struggle to regain power—to diminish alienation—is always bitter and uncertain since it must contend against the men and institutions which rule society.

We can now define power as the capacity of man or his creations to influence social existence. More precisely, it is the capacity of any dynamic system or structure, including the individual, to influence social existence. To be "dynamic" is to possess a vitality, an autonomy, which permits change, development and growth. When institutions, beliefs or individuals begin to lose their dynamic capacities and become rigid or unresponsive, their power is in danger.

Nothing in the definition requires individuals to have power over others. The man who is in command of his own social existence is a man of power. And experience tells us that his mastery is a manifestation of power in its rarest, perhaps supreme, form. Nietzsche wrote: "I have found strength where one does not look for it: in simple, mild, and pleasant people, without the least desire to rule . . . the powerful natures dominate, it is a necessity, they need not lift one finger. Even if, during their time, they bury themselves in a garden house."

All delegations of power do not increase alienation. Freedom reconciles man's social existence with his isolate qualities. This reconciliation is not possible without authority. Suppose a poor country is in the midst of famine. It may require a strong central power to establish priorities among crops, assign tasks and allocate resources in order to avert widespread starvation. In this situation the unwilling worker is not deprived of his freedom. For freedom can never include the power to starve other members of the society. And in any society wealth must be produced if men are to be liberated from perpetual toil. The weak must be protected from the strong, the individual from the crowd. The power exercised by institutions and ideologies serves freedom only when they act as the instruments of human will. Only, that is, when they exercise power but do not possess it.

It can now be seen that power is essential to freedom. The man totally without power, were such a state possible, has no influence upon his own existence. He is an object. A person with very little power is a slave. *Yet power and freedom are not the same thing, and among their differences is one which is a source of immense misery and danger. For although institutions and ideologies can possess power, only men can be free.* The transfer of power from man to his social creations almost always involves a loss of freedom. Imagine power and freedom bound together like the atoms in a simple molecule, as they move from men to an institution. The institution, however, can absorb only the power, leaving the linked particle of freedom immobilized, without the possibility of return. This, of course, is but scientific metaphor for the process of alienation.

Alienation is the diminution of human life through man's subjection to his own creations—an enslavement which begins, Marx wrote, "when the life he has given to the object sets itself against him as an alien and hostile force." It is alienation of the self from

the self, the transfer of the individual's powers to a social authority which does not contain him. An external will displaces the
will of the individual, incorporating some portion of his existence.
To the extent one's existence belongs to another—to an individual
or to an institution—his wants are no longer his own even if they
are experienced as matters of personal urgency and desire. Indeed,
an apparent contentment despite submission to an external authority is evidence that wants emerge from, and are created by, the state
of alienation. Although modern society has avoided many of the
failures which Marx predicted, it has brought an alienation more
intense and pervasive than he could have conceived.

We can glimpse the sources of this alienation in countries which
are enacting our past. An official of the Indian Government describes his participation in the construction of a new steel mill:
"Each one of us was helping build the future—a future one could
almost see, touch, and feel . . . One also felt that the plant now
had a life and personality of its own—quite apart from the men who
worked for it—a being that demanded the best from us and also reward, fulfillment—not the inward satisfaction of mastery, but
flowing from the inanimate mill to grateful men." In India this
panegyric is idealistic while in America it would be regarded as
nonsense. No executive vice-president of IBM would praise his
computer plant as an "independent" personality that "demanded
the best" from him. Because the rule of the machine is far more
extensive in America than in India, such a statement is inadmis-
sible.

The condition of alienation has little to do with happiness or
despair. One is no less a servant if he accepts or even embraces the
conditions of servitude. Such acceptance means that the power
which coerces has been absorbed into the structure of the spirit,
transformed into an aspect of individual identity.

A high official of the Johnson administration finally came to
doubt the war policies of his President. Yet he carried them out.
That, after all, was his job. He did what the machinery commanded, not with lackluster resignation, but with great efficiency
and elan. No less was expected from a man of his reputation. But
the President had his own problems, and so he fired the official anyway. Although the man was discharged brutally and without warning, he did not let anyone know this because that would have been

to betray the system or hint at doubt of its wisdom. When he left there was a White House ceremony. The President who disliked, fired and humiliated him, gave him a medal. The man wept. They were not tears of shame.

Although the concept of alienation describes an undeniable phenomenon of social life, the process of alienation is still mysterious. How does an individual become alienated? In what way do the imperatives and values of governing social institutions supplant individual autonomy? There is no definitive answer, but the discoveries of Freud and his followers provide at least two analogies. The first is the development of the "superego," formed when the child internalizes the values and prohibitions of his parents and immediate environment, which then act to repress some of his own instincts. Many such values are derived from the dominant ideology, from historical circumstances. (Some may be a necessity of all social existence.) Most study of the superego has been directed toward those forms of internalization which help to repress sexual drives. There is no reason, however, why a similar process could not incorporate commands whose function is to adapt the individual to the social process; whose consequence is not repression but displacement of the latent possibilities of individual will by the social will.

The psychic mechanism of "transference" hints at a second and even more interesting possibility. That mechanism was uncovered in an effort to explain why a psychiatric patient often developed a strong emotional attachment, even one of subjection, to the analyst. This bond is created, in Freud's terminology, because the patient invests the analyst with some of his own "libido." For our purposes, the description might be rephrased to say that the patient tranfers, at least temporarily, some of his own life force to the analyst. In a literal sense he is, by transferring or relating his own existence, receiving a changed awareness of that existence. Unlike superego formation, transference seems possible at almost any stage of life. Similarly, the individual expends his vital energies in work. He invests the objects of labor—both his personal product and the institution which contains his work—with that energy, i.e., with some portion of his active existence. That transfer creates a bond of identity between the individual and the economic process which has incorporated part of his life. Unlike the relationship between a patient and an unusually skilled analyst, however, that which is transferred is not returned. The individual has become alienated.

Loss of the individual's capacity to control social existence is dangerous as well as enslaving. The future takes on new dimensions of uncertainty, generating fear. Such fear may produce irrational recklessness, but the fearful more often become withdrawn and defensive, glimpsing the possibility of fresh dislocations in every change.

More than a century ago, Nietzsche traced the links between powerlessness and dissolution. He prophesied the need of the impotent to find scapegoats and villains, and to seek out those to whom they could feel superior. Many an American can today be persuaded to find the enemy in big business or the military-industrial complex. Others see it among black militants or student revolutionaries. Even though there may be some truth to such suspicions, they do not increase our understanding of oppression. Men do exploit others, but often as agent rather than master. This fact is not a moral exculpation; a social truth can be a personal lie, an institutional necessity can be an individual sin. Although a modern Secretary of Defense must support the President's policies, a particular Secretary of Defense is personally responsible for his actions. However, this kind of moral judgment does not constitute social analysis. It substitutes the question "who?" for the question "why?"

"Only the *weak* man wishes to hurt and to see the sign of suffering," writes Nietzsche. Twentieth-century man has validated this insight on a titanic scale. Nietzsche also preaches that although "the desire for destruction, change, and becoming can be an expression of overfull . . . strength, it can also be the hatred of the misdeveloped, needy, underprivileged who destroy, who *must* destroy, because the existing and even all existence, all being, outrages and provokes him." The violence which has traditionally attended American social conflict has usually been related to a purpose, directed at identifiable adversaries. Today, especially in large cities, we inhabit an ambience charged with random anger; frequented by violent acts which seem to have no purpose other than to express that anger. And public leaders are assaulted by the prototypes of impotent humanity.

As individual power wanes, the desire for a renewal of confidence becomes more urgent. The effort to satisfy this desire only strengthens the sources of alienation as the individual first accepts the goals and values which are eroding his power, and then—having persuaded himself that these are his true needs—intensifies the pursuit. The process feeds on itself. Nietzsche wrote that "The means of the craving for power have changed, but the same volcano is still glowing . . . and what one did formerly 'for God's sake' one does now for the sake of money . . . which now gives the highest feeling of power." The "craving for power" is not the only motive for the pursuit of wealth or worldly success. And, except in rare instances, such success does not satisfy the need for power. Indeed, the pursuit of external goods increases alienation, even though achievement can confer the illusion of control and confirmation.

We can find further evidence of dwindling power in the decline of moral action, that sensed responsibility which links an individual's way of life to its impact on others. There are growing numbers who do not apply their personal moral standards to their actions or occupations. Many would be surprised at the charge that they were responsible for the social impact of the organization which employed them. Their self-evaluation excludes this moral dimension. Yet an individual who is not morally implicated in the ultimate consequences of his activity necessarily views himself as a component in some abstract and unreachable process. If he does not will the result, it can only mean he has submitted to another will.

Our loss of power, the growth of alienation, is the consequence of decisive modifications in the conditions of human life; changes which are enforced and accelerated by an increasingly coercive and lawless economic bureaucracy. Yet, even though these economic relations dominate the social process they do not "determine" it in the manner described by Marx's doctrine of economic determinism ("historical materialism"), which remains the modern world's most significant and compelling explanation of social evolution. Economic relations sustain historical consciousness, but changes in those relations are given their particular form by the consciousness of the time in which they occur. The individualism necessary to capitalism also restrained the capitalist and undermined the forms of industrialism. The abolition of private property in socialist countries did not create a new communal consciousness. Instead, alienation was displaced from exploiting owners to equally remote and more powerful bureaucracies and their managers. In non-socialist countries commercial enterprise had its most expansive years after the decline of that hierarchical religious faith once considered its principal support. People can work harder, want more and buy with greater intensity without the opiate of sacred beliefs.

In every society economic relations coexist with other institutions: with politics, ideas, art, sexual mores. There must always be some link between these varied manifestations of social life. Within any society, economic activity is always fundamental, absorbing much of the energy of most of the people. That activity is not simply an exchange of labor and resources, but of human vitality and desire, of life itself. It establishes the structure within which people exchange themselves, out of necessity, or desire, or necessitous desire; and their return measures and defines the values and worth of their lives. Given the fundamental nature of economic life and its necessary compatibility with other aspects of society, it is almost impossible to disprove a causal relationship. One cannot deny or refute historical materialism from within the structure Marx has built.

Like other world views constructed by men of original genius, historical materialism can only be qualified by imposing the perceptions of another time upon the problems it seeks to resolve. The modern world has discarded or placed in doubt the revolutionary truisms of Marx's Europe: the possibility of a science of society, faith in the power of scientific reason and the belief that an idea in conflict with reason must be illusion. Historical materialism evolved from the nineteenth-century search for the *primum mobile*, a force which is the first link-in of causation extending to all results. So too, Wittgenstein points out, Freud sought for the "essence" of dreaming and the instinctual foundation for all individual behavior. Today the idea of determinism itself, of simple cause and effect, mechanical history within a mechanical universe, has yielded to interaction and feedback, probabilities and the relativity of observation. We possess an outlook which challenges or denies the existence of simple causation within any dynamic system whose consequences or product result from design, rather than from an impulse which initiates a chain of other impulses. Within this contemporary framework, society is not a thing, but a process in which material conditions, men, ideas and events continually clash and blend, each reinforcing and shaping the other. This process is not just a restatement of the dialectic which seeks to explain the emergence of new forces over historical epochs. It is a process which is in motion every hour of every day. The gulf between this concept of society and that possible to the nineteenth century is the distance between the steam engine and the computer. The circuits, the material construction of the computer, limit its capacity, but do not alone determine the answer it will give to a question. The computer must be programmed and that programming may, for example, fail to exhaust the computer's potential, depending on the programmer's skill and purpose and the state of the programming art. The question may be improperly put or framed with an inaccurate awareness of the machine's limitations. An inadequate response may stimulate the machine to correct itself or admonish the programmer. Nothing "determines" the answer, although capacity limits the machine's possibilities. Each component, human and electronic, is influenced by the other, and the structure of influence thus formed produces an answer. Within society economics is always dominant, but in society as process, as a dynamic system, causes and results can be different faces of the same thing.

Let us apply this view to a simplified précis of economic determinism.* To live, man must produce. He reproduces himself, and he wrests a livelihood from the material world. This second form of production requires tools—a bow and arrow, a windmill, a computer. The nature of these tools requires, or determines, a division of labor—a bowman, bowmaker and cook; someone to build an engine, buy it and run it; Norbert Wiener, Tom Watson and the Diner's Club. Perhaps technology alone does not determine the division of labor—tools need labor to work them and raw materials to work upon—but it is of decisive importance. Man is a toolmaking animal. The resulting division of labor, in all its immense complexities, can be described as the "economic relations of production." Marx writes: "In the social production which men carry on they enter into definite relations that are indispensable and independent of their will; these relations of production correspond to a definite stage of development of their material powers or production. The sum total of these relations of production constitutes the economic structures of society—the real foundation, on which arise legal and political superstructures and to which correspond definite forms of social consciousness. The mode of production in material life determines the general character of the social, political and spiritual processes of life. *It is not the consciousness of men that determines*

* Non-economic factors have a role in Marx's explanation of historical change. However, these factors, even if they are a significant present reality, were initially created by productive relationships and must give way once they become inconsistent with those relationships.

their existence, but, on the contrary, their social existence determines their consciousness." (Italics mine.)

"Economic relations of production" do not act in a vacuum or on inert matter. Our primitive ancestors were wandering hunters who sustained themselves as did many other animals. Yet they evolved a society quite different from that of the chimpanzee. In order to determine civilization, economic relations must act through and upon human beings, through individual capacities, instincts and drives. Since this is so, it would seem that the interplay between such relations and human nature is determining.

This particular difficulty can be minimized by asserting that human nature is itself shaped by economic relations† (until recently official Soviet biology extended this determinism to modifications in genetic structure), or one may reduce human nature to a rather uncomplicated drive such as economic self-interest. This last does not dispose of the problem but makes human nature a relatively simple constant, so that if society changes through history, as it does, it must be due to changes in economic relations. Marx himself tended toward both these solutions, with the important elaboration that economic relations did not act on individual nature directly, but on a class whose consciousness was shared by its members.

It is a historical misfortune that as Marx neared the end of his productive years, Sigmund Freud was still studying to become a respectable neurologist. For the later Freud revealed that human nature was the doorway to a labyrinth. "Self-interest" was two words, not one; and there were selves dominated by desires whose satisfaction could not sensibly be construed as an aspect of the defense or expansion of economic position. The human race seemed to incorporate instincts which were non-historical, which dominated every epoch in different forms.

If human nature is so intricately ambiguous, and if society is formed by the pressure of economic relations on human action, then it becomes impossible to disentangle modes of production, human nature and the scope of consciousness in order to assert that one of them determines civilization.

Moreover, the technology and science which shape the division

† This is true to the extent consciousness is shaped by economic relations. But consciousness is neither totally determined nor coextensive with human nature.

of labor are themselves an idea. The scientific method and technological approach are ways to think about reality. They are aspects of an ideology. Ideas and ideology cannot be described as a superstructure derived from economic relations if the foundation of those relations consists, in some important measure, of ideas. Nor can it be maintained that technology emerges spontaneously at a certain level of wealth or trade. Both the Greeks and Romans, at varying times, combined imperial conquest and colonies, with intellectual skills and capital at least equal to the resources of the Renaissance states and far greater than those of feudal Europe, both of which exceeded the ancients in advancing the technology of production. It is probable that the assumptions of scientific reason were so deeply embedded in the nineteenth century when economic determinism was being formulated that they seemed not an idea or a way of thinking, but a fact. We can see more clearly that technology is itself an attribute of consciousness, and one that has been dominant only in the post-Renaissance West.

Economic determinism is further undermined by the process of alienation. Let us assume that the institutions and ideologies to which men have become alienated were initially produced to serve the necessities of economic relations and the dominant class. Yet, as economic relations shift under the impact of new techniques of production, earlier institutions and ideologies do not compliantly adapt themselves to change. Through alienation they have acquired a power and vitality independent of human needs and interests. That strength enables them to survive and to influence social conduct after the conditions which produced them have disappeared. The maxim goes: "No army in the world can resist the strength of an idea whose time has come," nor, we can add, the tenacity of an institution or creed whose time has passed.

Marx does assume that emerging new forces must coexist in transitory struggle with the dominant interests of the receding present. That clash is revolution; its outcome predestined by the economic shifts which have produced it. But alienation implies something far more unexpected: Outmoded beliefs and institutions can influence the dominant classes to act against their interest; can, indeed, cause the entire society to undermine and perhaps destroy itself. History is replete with examples. The Greek city states retained their devotion to mini-independence despite the changed conditions of warfare and trade, until they all went down—oligarchs, tradesmen, philosophers, artisans and slaves. The nation state and the idea of nationalism were necessary to the early development of Western capitalism. In our own century the capitalists of Europe, as well as the workers, twice ravaged their societies and finally cast away their economic supremacy in thoughtless obedience to nationalistic doctrines, although the changed techniques of mass production, consumption and trade had already stripped away the economic justification for their behavior. Indeed, if Europe had not found in the United States a protective. Even after World War II, the European nations engaged in bitter and costly struggles to retain colonies whose economic role was obsolete. They wasted their substance at the command of a territorial imperialism which was actually inimical to the new "economic relations of production." Any doubt about this should be diminished by the examples of Germany and Japan which flourished largely because past structures were destroyed. In our own country, the war in Vietnam is yet another example of the way in which the alienation of a dominant class can influence it to engage in self-mutilation.

Even if we should assume institutions and ideologies to be determined by economic relations, once they gain an independent power, once alienation takes place, they become a source of social action. The economic future is born amid a living present still obedient to dying interests which are capable of retarding change or altering its direction. Perhaps in the long run the constructs of past alienation will fade, but by then there will be new "material conditions of existence" and the clash will continue. Pure economic determinism can thus be found only at the moment of social creation, a moment that must always be either myth or metaphor. From that point on, a civilization will be shaped by an interplay, a struggle, between economic relations, the human consciousness and those institutions which have incorporated the alienated fragments of human nature.

MARX: History is nothing but the activity of man in pursuit of his ends.

RESPONDENT: Society is also the activity of man in pursuit of his history.

The view of consciousness as the way in which existence is perceived, as a boundary to the formation of identity, reduces to a
tautology Marx's claim that social existence determines consciousness and clashes with his assertion that consciousness does not determine existence. Nevertheless, this description is not intended as
an exhortation to a changed awareness. That would be a counsel of
futility. The knowledge that consciousness excludes important and
definable elements of existence does not end their exclusion. The
reconstruction of self-perception is not an intellectual task. Understanding is not the equivalent of awareness, any more than the
ability to identify behavior as neurotic will eliminate the inner
conflict which has produced it.‡ Nor can consciousness be expanded
by an act of will, a mystic revelation, or as the result of some
benign cerebral mutation. For even though the modern consciousness is a cause of oppression, it is not a first principle. It is the
creature of the institutions and social process which it nourishes.

That consciousness is the consummation of an evolution which
began when an emerging commercial and technological life undermined medieval hierarchy, and which has continued for more than
three centuries as consequence and indispensable condition of
mounting productive forces. Consciousness can be modified only
through a drastic revision of the social process which defines and
continually re-creates it. The last third of this book discusses this
social process and its principal institutions, most of which are now
termed "economic," a designation which itself represents the ideological triumph of modern "economic science" over what was
once the subject matter of "political economy"; which speaks of
the transformation of philosophy into technology. But even the
most devoted econometrician would not deny, for example, the
social power of the automotive industry. The same is true for other
institutions involved in production and the creation of wealth.

‡ There is no psychological vantage point from which consciousness can be analyzed, since awareness of self is the starting point for all observation. There is no
experience to be relived, for consciousness has been limited by the absence of certain
experiences. The dominant position of psychoanalysis as a technique of explaining
behavior is itself sustained by the modern consciousness of individualism. It can
understand and heal individual existence only, not the afflictions whose source is in
the social process. Definitions of normality themselves originate in the dominant consciousness. Some of our individualism of behavior would appear insane or neuroti-
cally self-destructive to a medieval villager. (Even if we disapprove of such behavior
we ordinarily regard the actors as immoral or evil rather than as madmen.)

Moreover, no form of social organization can strip such institutions of their power over society. The function of society is to organize the material conditions of existence. Material conditions are those conditions which are not subjective. They consist of all relationships external to the individual, not only in work or consumption, but with the environment and with other human beings. Economic relations dominate the organization of those material conditions, i.e., the social process, because they supply fundamental needs and absorb most of the vital powers, i.e., the existence, of the individual. In a society without work, an automated utopia, economic relations would be a condition of the common life and not its ruler (unless the price of such an achievement had been the total enslavement of man to process). The portrayal of the modern economic process which follows is not offered as an aid to economic analysis, but as a description of the conditions of life within society. For, as we shall see, the necessities and the guiding interests of that economic process are imposed upon the individual as circumstance, value and desire.

This later discussion will enable us to move from the general concept of alienation to the concrete structures which are its cause, and to the varied ways in which individuals and groups are made to forfeit a portion of their existence. Even at this point, however, we can begin to dissolve generalizations by reference to the frequent observations in scholarly and popular literature of those values and behavior that conform to the purpose of the institution for which they work. Phrases such as "the military mind," "bureaucratic mentality" or the "organization man" are not metaphors but description of fact. Still, those expressions of alienation are only symptoms and outward forms of an oppression which cannot be so readily perceived, because we can no longer distinguish our own will from the will to which we have submitted.

Marx thought that changed economic relations would, of their own force, restore social existence to consciousness and make possible the human community which was the goal of utopian communism. Communism, he wrote, "is therefore the return of man himself as a social, that is, really human being, a complete and conscious return." Later we will touch upon some of the reasons for the failure of this expectation. That failure, however, does not contradict or qualify the conclusion that human freedom requires a consciousness coextensive with human existence, and that we can re-capture our own existence only by an assault on the material society which imprisons it. It should, however, be a warning that we cannot know where to strike and to what purpose until we understand the process which defines and enshrouds existence, and the manner in which it denies us our freedom. And even the most far-reaching and purposeful changes in economic structure will not, by themselves, create the conditions of freedom unless they are accompanied by knowledge of what we should want, the needs of the "deepest self." Without this, the most cataclysmic of revolutions can only succeed in changing the location of the prison.

"The hunt for happiness will never be greater than when it must be caught between today and tomorrow."

Nietzsche

PART IV

AMERICAN ECONOMIC CAPACITY—THE

MATERIAL ABILITY TO SATISFY HUMAN

WANTS

> Gaily bedight,
> A gallant knight,
> In sunshine and in shadow,
> Had journeyed long,
> Singing a song,
> In search of Eldorado.
>
> But he grew old—
> This knight so bold—
> And o'er his heart a shadow
> Fell as he found
> No spot of ground
> That looked like Eldorado.
>
> And, as his strength
> Failed him at length,
> He met a pilgrim shadow—
> "Shadow," said he,
> "Where can it be—
> This land of Eldorado?"
>
> "Over the Mountains
> Of the Moon,
> Down the Valley of the Shadow,
> Ride, boldly ride,"
> The shade replied,—
> "If you seek for Eldorado!"
>
> Edgar Allan Poe, "Eldorado"

CHAPTER 1

Freedom is defined in relation to historical conditions, as the enlargement of human existence to the limits set by the possibilities of the time. Capacity tells us what is possible. The capacity to eliminate poverty exists even within our current economic process; that is, it could be exercised without an important alteration in our dominant "relations of production." Other afflictions will not yield to so propitiatory a remedy. The structure of society itself imprisons capacity, intercepting every effort to place our powers in the service of human freedom.

The capacity which contains our possibilities consists of material resources, human skills and technology—including the knowledge which can redirect and expand technological achievement. It is physical capacity. That physical capacity is compounded of two distinct elements. The first is productive power*—resources and

---

* "Productive power" rather than the "capacity to create wealth." We can produce things which are not wealth. Whether or not they are wealth, i.e., whether they have economic value, is determined by the existing economic process, particularly the market structure. Therefore, terms such as "wealth" cannot be used to describe a capacity independent of present relationships. As we shall elaborate, the use of such terms is an important technique for concealing the dimensions of actual capacity. Productive power is not an entirely satisfactory substitute. But our entire vocabulary is entangled in the present social process, and the best that can be done is to choose phrases with the most neutral content possible, understanding that they are being arbitrarily stripped of connotations derived from the dominant economic ideology.

the technology of production—which is largely, but not exclusively, a measure of how much we can produce. The second element consists of the possible uses of production—the technology of goals and the necessities of choice (including both present possibilities and our present ability to direct the future development of productive power). For example, statements that we can eliminate pollution or reduce the amount of necessary labor imply the assertions that (a) we know how to do this and (b) we can do so without sacrificing other objectives more important to human life. Each of these two elements—productive power and possible use—influence the other. Rising productive power reduces the need to choose between desirable goals and often, but not necessarily, increases the variety of possibilities; while some uses of production are more likely to lead to increases in productive power. (In the long run all uses make some contribution to an increase in productive power.)

It is clear from this definition that physical capacity is not a measure of how much we can now produce or what choices can now be made. (It could, for example, be defined in terms of our ability to increase leisure time.) Capacity exists, but as the description of a present potential. It does not have a material existence; that is, we cannot point to it, or sketch its contours with indisputable logic. It is what we could accomplish were the society organized to serve the freedom of its members. Since no such society exists, any description of capacity must contain assertion and prophecy. Yet these uncertainties begin only when we try to establish the magnitude of disparity. For it is undeniably clear that we possess far more expansive possibilities than we can hope to achieve within the present structure of society; that society's ability to satisfy human wants is far less than its capacity.

We can clarify this distinction between capacity and ability by analogy to individuals who are made less than they might have been: Individuals, for example, whose inborn talents—those contained in genetic structure—are stifled by forms of mental illness which are creations of social reality. In a different society they might have escaped the dislocating experience which has imprisoned them. The world of the "healthy" is similarly populated with many whose capacity has been aborted by the impositions of their society.

The capacity of individuals is destroyed not only by the physical impairment of function. Values and ideology also compel the suppression of capacities whose use is inconsistent with the imperatives of social structure; e.g., an individual whose vitality is consumed by the desire to increase income cannot realize a potential for play or human intimacy. Of course, we cannot separate the individual from society in order to know precisely what has been perverted or destroyed. In this sense individual capacity is an abstraction, but one which represents a reality affirmed by the common experience and understanding and by what we know of biological structure. The same is true for the physical capacity of a society. We cannot make an "econometric model" of our unused capacity or describe it to the satisfaction of a computer. Nor can we offer scientific proof for the superiority, i.e., more liberating qualities, of values which support the choices involved in any description of physical capacity. Yet we do have persuasive evidence for the existence and general dimensions of our present capacity. And we also know that history is strewn with societies which were unable to realize the possibilities latent in a capacity which they did not even perceive.†

In 1940, the American Gross National Product was approximately one hundred billion dollars, a few billion dollars less than it had been eleven years before.‡ About 15 per cent of the labor force was unemployed. Five years later the GNP was about 212 billion dollars and almost everyone was working. There had been no discovery of unsuspected resources or of a prodigious new technology. Instead, we had gone to war. The urgencies of conflict shattered obsolete economic relationships and ideology, liberating a capacity which had been latent during earlier years of Depression. Could we then have made the same productive changes before the war? Only if we had been a different society, with different relationships and values; only if we had understood what transformations were necessary and had the power to make them.

† Even as abstraction, capacity cannot be completely separated from social structure. In order to be used, capacity must be organized and all forms of organization exert restraints. Moreover, even the most drastic revolution cannot immediately impose totally new forms of consciousness and belief. There is no escape from the fact that capacity always changes more rapidly than the social relationships which created it.

‡ In current prices. In years subsequent to 1929, GNP had dropped as low as fifty-six billion and unemployment had risen to a high of 25 per cent—both in 1933.

Today we also have the capacity to meet wants which we are unable to satisfy. Those wants are less well-defined, more ambiguous than the needs of a society in depression. Many of them are not material in the traditional sense. Still, any hope of meeting them depends on our physical capacity. It is the inescapable foundation.

That physical capacity is not like some buried vein of gold awaiting the moment of discovery. It is present as a force continually straining against the society which binds it. This necessary opposition supported Marx's expectation of capitalist collapse: "The productive forces at the disposal of society no longer tend to further the development of the conditions of bourgeois property; on the contrary they have become too powerful for these conditions, by which they are fettered, and as soon as they overcome these fetters, they bring disorder into the whole of bourgeois society, endanger the existence of bourgeois property." As prophesied, the productive forces of traditional capitalism became too powerful for the society which contained them. However, as we shall see, the resolution was not utopian communism but a bureaucratic economy which today stands in opposition to the even more powerful productive forces that it has created but failed to liberate. That fact produces a general awareness of contradiction whose consequence is discontent and social unrest. This contradiction is not generally perceived as an opposition of capacity to economic structure, nor can one readily identify the precise sources of oppression or the objectives whose attainment would enlarge freedom. For not only capacity but our awareness of capacity is directed and limited by the social process.

As a nineteenth-century scientist it was natural for Marx to believe it possible to move from description to prophecy. Where his age saw certainty and logical progression, the consciousness of the late twentieth century glimpses ambiguity and choice. Contradiction must finally be resolved, but the fact of contradiction and the necessity of resolution only instruct us in the reality of oppression and the possibilities of freedom. The failure to use capacity is always a result of alienation; unalienated existence cannot coexist with unused capacity as material reality.

Marx was also a utopian, who in the urgency of his millennial desires ignored his own admonition that "mankind only sets itself

such problems as it can solve." The problem he set—a reconciliation between man and his creations—could not be solved. It
was beyond the capacity of his time. Individuals can be utopians,
but societies are limited to the historical possibilities of freedom,
and capacity is the most important measure of those possibilities.

The last third of this book discusses the functioning elements
of our economic process and, in so doing, accumulates evidence
of our capacity. In order to describe denial one must specify that
which is being denied. First, however, let us sketch some of the
productive forces which have emerged in postwar America. Since
those forces exist within our present society and are confined by
the dominant relationships of power, they hint at the extent of
our power to enlarge freedom. This section does not aim at a complete or comprehensive description of this Platonic economy, the
reality whose obstruction shadows our existence. It is meant as
suggestion, almost as metaphor, of a capacity which is clearly more
expansive than the reach of our time-bound understanding.

CHAPTER 2

Ye fools and blind: for whether is greater, the
gold, or the temple that sanctifieth the gold.

Matthew 23:17

A small piece of uranium 235 will silently emit radiation until,
over eons, it transforms itself into inert matter. But if enough
uranium is amassed the energy will rise as particles from one atom
smash into another, creating controlled power or an uncontrolled
explosion. The economic counterpart to this process began to dis-
close itself through the same events which revealed the temporal
applications for unstable atoms. And the past twenty-five years
have been dominated by the competition between these two offspring of World War II: the murderous Cain and the fruitful
Abel.

In 1932, two months before his election, voicing a widely shared
conviction, Franklin Roosevelt told the Commonwealth Club of
San Francisco that "our industrial plant is built . . . our task is not
the discovery or exploitation of natural resources, or necessarily
producing more goods." Since we had approached the limit of our
capacity, if indeed we had not "overbuilt," prosperity could best
be restored by making more effective use of what we had, finding
foreign markets for our surplus production, and redistributing
wealth more equitably.

The early policies of the New Deal were based on this evaluation, and as their futility became manifest, the transition was
made to what Arthur Schlesinger, Jr., has described as the Second
New Deal. In its first year, the Roosevelt administration spent a
little less than the Hoover administration in its last. In the eight
years from 1932 to 1940, the federal budget crept upward from
4.6 billion dollars to 9 billion; and the Depression still continued.
In the next five years, the budget went to 98 billion dollars, the
Depression was over, and the United States had become the
wealthiest society in world history.

> Jim had borrowed Sam's good gold and didn't want to pay;
> The only idea that he had was to give poor Sam away.
> He sold out Sam and Barnes and left their friends
>   to mourn—
> Oh, what a scorching Jim will get when Gabriel blows
>   his horn!
>
> "Ballad of Sam Bass"

Despite the colossal wartime growth, apprehension remained.
The memory of the Depression was fresh, and probably only a
minority believed that the prosperity induced by war would survive the return to peace. Rarely, even in America, has pessimism
been so abjectly humbled. The national income today is five
times what it was in 1945. And with 5 per cent of the world's
population, we consume about 40 per cent of all goods produced
in the world. Such a concentration of consumption would have
been inconceivable before the industrial age, when most production was agricultural and locally consumed. And from the beginning of the industrial age until the end of World War II, no
single country consumed as much as 10 per cent of the world's
goods. As for the absolute dimensions of American wealth, it is
within reasonable limits to calculate that our production in one
year is equal to the combined production of the Western world
from the beginning of recorded history until some time in the late
nineteenth century.

In retrospect it is clear that World War II not only ended the
Depression, but initiated a new period in economic history. Many
economists would agree that if Roosevelt, in 1933, had begun to

spend a hundred billion dollars a year on tanks, planes and guns which he then transported to ships and carried to the mid-Pacific to be dumped overboard, the Depression would have ended sooner. For that is essentially what was done in the forties. Of course, the products were used first, but the use did not create wealth. (Under other circumstances, weapons have been a capital investment in the acquisition of raw materials or markets.) The fortunes of war made the government a wasteful and large-scale consumer, and that government spending precipitated the advent of the modern economy. In the seven years from 1938 to 1945 the GNP more than doubled. In that same period, government spending rose from 12.9 billion to 82.8 billion dollars, while private investment only increased from 6.6 billion to 10.4 billion. With evenhanded ignorance Admiral Yamamoto had summoned from the pregnant deeps both the eight-million-car year and the Sony transistor empire.

Divested of qualifications which are both necessary to understanding and misleading, the outlines of the modern economy assume a powerful simplicity.* Individuals wish to acquire goods. Manufacturers increase production to meet the demand. This means more jobs and higher earnings, which are distributed to the workers, shareholders and to the corporation itself. The newly employed and the recipients of increased earnings have more money to spend, either as consumers or investors. Production responds, continuing the upward spiral.

In the industrial age such a continual upward movement was believed unlikely or even impossible. The market system was thought to be a device for distributing a limited number of goods, that is, prices were set when people bid for a restricted supply of commodities. Many argued that the demand for goods was limited or tended to stagnate, and would fall behind supply, compelling manufacturers to curtail production, lower prices, eliminate jobs, reduce wages or take all of these measures in combination. Much of the theory behind large-scale government spending or its Keynes-

* Many of these qualifications become apparent in subsequent discussion. As the process of growth is self-reinforcing, every result is, in part, a cause. E.g., consumers must be enabled to express increased demand, through investment or by some other method of multiplying the resources available to consumers. This outline starts from consumption because its relationship to growth is more certain and more efficient. Moreover, consumption by government initiated modern growth.

ian counterpart—the tax reduction—consists of the assumption that this impasse can be avoided if government prods a stagnating demand by increasing its own consumption or by placing more money in the hands of individuals and/or corporations. These principles are still an aid to understanding. Demand can stagnate and investment can decline. The government can increase spending and reduce taxes in order to stimulate the economy unless demand and the response to demand are restrained by circumstances other than income levels. The difference, however, is that these theories now seem to be descriptions of certain conditions rather than economic laws, possibilities rather than necessities.†

Many important changes converged to shape the new economy. This discussion mentions only four—technology, bureaucracy, credit and velocity. All of these can help us avoid that serene cul-de-sac called equilibrium, where supply equals demand. The most effective way to pursue this objective is to keep demand ahead of supply, so that new and expanding wants constantly press against production. But it can also be helpful to increase the supply even where there is no present demand, for a new supply of goods can create its own demand. I am writing this in northern Maine where all but the poorest families own, or aspire to own, a snowmobile. Yet only a few years ago there was no demand for snowmobiles. Skis and snowshoes were the only instruments for the snow traveler. It is possible that purchasing power has been transferred from something else to snowmobiles, and that the total level of demand has not been raised. Yet in the modern economy this conclusion is not inevitable. As we shall see, a new product can raise the total level of demand. (For example, one way to buy something without forgoing other purchases is to spend money one doesn't have by borrowing against future income.) It is not easy to make more out of less, to perform the alchemy of economic growth. The phenomenon of growth is as old as industrialism, but the expansion of the past quarter century is of a different order. It is the creation of

† The process of expansion is a potential which can be hampered or even arrested by faulty government policies, industrial mismanagement, the uneconomic use of resources and technological stagnation. We are currently afflicted by all of these, the most important being the rigidities and the misuse of resources intrinsic to the large economic institutions which we shall examine in the next part. The swiftest and most far-flying jet is unlikely to reach Paris if someone has made holes in the fuel tank.

productive forces whose potential for future growth is both limitless and protean. Those presently constrained forces are capable of a rising national achievement directed to the satisfaction of an immense variety of human wants—submarines or pure air, highways or communities—providing an unprecedented ability to choose the conditions of social existence.

The seeds of this indifferent leviathan began to germinate during the presidential administrations of Ulysses Grant and Grover Cleveland: the telephone of 1876 and the internal combustion automobile of 1887, the evolutionary predecessors of modern technology and economic organization. Even as the industrial age was gaining ascendancy, it was evolving the means of its displacement. With a coincidence which, given the state of our knowledge, must be thought poetic rather than significant, both of these inventions came in years when modern crisis was being shaped. In the year of the telephone, 1876, the presidency was exchanged for withdrawal of troops from the South and an understanding that the federal government would ignore its responsibility for the new constitutional rights of blacks. And in the year of the automobile, the United States leased a naval station at Pearl Harbor from the kingdom of Hawaii, taking a major step toward becoming a military power in the Pacific (and Heinrich Hertz propagated a beam of electromagnetic waves, which were to reorganize the world and change science's conception of the universe).

The most significant traditional function of technology is to increase productivity, thereby multiplying the economic power of investment; at least as long as the value of a technological change stays ahead of its costs. Although continuing to serve this purpose, the process of modern technological change has assumed a character radically different from previous invention. Much of the technology in the industrial age was designed to process raw materials and/or to extend and amplify physical strength. The reaper, sewing machine and Bessemer converter improved our ability to extract and process the resources of nature; while the cotton gin, linotype and steam engine took over the work of hands and muscles so that, even today, power from engines of all kinds is measured in horsepower. But recent technology has tended to extend our senses, our ability to hear and see and even that synthesizing sense, the ability to think. Earlier technology developed methods of using energy to power engines which, in turn, could move, shape and carry physical objects (railroads, pneumatic hammer, steam pumps, etc.). Much of today's technology uses energy itself as a vehicle to carry words and pictures, information and ideas. It moves, transforms and amplifies, not physical objects, but individuals and what had been regarded as the elements of individual existence—sense and mind. This potential was present in earlier forms of transportation. But the automobile was the first vehicle designed primarily to carry people, and it led to a greater increase in mass mobility than the total changes of all previous history. The telephone made another kind of mobility accessible to the general population. The altered nature and direction of technology, combined with the speed of technological change, which is itself a consequence of changes in the nature of technology, has had a transforming impact on the capacity of our society.

The new technology, for example, has lessened our dependence—actual and psychological—on the materials of nature. The supply of raw materials and human labor were among the most important limitations on the productive power of the industrial age. Raw materials were often hard to get, relatively expensive and thought to be limited. One of the classic ways to increase national wealth was to acquire a new supply of natural resources either by discovery or conquest. Indeed, as late as 1941, the United States and Japan entered a conflict at least partly precipitated by a dispute over access to the "strategic" rubber and tin of Indochina.

The manufacture of textiles had been the first great breakthrough into the industrial age. Around the squalor and exploitation of the British mills were fought the bitter opening battles over automation, woman and child labor, working conditions and dismal wages. The wool came from sheep, silk from worms and cotton from the distant fields of Egypt or North Carolina. It was in the mill towns that Karl Marx made observations of capitalism, and workers began to sing of the industrial paradise to come:

> "Where the mills are made of marble
> And the machines are made out of gold
> Where nobody ever gets tired
> And nobody ever gets old."

Today many of our fabrics are chemical synthetics, while the application of machinery, chemicals and hormones to agriculture allows us to produce all the wool and cotton we are willing to pay for. Meanwhile, many of the descendants of millworkers spend the bulk of their hours in houses made of wood and plastic. Their fatigue is more likely to be nervous than muscular, but everyone still gets old.

Each discovery of a technological substitute for a significant natural resource is equivalent to the kind of discovery which once made men and nations rich (or which, during prehistory, gave its name to the age). The volume of such discoveries over the last quarter century has led to the justified conviction that most raw materials could be replaced once it became necessary and/or profitable to do so. Even oil, the international soldier of fortune and revolution, can be replaced over a period of time by nuclear, chemical or solar energy; or synthesized from the almost unlimited supplies of hydrogen and carbon.

Modern technology has also managed to create new "natural resources," i.e., it has synthesized natural materials and phenomena in order to create resources which add to productive power. IBM, for example, is not only one of the world's largest corporations, but its relative importance within the modern economy is even greater than the statistics of size. The raw material on which this industry has been constructed is not the metal from which computers are made, any more than the raw material of iron is the fire in the smelters. The natural resource, the primary substance from which computers are manufactured, consists of electricity, programs and circuits formed of other technological creations. It is energy combined with a specialized system of logic. The mega-industries of photography and Xerox depend upon light and chemicals. Technology has transformed hitherto valueless substances, and even immaterial processes, into the raw materials of important industries. The characteristics and qualities of these new natural resources demand fuller investigation. Some of them, like light and logic, are theoretically unlimited. Moreover, technological raw materials tend to be more efficient than traditional natural resources since the supply can be planned to mesh with the needs of production, reducing the economic hazards of scarcity and surplus. Through its capacity to devise substitute materials and create new ones, technology reduces a classic limit to growth, continually providing new wealth of the kind Columbus sailed to find and Standard Oil struggles to command. It is the philosopher's stone.

This technological evolution helps explain the postwar dissolution of colonial empires. The decreasing importance of traditional natural resources combined with new techniques of manufacture and international trade—themselves partly a result of technology —made it more economical for advanced nations to buy what they needed, without bearing the burden of government. Nothing is more instructive than the experience of Japan roaming the Pacific in search of land and material wealth, defeated, confined to its islands, and now the third richest country in the world.

Technology has also reduced the importance of the size of the labor force as a natural limitation on economic growth. More important than existing automation is our knowledge that it is technically possible to build machines which could accomplish many, perhaps most, of the tasks now performed by workers. This has not been done because, in many cases, men are cheaper than the cost of automating and because of important deficiencies in the economic structure, which we shall examine later. Nevertheless, any proposition that the amount of available labor is an inherent or inescapable limit to production is either gone or deformed beyond recognition.

In addition, technology continually bestows new objects of consumption on a population made receptive by the modern techniques of creating demand. Some of our largest corporations such as IBM, Xerox and Polaroid owe their existence entirely to a demand for products which did not exist or for which there was no market when World War II began. Other giants such as General Electric and RCA flourish on the continual innovation of novelty. Since the individuals who desire these goods do not want to give up other things that are important, the economic structure allows them to extract the additional resources. They can, for example, borrow or demand higher wages.

The principal stimulus to wage demands, for example, is not an abstract calculation based on a just division of the returns from increased productivity, but the desire to improve a standard of living whose requirements are continually redefined by the appearance of new products. The existence of television preceded its incorporation into the essence of American life.‡ Who bears the cost of higher wages and the risk that those who borrow may default? To an increasing extent the answer is almost everybody, which means almost nobody who profits directly from production. Most large industries have the power to raise prices to cover higher wages. While credit now exists on so large a scale that failures to repay can be statistically predicted and the loss compensated by higher interest or calculated as a cost of doing business and reflected in higher prices. (In addition, the general public bears a large part of the risk through a tax structure which allows interest and bad debts to be deducted.) When society as a whole pays for higher wages and dishonored debts, then wage costs and credit risks have been socialized. This form of socialism is also regressive, for those who are outside the organized wage system or whose economic position bars them from credit—the poor and unemployed—must share the costs but receive none of the benefits.

The products of technology help to support an entire "industry of the new," an industry whose growth depends upon a flow of fresh commodities, e.g., advertising and television. In addition, although jobs are lost when a product is displaced, the new producer creates employment and often requires new construction and new machinery. Even if demand were constant, innovation would increase investment. Some of the wealth-producing power of technology comes from change for the sake of change regardless of the value of the result.

The structure and achievements of modern technology have confirmed the assumption that there is no limit, theoretical or practical, to the technological process. Change can follow change, invention can lead to invention, affirming Macbeth's exclamation: "What, will the line stretch out to the crack of doom?" Innovation itself has become a product. It can be planned, and we can be confident of finding technological solutions for those difficulties to which research is addressed. With adequate investment we could be assured of a continual flow of wealth enhancing technology, capable of being directed to the satisfaction of a large variety of individual and social wants. The reason our technology lags far behind possi-

‡ Control over demand is one of the principal characteristics of the modern economy. See Part V.

bility is the indifference or hostility of large industrial bureaucracies to technological change and the imposed ideology of an economic process which confines the direction of innovation.

A second factor of the new economy—economic organization or bureaucracy—is itself a creation of technology. I will not summarize the analytical descriptions of J. K. Galbraith's *New Industrial State* (which replaces his "countervailing power" with integrated power) or the insights of Adolf Berle and Gardiner Means. A few observations will help make the point. The term "bureaucracy" has special relevance to the description of current forms of economic organization. It implies diffusion of authority with complex procedures tending toward rigidity. It connotes devotion to organization as an end, rather than as the instrument of some external purpose. We will examine these institutions in some detail, for they dominate our society. However, such structures also demonstrate the technical possibilities of a decentralized form of economic organization which would permit long-term planning and the efficient allocation of resources. The new technologies of economic organization make it easier to uncover new markets and sources of supply, reduce dependence upon the vagaries of market forces and can influence demand to conform with the goals of production.

Matched to technology modern economic organization is capable of meeting nearly all our material wants. It can expand production to meet rising demands. It can innovate where innovation is necessary and use its own reserves of capital, along with its privileged access to the capital structure, to invest in almost any kind of production. It could, therefore, be modernizing cities, ending pollution, building homes and expanding schools. Moreover, such changes in the direction of production would not require an economic sacrifice by the society as a whole. The purchase of clean air for a city would stimulate the economy at least as much as the acquisition of a missile or a truck. Out of the price would come wages and earnings. From wages and earnings would come consumption and investment. Expansion would continue. Twenty-five years ago we did not have a computer industry. Its development has required enormous investment. Yet the American people were not advised in 1945 that they must choose between computers and new cars. Had that choice been made there would be no computers.

The same principle holds for those needs we call "public." The necessity of choice does not inhere in the nature of production; it is imposed by an economic process which directs the resources of society in its own interests. However, the possibilities inherent in the technology of economic organization cannot be realized within the present structure of economic power. For us that structure remains a construction whose consequence is oppression and whose liberating possibilities are untouched.

A third element of the new economy is the epidemic expansion of credit, especially consumer credit, or what might be called private deficit spending. We have seen how the public spending in excess of revenues—which was compelled by war—generated modern economic relationships. In the early 1960s, the government cut taxes deliberately to create a deficit, hoping to increase economic growth. This measure is thought to have worked, since we began our largest sustained peacetime expansion at about the same time. Belief in a relationship between public deficits and increased economic activity is no longer a tenet of political ideology but a matter of economic dogma for conservatives and liberals alike (although not all agree that deficits are the best way to stimulate the economy).

When the virtues of public thrift were still being seriously maintained, proponents often argued by analogy to the ruin which threatened individuals who lived beyond their means. It was hardly noticed that household budgets were also going seriously out of balance. Individuals who spend more than they have, must borrow. They make loans, open charge accounts, buy on installments or select from an increasing array of alternative credit devices. Such individuals are engaged in their own deficit financing. On a large enough scale this excess spending should have the same kind of impact on the economy as a government deficit. And the scale is very large indeed. In 1950, private debt, corporate and individual, was about the same as public debt—around 240 billion dollars. Today, the total net private debt is over one and one-half trillion dollars, almost triple the combined debt of every government in America. Outstanding consumer credit, the amount borrowed to buy consumer goods, is over 160 billion dollars. This private debt has grown steadily over the past twenty-five years, and at a faster rate than public debt, affording a continual stimulus to economic activity. The acceleration of private debt accompanied a growing confidence in the peacetime durability of prosperity. For large-scale private borrowing is only possible when consumers and business share a general expectation that expansion will continue. They are spending in anticipation of future income and usually in anticipation of increased income. Individual consumers did not think they were living beyond their means. They were simply buying today what they could afford tomorrow.**

Only in the last half dozen years have we begun to remove some serious restrictions on the expansion of consumer credit. For even though the economy as a whole was certain to rise and most individuals could be counted on to repay their debts, a particular retailer or business was not protected from a disproportionate share of costly defaults. This meant that credit had to backed by a personal evaluation of a consumer's "credit worthiness," or not extended at all. Central credit bureaus and the credit card—consequences of computer technology—are solving this problem (and creating possibilities of coercion which can only be avoided by some form of public control). By placing a large number of individuals in a single credit system, the proportion of defaults can be statistically predicted. That loss is paid for through higher interest rates or by increasing the cost of credit services, which the seller passes on in higher prices. If a large proportion of businesses refused to use these new services the system might unravel. But the reverse is happening. A credit card, for example, is often honored where a check is unacceptable, although checks retain their conventional economic description as "money."

As the private deficit rises, the consequent demand stimulates economic expansion. Growth produces the increased income which justifies past borrowing and provides a higher platform for the next round of credit. Nor is there any theoretical limit to this process, at least if interest charges stay within bearable limits. By borrowing against future growth we help to bring it about. The miracle of the loaves and fishes has been transformed into an economic process.

Private deficit spending is a manifestation of the modern economy's capacity to respond to demand larger than accessible wealth,

** Recent increases in private debt reveal another stimulus—the belief that prices will rise. The recent inflation has contributed to expanding industrial profits, which is among the reasons strong measures of control have not been applied.

to create wealth from the expectation of gain. The present condition of society and the necessities of the existing economic process depress demand far below this potential, while many of our material needs cannot be satisfied because there is no economic mechanism which permits us to express them.

Velocity as a component of the economy is a creation of modern technology and economic organization. But the accelerating velocity of people, goods, information, ideas and economic transactions has independent economic meaning. It was once thought appropriate to describe the economy with the allegory of a runner who lost more energy the harder he ran, until, finally depleted, he had to stop. Our recurrent experience of growth and depression seemed a command of natural economic laws. Only a few years ago some official economists explained that the economy was "overheated," implying that there was too much investment, expansion and consumption. In other words we were getting rich too fast and, like the runner who exceeds his capacity, were threatened with serious damage.††

Around the turn of the century physics discovered a law of nature which provides a more appropriate analogy: The faster an object goes the greater its mass becomes, until, at the highest possible speed, its mass is infinite. Modern economic growth has been fortified by the ability to increase the rate at which we conduct the billions of transactions and relationships which constitute economic life. As a result of that acceleration, more goods can be produced and more bought; more workers can go where labor is needed; more supplies can be transported to factories and more goods to market; more ideas can be absorbed and put into practice; while more information can be assembled and used. Among the ten American corporations with the largest revenues, three of them—AT&T, General Electric and IBM—are wealthy to a large extent because they enable others to hasten activity. Three others are automobile companies who must count this among their services. Economic process, like all purposeful human activity, is com-

††An economy can't grow too fast, although the process of growth in today's economy can produce painful distortions, such as inflation. Indeed, sustained economic growth within the present economic process will require permanent regulation of prices, if, indeed, such growth is not foreclosed by the tendency of the modern economy toward stagnation.

pounded of both materials and time. If resources, demand or other economic materials are limited, then rapid consumption precipitates scarcity and stagnation. To the extent such limits are no longer necessary, acceleration of activity adds to growth. Of course, particular materials are limited. There is, for example, some end to the demand for automobiles or to the supply of oil. But these limits determine the content of growth. They do not bound growth itself, although from within the confines of contemporary society they may appear as absolute barriers. However, the velocity of any object consists of direction as well as speed. As long as the economic structure limits the direction of economic activity we cannot realize the benefits contained in the principle of acceleration.

One cannot scientifically prove the existence of a physical capacity greater than our present ability, and it would require a far more extensive discussion to persuade those who are not already inclined to agreement. Yet it is undeniable that the events of the past three decades, in addition to increasing our wealth and productive power, have fundamentally modified the economic process itself. Human needs, the foundation of economic demand, now lack any discernible limit. Wartime experience and postwar growth demonstrate that productive capacity can be expanded to meet rapidly rising levels of demand. Technology has already abolished many of the restrictions imposed by the limited supply of natural resources or labor, and could eliminate many of the remaining dependencies. Innovation itself is no longer the consequence of fortuitous discovery, but can be planned and anticipated. A sufficient investment of skill and money could produce a technology to reduce the amount of necessary labor and to resolve many of the material problems which obstruct the enlargement of human life. When these realities of the new economy are matched to the possibilities of modern techniques of organization it becomes possible to allocate resources toward the fulfillment of nearly any material desire. We could rebuild cities, restore nature, end poverty, and in the process add to our total wealth, although that wealth would take different forms. It would be social wealth defined by the qualities of a free existence; it might be measured, for example, by decreasing the hours of work as well as by increasing the volume of production. We do not do these things because our society is dominated by economic structures and an attendant ideology which confines our capacity within a pattern of activities designed to maintain and strengthen ascendant structures. That imposed pattern is at variance with the most urgent human needs; indeed, it is responsible for the oppressive conditions from which those unfulfilled needs arise.

CHAPTER 3

Your fevered glimpse of a democracy confused and foiled with
an equality not equal to the envy it creates.

Edwin Arlington Robinson

You do everything for the niggers and nothing for the Indians.

Indian representative to Massachusetts
Commissioner of Public Works

The most traditional form of bondage is that imposed by material
necessity. Hunger and deprivation are historical constants but the
nature of poverty—its form and its relationship to the possibilities
of freedom—depends upon the particular conditions of each society.
American poverty and the barriers to its elimination are consequences of the same social process which dominates the life of every
citizen.

All poverty is "structural," not the consequence of natural or
divine law, but of the man-made social order. In our society, for example, a man whose hay field was found to contain oil would become rich, while one who spent his days at a market place arguing
about the nature of truth and justice would receive nothing except,
perhaps, a sentence for vagrancy. Yet, the philosopher, as an individual, is at least as economically productive as the landowner.

Those who produce in some ways (running a factory or concocting advertisements) earn large incomes, while other producers become destitute, e.g., the inventor who didn't protect his rights or the farmer who can no longer compete.* The existence of economic "worth" is not a transcendent fact, but the expression of these social values which are enforced by the economic process.

Where resources are limited, some poverty is unavoidable. In a competition conducted under conditions of scarcity some must win and others lose. But those who come out ahead do not "deserve" their reward in any abstract moral terms. They have the strength to command wealth, that is, they have what the society values and can be made to pay for.

Some poverty can be justified in a society of limited resources which must concentrate wealth as capital for investment. However, in such societies one invariably finds interests which command a share of wealth in excess of the concentrated accumulation needed for growth. The result is a surplus of poverty in excess of economic requirements. This power to command wealth—economic strength —is conferred by the ideology which sustains a particular social structure. Since "surplus" poverty is an imposition on present weakness, those who determine the components of economic strength— what shall be valued and rewarded—are those who are already strong.

Within our own social structure wealth is not distributed either to people or institutions in amounts proportionate to their contribution to the creation of wealth or the prospects for growth. The clearest examples are the inheritance laws that can confer a substantial economic value on an individual's submission to birth and which are indifferent to the recipient's present capacities or future plans. Large farmers are subsidized for not producing and shipbuilders are paid to construct ships which we could purchase less expensively from others. Although the historic economic and investment functions of large banks have been severely reduced in recent decades, they are making more money than ever. And, as we shall see, the rewards bestowed by the large modern, economic

* In some socialist states the principal object of competition is authority over wealth, rather than wealth itself. This makes necessary a different description of the underprivileged, but has not eliminated the category. The alienations of all advanced societies, socialist or not, are similar. If money is not power, then power is money.

bureaucracies bear an increasingly more tenuous relationship to economic productivity. Such uneconomic rewards are infiltrating every aspect of our economic life, increasing that proportion of social wealth whose distribution is arbitrary. Those excluded from an arbitrary distribution are not being punished for their inadequacies. They are the victims of superior strength.

The existence of material deprivation is not always an exhortation to social action. Even so, poverty is always a consequence of social structure, i.e., of social choice. Poverty in America is not the consequence of scarce resources, the need to concentrate capital for future growth, or the economic inability to end it. The American poor are oppressed, the victims of a material deprivation imposed by the relationships of society. In other periods, poverty as oppression could be explained as the rational pursuit of self-interest by the forces of production. This does not explain the persistence of poverty in our society. The elimination of poverty—an equivalent to the creation of consumers—would greatly expand the market. (Automobile companies, for example, would be among the first to benefit. If they followed the logic of self-interest, they would establish full-time Washington lobbies for poverty programs.) Indeed, our failure to continue the process of augmenting the number of consumers is a principal cause of today's relative economic stagnation.

Clearly poverty could be ended without degrading or impairing the life of the non-poor majority. When to this fact is added the knowledge that the elimination of poverty would enhance the well-being of the entire nation and strengthen those economic forces which now dominate the society, one seems to stand at the verge of a radical social disorder.

Americans have often conceived of justice as equality of opportunity, a standard which came naturally to the occupants of an abundant continent free from the settled inequalities of Europe. Yet the phrase itself is a vacancy, given content by the changing elements of the social process. Although one can most easily observe the decisive influence of social structure on the injustices created by material inequality, it also confines individuals at every level of society. Opportunity itself, what is to be pursued, is defined by the rewards and values imposed by dominant economic institutions. That everyone can have an education, a job, make money is not the equivalent of the assertion that everyone can seek to extend his powers and inner resources. The traditional assertions of opportunity can be retranslated: Everyone can have an education if he goes to schools which destroy curiosity and imagination. Everyone can have a job if he gets a degree, settles for a life-draining urban environment and accepts the values and requirements of ruling economic institutions. Everyone can make a living if he possesses or acquires skills which are rewarded and neglects those capacities which have no market. To the extent these demands and the institutions which impose them are oppressive, i.e., do not constitute necessary sacrifices on behalf of higher human values, equality of opportunity becomes the liberty, and at times the desire, to choose one's form of bondage. Since freedom is defined by historical possibilities, it is continually narrowed as we increase our material ability to liberate the repressed and suspended functions of our nature. We are made less by the magnitude of denial.

CHAPTER 4

A *Story from a Future Edition of the* Wall Street Journal

The first public offering of Blacks, Inc., was oversubscribed in a matter of hours yesterday as institutional investors snapped up large blocks of the new issue. By closing, shares had risen to 32½ from the offering price of 25. Seasoned observers expressed little surprise at the enthusiasm, even though the company has not yet begun operations, pointing out that few businesses had begun with such optimistic prospects. Economists were almost unanimous in their predictions of rapid growth and high profits.

The president of Blacks, Inc., Rangeley T. Oquossoc, said he was pleased with the day's trading and was confident that no investor would regret his purchase. "It's a blue chip with high growth, what more can you ask," he asserted from his Harlem home.

The new company has an exclusive contract with both the federal government and the Poverty Authority recently established by agreement of all fifty states. Under the contract, Blacks, Inc., has agreed to spend at least thirty billion dollars a year to eliminate poverty. Its activities will be almost wholly concentrated in two fields. The first of these will be general and vocational education and special skill training. Second, it will create jobs through loans to businesses and, where appropriate, direct contributions to the capital investment of private companies. In return, the federal and state governments have agreed that Blacks, Inc., will receive all the tax revenues produced by its programs, all reduction in public aid made possible by its efforts, as well as the corporate taxes on all profits which are attributable to increased consumption by those it has helped. There is also a special bonus arrangement to cover general increases in national wealth.

Asked to explain the arrangement, the buoyant Mr. Oquossoc said, "Look, it's a sure thing. But it's very complicated so I'll just give you a general idea. There are about six million heads of families who are poor and about five million poor people who aren't living with any relatives. Incidentally, about 75 per cent of them are white, which makes some folks ask why I call our company Blacks, Inc. We thought it would encourage investors . . . blacks inc . . . not in the red . . . get it. Well, anyways, a lot of those poor folks are old folks, and there isn't much we can do for them. That's up to the government. As for the others, which is most of them, we figure it will cost about forty thousand dollars to put a man to work. That includes training and creating the job. It's a pretty conservative estimate, and we may be able to do it for less. The most any state spends on education per pupil is about one thousand dollars per pupil. We'll bypass the regular school systems and set up our own and we'll have a lot of apprenticeship programs. The regular schools aren't much good, you know. Also we'll create a lot of our jobs in the service industries, like mechanics, plumbers, clerks. That's where the real growth is, and it costs a lot less to create a job like that than in manufacturing. Some of the time it'll cost hardly anything. A good low interest loan to a business will do the trick. But using the forty-thousand-dollar figure, let's suppose we work with a million poor people a year. That's forty billion dollars, which sounds like a lot of money. But, remember, when you build a new factory you don't count the entire cost in one year. You spread it out over the period of time that factory will produce for you. So we'll amortize our cost over thirty years, a good round number for how long we can expect our investment to produce . . . by which I mean how long a man will work. That gives us a cost on that million people of 1.3 billion a year.

"Now once a person is trained and working, his family income, on the average, should be about ten thousand dollars a year, which is now the median family income for the United States. And that's a low figure because it is the median for everybody, not just for those who are working. Now when our client was poor he wasn't paying any taxes to speak of. With his new income he'll owe about one thousand dollars a year in federal taxes and one hundred dollars in state taxes, which all goes to us. Also he'll have about five thousand dollars more to spend and, if he does like the rest of us, he'll spend about 90 per cent of it. That means forty-five hundred dollars more sales for business and, at a modest 10 per cent, about four hundred and fifty dollars in profits, of which 52 per cent goes to us in taxes. Public aid is a little more complicated, but we figure that for every million people we put to work, all kinds of assistance programs can go down about one and one-half billion dollars a year out of the about twenty billion dollars a year, which we figure is because of poverty. Don't forget that during World War II, when a lot of people got jobs, the same kind of public aid dropped about 65 per cent. Now if you multiply all that out—increased taxes and less public aid—you get about 1.9 billion a year.

"There you have it. Cost is 1.3 billion and profit is 1.9 billion. It's a profit of about 46 per cent. Pretty hard to beat, isn't it? And it'll probably be even more. Because history proves that as more people go to work, median income goes up, and if it does we make even more. If taxes go up, we do even better. And if *that* doesn't happen it'll be a surprise to all of us."

Asked about the special bonus arrangement, Mr. Oquossoc replied, "Well, that's sort of arbitrary. But, you know, if you get a few million more people working, all sorts of things start to happen. Profits go up and wages go up and so do tax receipts. In other words, eliminating poverty makes everyone a little richer and so it's only fair we should get something. That's the whole story of this country," Oquossoc said. "As more and more people went to work everyone got richer. Remember, the rising tide lifts all the boats."

When asked why no one had established such a business before, Mr. Oquossoc explained, "No one ever thought of it."

PART V

THE STRUCTURE OF ECONOMIC BUREAUCRACY—ITS DOMINATION OF THE SOCIAL PROCESS

The Guardian Prince of Albion burns in his nightly tent:
Sullen fires across the Atlantic glow to America's shore,
Piercing the souls of warlike men who rise in silent night.
Washington, Franklin, Paine & Warren, Gates, Hancock,
          & Green.

· ·

Washington spoke: "Friends of America! look over the
          Atlantic sea;
"A bended bow is lifted in heaven, & a heavy iron chain
"Descends, link by link . . . to bind
"Brothers and sons of America . . ."

                  Blake, "America"—A prophecy

CHAPTER 1

One fall day I interrupted work to help make apple cider. A dozen
or more pickups, jeeps and cars hauled sacks and bushels of apples
from Franklin County homes to a cider press in a friend's barn. Our
concourse of non-farmers contained one printed poet, two still
unread, a couple of prose writers, an authority on education, a re-
tired politician, two musicians along with the women who made
up their expanded "family"—emigrants, dropouts, ideologues of
the natural, and those who wanted fresh cider. Most had come to
rural Maine from other lives and places, the move eased by voca-
tions which could be pursued away from urban centers. Most of
the women were there because of the men who brought them.

The unloaded apples were poured onto a wooden chute which fed
a power-turned cutter. Apple fragments were raked and tamped into
thick squares wrapped in cheesecloth. Five squares—about twenty
bushels of apples—were stacked on the base of the press and cov-
ered with a layer of thick timbers beneath a metal plate which was
welded to a huge screw fixed in a supporting beam. As the screw
was turned the descending plate crushed the juice into a wooden
vat, from which it was dipped, strained and reloaded into barrels,
jars and plastic milk bottles. It took three men to force the screw
through its last turns. Their final grunt signaled that the process of
production was over; the process of acquisition could now begin.

As any philosopher knows, the entire weight of human history sat on the production of this cider. The millennia evolved social forces which urged individuals to the barn. The powers of modern technology had induced them to find merit and sensuality in obsolete techniques. Affluence enabled them to spend labor far more valuable than its produce, to ignore the roadside stands whose cheap and equally fresh cider had been pressed, not for pleasure, but out of economic necessity. Even the apples had a history. They were immanent in spring blossoms; their size and sweetness dependent on the chances of sun and rain; their future at the mercy of passing deer. Apples and we—a process of organic intricacy. All the same, the cider I tasted and acquired was pressed by those men, in that press, on the seventeenth of October in George's barn. A single bolt of lightning on the previous night would have stripped the forces of history and the dynamics of society of the power to produce even one jar of that particular, tangible and distinct cider. Unless, of course, we found an identical press. But old presses like that, in good condition, are not easy to find.

Will and idea, economic relations and genetic decrees manifest their power through a social order. The struggle for increased freedom must be mounted against existing structures, and not the historical forces which created them.

The struggle to re-establish harmony, to make a revolution, is always difficult and uncertain, contending, as it must, against the powers and goals of past generations which have congealed into institutions and a way of life. That social order resists the pressures set up by changes in the underlying realities of power and interest. Since material capacities created by modern generations are far more extensive than the achievements of earlier centuries, the social order which embodies them has more formidable powers of resistance. It is not only a structure, but a process of such incredible complexity that it baffles the traditional search for the agents of oppression—rulers, the dominant class. "Everyone will be carrying out orders," writes R. D. Laing. "Where do they come from? Always from elsewhere."

CHAPTER 2

> (T)he . . . development of the productive forces . . . comes
> to a standstill at a point determined by the production and
> realization of profit, not by the satisfaction of human needs.
>
> Karl Marx

> Chicago was intended as a town of export for corn, and there-
> fore, the corn stores have received first attention. When I was
> there they were in perfect working order.
>
> Anthony Trollope in 1862

> We're all caught in a friggin whirlpool.
>
> Elden LaBelle, former proprietor,
> Riverside Inn, Kingfield, Maine

As the ensnarled, though rebellious, heirs of scientific reason, our
search for comprehension of economic order requires us to probe for
constituents and their connections. Yet the whole will elude us. We
are legatees of four centuries of progress toward dominion of the
particular; trained to see reality in the concrete and fragmentary,
until unity, the totality, is replaced by category—a device, a metaphor, which permits us to ignore disparities beween elements of
reality so we may better fulfill certain purposes and be permitted a

consoling belief that our mind is understanding and describing the world rather than using the world to describe itself. It works, i.e., it has practical results for many pursuits, especially technology. But it does not explain the structures through which men organize and contain their social existence.

The words "economic order" and "economy" are themselves categories of convenience, which tempt us to regard the plexus of activities and events which they categorize as a self-contained system, an organic unity. If we succumb, then we must also accept, often unknowingly, the ideas and relationships of interest which are not contained by that category but which, in the reality of the whole, support and interfuse the economic structure. That structure mirrors and forms, is part of, every feature of the human community: New York's choked cross-town streets and the solitary anxieties of an Aroostook County potato farmer; the possessed violence of the addict and the Inaugural Address of a new Chief; the self-expunging intensities of orgy and the tendered masteries of the turnpike.

We can repair and reform the economic structure. But an assault on the structure itself, on the indispensable elements of its present functioning, requires us to question and endanger the assumptions of society, that is, the nature and quality of our own humanity.

In conversation not long ago, a political leader said, "But in a free society, how can you really control technology?" By which he meant not simply the protection of health or life, but the actual prohibition of technological developments and the production of innovations if you were averse to their social consequences.

His dinner companion replied, "But if you can't choose, then you are not a free society." The discussion moved on, leaving an issue more basic than it appeared to the participants. Our questioning politician was thinking of the liberty to innovate, create and make the results available to the citizenry. Over the centuries, that liberty has acquired a protective nimbus composed of other liberties—freedom to think, academic freedom, freedom of inquiry, the people's freedom to choose the new. Yet it is clear that the nature of modern production has given, perhaps imposed, that definition of freedom. Long before Marx, Voltaire said, "The commerce that has enriched the citizens of England has helped to make them free, and that freedom in turn has encouraged commerce; this has produced the greatness of the state."

The response of the statesman's companion implies another concept of freedom—the freedom to decide how we want to live, to determine the nature of future relationships and environment, freedom even to retain the present—and to prohibit the technology which obstructs these desires. This definition, like the other, is a metaphysical construct. It is also a consequence of our present condition and economic order. Otherwise one could not conceive it, even as abstract possibility. This idea of freedom has its source in the destructive failures of our present structure and in the stifled and untapped physical capacity to create a stronger, more flourishing and freer economic order. It is contained and determined by the oppressions which are imposed by the present order and also by its enlarging possibilities. Which is always the case. Marx wrote that "mankind always sets itself only such problems as it can solve." A problem appears only when there is a solution. Before that, it is destiny.

The politician's idea of freedom conforms to the modern system of production. Today nearly all technological inquiry and much science require capital investment. The direction of that investment helps determine what shall be thought about and what discoveries will be made. Intervention in such decisions is the replacement of one set of imposed priorities and directives with another. To bar such interventions as an infringement on freedom is to sustain the existing distribution of the power to decide. But this relationship does not, by itself, explain the social authority of this idea of freedom. As we have seen, it is an idea which had its origins in the struggle of science and commerce against an enshrouding medieval order. It was once the banner of revolution, the bearer of a widening freedom. It is tied to the ensuing centuries of scientific reason and technological development. And it is also linked to accelerating individualism. The freedom it assumes belongs to the inventor, the producer, the consumer—as individuals. It does not speak of community freedom or that of the society or group, not because of omission, but because this freedom does not contain them. It is of a different order, belonging to a distinct world view. The idea is incorporated in a social structure which does not have a mechanism for weighing technological change against social change and making a choice. If society does not provide ways to choose, it excludes the choice itself from its idea of freedom.

So too, nearly all the forms of public debate are a visible outcropping of assumptions and values structured by the reinforcing pressures of history and material reality. We have now decided upon a volunteer army. Yet can it be claimed that prospective recruits volunteer for those conditions of social and economic life which tempt or drive them toward military service? We can only say that if we accept as given the present distribution of income, the relationships of power and interest which impose that distribution and the social framework which limits alternative opportunities—then recruits will be volunteers. Another perspective would see the volunteer army as a consequence of the greatly increased economic power of the middle class, especially the more affluent and educated of that class, being exerted, as is traditional, in their own interest. The more philosophically inclined can view the establishment of a large professional military as part of our progression toward centralized authority. All of these modes of analysis are correct. Indeed, they are all related, not just linked but as distinguishable revelations of the same process.

The language of economics contains words which seem to describe facts, objective phenomena, but which really express the ruling forces of our cultural process. There are general terms like "wealth," "prosperity," "growth," and the narrower, more technical symbols—"market value," "exchange," "Gross National Product." "Prosperity" and "growth" tell us little of what is happening to the lives of individuals in the society; only how well the present structure is doing by its own, intrinsic scale of measurement. I do not mean the obvious opposition of the economic or material to the non-economic or immaterial. Rather, what is economic, what is to be counted, is a matter of values and interest and not of necessity. For example, we add to our economic wealth when we produce a car, and not when a city sets aside land for a park. Even if it could be proven that the presence of a park so uplifted the morale of nearby residents that their work output rose 10 per cent, it would not enter into calculations of growth, prosperity, etc. For it has no market value. Nevertheless, people want it. But the market structure we have inherited provides no mechanism through which that desire can be translated into economic demand. Therefore, even if people want the park and use it, if it adds to their income by permitting a reduction of other expenditures for recreation and transportation, it is not growth. Yet society has produced a material object which enhanced happiness, raised income and perhaps even added to productivity.

If the discourse and definitions of economics are not simply descriptions, intellectual analogues of material reality, neither are they arbitrary and changeable. They are the manufacture of a commercial-industrial society, fashioned to justify the dominant interests and modes of production. This is true of Marxist economics as well as the liberal, or market-place, economics which has dominated Western society from Adam Smith to Keynes. Both are ideologies of emerging industrialism, germinated by the struggle between the new industrial system and a dying feudalism, between businessman and aristocrat, a new middle class and the old upper class. These ideas, however, are not condemned by their origin. When society evolves new ways to create wealth, a redistribution of power, then a new economics is needed. The concepts and rules so evolved are useful, but the terms which often sound technical are also ideological, deriving from the relationships and necessities of the time. They cannot be given a different content by fiat or consensus, only by shifts in the order they describe and serve.

An Indian from a small lost tribe on the Nhamunda River—a tributary of the middle Amazon—was taken by a benevolent missionary on a round trip to the ocean coast a thousand miles away. He arrived during a storm and stayed on the beach for only an hour before it was time to return. That night the villagers gathered to hear him describe the sea. "It is not very big," he said. "I stood on one bank and I could see the other, which seemed to be like a wall of clouds; perhaps it was white rock. The sea was not flat like the river but made up of huge walls of water, taller than this hut, which rushed toward me and then as they neared, toppled with a sound like the thunder. Its colors were dark, almost black, with many fragments of white. No place for a man," he ended, and the others nodded.

The historical confinements of language and thought are so obstinate that we are persuaded to view the sources of our oppression as aberrations, monstrous malfunctions or, if so inclined, as the triumphs of powerful conspiracies, rather than as the expectable consequences of our economic process and the society which contains it. We have, for example, experienced a decade-long debate about the problem of the cities. It seems bewildering that an affliction which has kindled so enduring a consensus of outrage continues to deepen untended. Except there is no problem of the cities.

A century ago Anthony Trollope, after describing the disheveled life of early Chicago, explained that "Chicago was intended as a town of export for corn, and, therefore, the corn stores have received first attention. When I was there, they were in perfect working order." The impulse for the origin and growth of our cities came from trade, commerce and finance—the animating activities which encompassed the urban purpose. Cities were populated with those engaged in directing enterprise and commerce, neighbored by legions of cheap labor for business, services and construction. The economic function of the city depended upon its residential function. In the last several decades a multitude of changes severed that relationship. The spread of affluence and the automobile, improved communication of information and entertainment, new roads and the disappearance of restraining ties to neighborhood and ethnic groups, all lured, encouraged and provoked those from the upper levels of business to leave the city. They found it unnecessary and increasingly less desirable to live where they worked. At the same time, the need for cheap unskilled and semiskilled labor steadily dwindled. The residential city was no longer necessary to the economic city.

As the conditions of urban life decay, as "the little streets are hurled upon the great," the mechanisms of commerce and finance can still function and flourish. The horizons of our "decaying" cities are pierced with new commercial towers; a bureaucratic architecture to celebrate the precepts of the age. The same officials who plead the desperation of urban life struggle and scheme to populate the city with more of those stone-steel hutches which draw strangers to the city in the morning and cast them forth at night; feeding the process which destroys—because it does not need—the life-sustaining amenities. The city is not in trouble. It functions as well as its purpose demands. Only life is in trouble. Unless a different economic order alters the urban purpose, decay will continue. Indeed, economic institutions may soon find they too can function outside the urban center. The necessary technology already exists. After centuries of urbanization we may be ready to go "back to the land," except, of course, the land will have to be paved.

Observations such as these on the cities intimate the existence of a world beyond the necessary and arbitrary constructs of analysis. A precautionary awareness that any analysis of the modern economy—including the descriptions of this book—requires us to participate in universal falsification may clarify the effort to approach, if not the truth, the understanding which must precede change.

CHAPTER 3

THREE FULFILLED VISIONS:
1. Centralization of the means of production and socialization of labor at last reach a point where they become incompatible with their capitalist integument.

Karl Marx

2. The people who own the country ought to govern it.

John Jay

3. While we have land enough to conquer from the trees and wild beasts we shall never go abroad to trouble other nations.

John Adams in Holland
during the peace negotiation

"The owners of mere labor, the owners of capital, and the land-owner," wrote Marx, "whose respective sources of income are wages, profits, and rent of land, or in other words, wage-labourers, capitalists and landowners, form the three great classes of modern society based on the capitalist mode of production." All of these classes which Marx described can be found in modern society, but they are no longer the "great classes." The description does not include the managers of industry, custodians of capital, leaders of

unions and the millions of highly trained, educated and professional workers whose necessary skills give them a more powerful
claim on the economy than "mere labour power" could hope to assert. Nor does Marx admit the leaders of the state who not only
serve the private economy but themselves manage a large and
powerful economic enterprise, a vested interest. Yet these unlisted
groups, these "classes," dominate the modern economy. They
have arisen from a division of ownership made possible by
technology.

Since Berle and Means described the modern corporation, the
separation of ownership from authority over industry has been
part of the common understanding. These insights can be extended by approaching them from a different vantage; by examining the concept of "ownership." It is now apparent that ownership is not elementary, not an irreducible unity, but a cluster of
relationships between individuals and property. And those relationships are separable: that is, the attributes of ownership can
be divided among individuals and groups, resulting in a redistribution of economic power.

What is "ownership"? To say that one owns a car is a statement different in kind from the assertion that one has driven or
wrecked a car. The last two are descriptions of external physical
realities. The first asserts a legal status, an enforceable convention.
(In a society without laws or enforced customs, one would own
what he could defend, and ownership would then be a description of physical reality.) As such, the meaning of ownership is
historical and social.

We can more easily understand the modern meaning of ownership if we first examine what it meant during the industrial age.
Ownership implies value. One can possess and claim to "own"
something which is totally valueless, but the statement has no
economic meaning. Imagine a man enamored of a small piece of
sandstone which he displays in his home. To say he owned something that no one else wants is merely to assert that it is in
his possession. If he talked about the stone long and provocatively
enough to arouse the desires of others, it would take on value.
That's the history of advertising.

Value depends largely upon the possibility, actual or potential,
of exchange. There are few exceptions. A wizard might have

magical powers which only he could exercise. Nearly any social use of those powers, however, would be exchangeable, if only as entertainment. So, too, a man cannot exchange the thoughts which are his own—at least in the absence of extrasensory perception—but if he gives them a social form, through language or action, the product can have exchange value. In these cases, although the process is inseparable from a particular individual, its product is not. If no social use is made of the process, then the idea of ownership is irrelevant. It is like owning your dreams.

As only things of value can be owned, ownership included the right to that value. And that right must be exclusive to the extent of ownership. If non-owners have a right to the value of property, then no one owns it, although someone, or everyone, may have a right to possession. In this sense Marx described workers as owners of mere labor power, capitalists as owners of capital, and landowners as owners of land. Each of them received the value of their property in distinctive ways (wages, profits and rents) but it was their property—what they owned —that made them members of a class. They would remain members of that class even if temporary economic conditions made it impossible to receive any value for their property. (If such conditions were permanent their property would be valueless, their ownership destroyed.) There was also a middle class which owned an assortment of special skills and strategic positions. Since Marx believed this group was doomed he did not elaborate its class qualities in great detail. But the principle was the same.

The exclusive right to value was a logical principle of an economy based upon ownership. At some point, however, this right was enlarged: The owner could exclude all others from the property itself. An owner could shut down a factory, keep his land idle, bury his capital; he could withdraw his property from the society and renounce its value; and still bar all others. This was power and not economics. The economic relationship of ownership, a creation of the social structure, was fortified until property became an extension of its possessor's own existence. This was an enormous leap into alienation.

One could argue that the creation of ownership, the exclusive claim to value, would enlarge the total wealth of society. But the right to exclude meant that individuals would have the power to strip mankind itself of value and benefits. Ownership so defined was more than a function or relationship. It was sovereignty, and the ideology which sustained it was a faith.

This change in the content of ownership reflected the related increase of individualism. In any hierarchical society—where people are also part of some organic whole—it would be monstrous for an individual to claim the power to exclude the entire society from value by withholding or destroying the value of property. Yet even those landowners and emerging capitalists who sought to realize the full value of their property did not oppose the expansion of ownership. For if society was allowed to assert a claim to unused property, there was a danger that the use of property might also be measured by standards of public welfare or economic reason. It was necessary for the productive owner to protect the unproductive so that his own position would be secure. Nevertheless, this was the most vulnerable point in the structure of capitalism, and the power to renounce value, although still present, has been progressively reduced. Today, for example, the failure to use capital, to invest, is punished by a partial expropriation in the form of higher taxes. (And the managers of modern economic enterprises do not have the power to exclude.) While in a modern underdeveloped country, the unproductive landlord is the first object of revolutionary attack. It is through the weakness and irrationality of his position that the idea of expropriation gains entrance.

Ownership is a right to value, not value in itself. The right to value necessarily contains a personal element: the right of the owner to share in the determination of value—to set prices, bargain, determine use, decide whether to sell now or later. Naturally, the scope of that right was limited by economic conditions, by the power of those on the other side of a transaction. In the case of the worker, the right of determination could be almost nonexistent, although he could refuse to sell his labor at the going rate. This right is not a usurped addition to the concept of ownership; it is implicit in the right to value. No economic system can determine value automatically and with mathematical precision. How to receive the full value of goods always involves some degree of judgment and choice. If someone else is allowed to make that choice for the owner and without his consent—even if the owner is entitled to the full proceeds of the exchange—the right to value is diminished. (One who acts at the direction or consent of the owner is either an agent or the recipient of a gift; both relationships are consistent with ownership.) Even the simplest judgment— whether to sell now or later—depends not only on prediction but on the total economic situation of the property owner. One could posit a concept of ownership which vested a right to value severed from authority over property. However, the meaning of ownership is not revealed by a logical investigation of semantic possibilities. It is a legal relationship which evolved to forward the purposes of a changing economic process. One of the principal economic functions of ownership was to distribute authority over property in order to stimulate the creation of wealth. That authority was a necessary support for the power of those men, institutions and forces who came to dominate commercial and industrial societies.

In addition, among the ideological principles of private ownership is the assumption that those who hold economic power will use it to benefit themselves, to pursue their self-interest. That ideology is itself a recognition of the psychological imperatives imposed by an economic order based on ownership. One must, therefore, expect that a person with power to transfer another's property without consent will appropriate some of the value. Historical experience validates this expectation; loss of authority over property leads to a reduction of value, and is, to this extent also, a constituent of the right to value.

Authority over property came to be regarded as the principal quality of ownership. As summarized by the standard nineteenth-century treatise on British jurisprudence, "Ownership of property might be described accurately enough in the following manner: 'The right to use or deal with some given subject in a manner, or to an extent, which, though it is not unlimited, is indefinite.'"

Since the power to dispose of property is part of the right to its value, a transfer of that power is a partial transfer of ownership, and the retention of that power is necessary to ownership.* This attribute of ownership is the link between value and economic

* This is why, for example, we provide legal or constitutional authority for the power of eminent domain, recognizing it as a qualification of the right of ownership.

power. It is the use of wealth which shapes society, not its mere existence, although the level of wealth helps determine the framework for possibilities and oppressions of any particular society; i.e., the fact of wealth can make society affluent, but what happens within an affluent society depends upon the use of wealth.

Within industrial society significant economic power—power over and within the economic structure—was that conferred by ownership of the instruments of production. Plows and factories can be sold. They have exchange value. But that value is largely established by their capacity to help create other goods of value —crops or cars. Although this capacity is the basis for value (as scarcity is for the value of a jewel), value itself is established and realized through exchange. The instruments of production are not simply put to use, they are consumed in the process of production. They are used up, merged into the object of production or worn out. The owner of a factory exchanges raw materials, human energy, buildings and machines for goods. The power of an owner to use, or direct the use of, instruments of production is equivalent to the individual's power to exchange his goods. For the same reasons, personal control is inherent in value; it is part of the right to value and is that attribute of ownership which yields economic power.

Labor power is an essential part of the productive process. But when Marx wrote, the value of labor power was dispersed among millions of owners, while the value of factories, machines and raw materials was concentrated. The calculation of wealth requires a simple addition of values, but the economic power which such wealth creates proceeds in some kind of geometric progression. In Kingfield, Maine, where this is being written, the owner of the wood mill—the town's only industry—probably has net assets of around one hundred thousand dollars. Some of his workers (who are not unionized) probably have net assets of around ten thousand dollars. Those workers do not have one tenth of his power; they have no power at all, and he has a great deal.

Economic power, as we have seen, is a consequence of the right to value; its exercise is an attribute of ownership. Concentration of ownership brings a disproportionate aggregation of economic power. It is a kind of alchemy: the piling up of impotent units transmutes the accumulated mass into a source of great power. But how does one thing become another? Ownership is robed in power by the entire structure of economic relationships, values, ideology and politics which constitute the social process. The nineteenth-century worker, for example, was impotent because he owned such a tiny fraction of the available labor power. If the economic structure had made it possible to own a great deal of labor, or all of the labor resources available to a particular factory or industry, that ownership would have yielded a great deal of power. This is why men once fought to dominate the slave trade, and why modern labor leaders are invited to spend time at the White House.

This analytical sketch revises the observation that power and ownership have been separated in the modern state. For if authority inheres in the right to value, and is thus an attribute of ownership, it cannot be split off leaving us with authority in one place and ownership in another. If so, what remains is not ownership at all, but something else with the same name. Instead, we have divided ownership itself, permitting the attributes which compose it to fall into different hands. This is not an argument over labels. The division of ownership is a division of claims on value and brings with it a division of economic power. And when economic power is divided, it is diminished.

For an illustration we must adopt a perspective which belongs to twentieth-century consciousness and look upon *ownership not as a fact, a fixed state, but as a process, an element of a dynamic system whose essence resides in function and not existence.* A computer is such a system. It can be assembled from distinct modular units; one for memory, one for reading programs, etc. Together these units make up a computer; but if disassembled none of them can do some proportionate fraction of what a computer can do. They are no longer parts of a computer, for one cannot be a part of something which does not exist. Their functions of memory, calculation, etc. are attributes of the concept "computer." By separating those attributes the total power has been greatly reduced or even eliminated.

A political example of this principle is furnished by the history of the constitutional division of powers, reinforced by a system of checks and balances which was designed not only to separate the power of the state, but to reduce it, to prevent government itself from becoming too powerful—through a division of the attributes of political sovereignty. The modern fusion of once separated functions has not simply transferred power to the Executive at the expense of Congress, but has increased the total power of the state.

A division of ownership, by dividing economic power, also reduces it, so that the total economic power in the system is less than it was. We are, of course, speaking of the power of human beings; for the factory continues to disgorge its products, command resources, shape our civilization. And as economic relations take institutional form, we have necessarily designed a structure to institutionalize human impotence. It is called bureaucracy: the limitlessly tolerant servant-master of advanced societies, it is perfectly willing to be called communist in one place and capitalist in another—so long as it is allowed to function.

"Bureaucracy" is not a pejorative for unloved organizations. It designates a determinate structure and manner of function—a process. At least two conditions are necessary to bureaucracy. It must, first, be relatively independent of the desires, special purposes or insanities of particular individuals, including the transient holders of supreme headship. Secondly, it must be large; large enough to permit and justify internal regulation through "policies," "procedures" and "standards," able to dilute and restrain the consequence of personality with the rule of law. Function and size thrive in mutual dependency, in inorganic analogy to soul and body, mind and matter. Once bureaucracy becomes a dominating form of organization, its attitudes and values are diffused through the society. In this way a single mind can become a bureaucracy.

CHAPTER 4

Not all industries are bureaucracies, just the important ones. Of the more than one and a half million American corporations, one tenth of 1 per cent possess more than 55 per cent of all corporate assets—over one and one-third trillion dollars. Even these figures churlishly understate the economic importance of the supercorps. Their behavior bounds the behavior of most smaller units, and all are implicated in their fate. Should even a single major American industry collapse—were that possible—it would be a far greater economic disaster for us than, say, the bankruptcy of Britain, the fall of France or the discovery that there was no gold at Fort Knox. (The last might be a relief.) Given the scale of the American economy, that is concentration enough to stagger the night thoughts of any nineteenth-century Marxist. If this were really a concentration of capitalist wealth and power, the system would have collapsed into the state as Marx predicted. Let us rather describe it as a concentration of productive capacity.

Of course, one can also measure corporations by market value, revenues, profits, etc. It also makes a difference whether you include all corporations or just manufacturing corporations, thus excluding banks, insurance companies, etc.; although it would seem a little strange to neglect the holders of capital in an analysis of capitalism. But whatever method you choose the conclusion is the same—a concentration of dominant economic and productive capacity in a few large units. And the pace of concentration has been accelerating over the past decade.

The concentration would be even greater if we grouped companies according to shared interest and action, rather than by corporate charters. It makes more sense to think of the automotive industry as a single economic unit rather than as an industry dominated by three major companies. These companies produce essentially the same product in the same way. They never indulge in serious price warfare or technological competition. Their shareholders overlap—increasingly so with the growth of institutional investors—their managers are cut from the same pattern, they sign the same contract with the same union and prevail upon the same agencies of the same government. It does not take a trinitarian metaphysics to see that viewed from the perspective of social welfare or economic science, functionally, they are one.

The ideological justifications for economic competition are not metaphysical but functional: to vivify the economy by, for example, rewarding superior performance—innovation, efficiency and energy —and by permitting the purchaser maximum value for his money. Corporations are functionally distinct only when they are competitive, or at least when large elements of competition remain. Company names and corporate charters tell us only about economic history and the law, disguising the economic structure. In the world of the megacorporations there is little functional difference between monopoly and oligopoly—between telephones, computers, automobiles, steel and oil. Indeed, the oligopoly has the economic power of a monopoly without providing the same temptation to public regulation. For one corporation to absorb the others—to create a monopoly—would bring great dangers and almost no advantages. Those who managed the takeover could not even be sure that their salaries would increase. Nor would stock necessarily be a better investment.

A functional analysis of the economy would expose a prodigious concentration of assets. We would see that the few corporations with more than half the assets are really only ten to twenty bureaucracies. We would also find that many smaller companies function as parts of the same structure. Such an analysis would require an exploration of actual differences in product, prices, innovation and the effort to expand a share of the market. Viewed this way we would find immense and accelerating concentration, already over-flowing national borders. Any other kind of analysis is a study of names.

Who owns these economic brontosauri? Economic literature generally agrees that the managers are not owners. Yet, as we have defined ownership, managers do possess one of its attributes: the power to use and direct.* Certainly no one else does. They are part owners, although their power has been greatly limited by its division from the other attributes of ownership.

Our search then turns to the legal "owners": the holders of common stock. More than thirty million people own stock in American companies. Many, perhaps a majority, hold shares in the larger companies. All of the economic bureaucracies have legions of shareholders. Corporate charters and corporation codes seem to agree that these shareholders own the company. Yet a shareholder cannot exchange his stock for an equivalent fraction of a corporation's assets. Neither can he demand an equivalent portion of corporate earnings; that is, he has no right to the value of the company. Yet ownership is a right to value; those without that right are not owners. If a security was, in fact, a claim to value of the company its price would tend to affect the present or rationally foreseeable assets or earnings of a company. It does not. For example, IBM with assets of around eleven billion dollars has a market value (total cost of all shares at the current price per share) of over forty-six billion dollars, while AT&T with over sixty billion dollars in assets has a market value of less than thirty billion. This is an extreme illustration of the fact that the market value of almost all large companies has no fixed relationship to its assets. And the same is true of earnings. A company like Xerox, with earnings of around two and a half billion dollars, has almost the same market value as General Electric with earnings of over ten billion dollars. Nor can any purchaser of stock in Xerox anticipate that its earnings will ever equal those of General Electric. These disproportions would only surprise one who assumed that a share of stock was actually a claim on the value of a corporation.

Forbes magazine says of market value that "there are few

---

* Somewhat qualified by the limiting authority of directors, etc. But those limitations are themselves the consequence of institutional structure.

figures more ephemeral, more shifting, more dependent on matters that are frequently out of management's control." The nature of the securities market is such that the value of stock is as much a matter of metaphysics as industrial worth; more the product of alternating greed and timidity, passionate expectation and chilled detachment than of economic expansion and decline. There is some relationship between the value of securities and the strength of the corporation that issued them. Shares in a bankrupt company would be worthless. However, we need not analyze this relationship—analogous to the link between the value of the dollar and the strength of the economy—to establish that one who buys stock in an economic bureaucracy does not possess any fixed or proportionate claim to the value of that corporation as expressed in earnings or assets, present or future.

The fact that dividends are issued does not qualify this conclusion. After taxes and costs are deducted from corporate earnings, about 75 per cent of what is left goes back into the corporation. This is known as the "cash flow," even though it doesn't flow anywhere. The remainder is for dividends, whose size is determined by management and not shareholders. Functionally, dividends are designed to help maintain a market by giving shareholders some return on their capital. Shareholders receive less for their money than bondholders, but they are recompensed with hope.

Since shareholders have no right to the value of the corporation, they do not own it. If some Tibetan monk were moved to study our economy as a penitential exercise and was restricted to a volume containing the law of corporations, he might well conclude that shareholders did own them. He would discover that shareholders had a legal right to set policy, hire and fire managers, even to dissolve the company and distribute the assets. He would not understand that his studies were historical; the exploration of a legal structure which was the residue of a receding social reality. The broadening of stock ownership to large numbers of the general public has made it impossible for shareholders to exercise their legal powers. Ownership has been nullified through dispersion.

Some seem to believe it might be possible to organize shareholders, to re-establish shareholder power through unification. Among the many fatal barriers to this hope is the fact that stock in a particular company represents only a small fraction of the income or economic interest of most shareholders. They can neither hope nor afford to give that company the attention required by any sensible exercise of power. Moreover, if it were possible to organize shareholders they would be even more intent on short-term profit and growth than management. That is the nature of their interest. As shareholders, they do not represent the consuming interest, much less that of the entire citizenry. A shareholder democracy would be more rapacious, shortsighted and anti-social than an economic bureaucracy. However, such arguments are academic, for the ownership necessary to "shareholder power" no longer exists.

If shareholders do not own the company, what do they own? They own stock. In some fashion that stock is backed by the corporation. But, since their only right is to the value of that stock as determined by the market, stock is all that they own.

If the shareholders don't own the corporation, and if the managers don't own it, then who does? There seems to be only one remaining possibility. The corporation owns itself. The relationship is not comprehended in Marxist categories, but Marx was too much of a nineteenth-century humanist to follow the paths of alienation to the end.

CHAPTER 5

Marx's attack on religion was invested with the righteousness of a prophet who perceives a corruption of the faith. The powerful attraction of Marxism derived from its awareness that the expanded material possibility of satisfying traditional desires had converted inevitability to injustice. It accommodated the censures and prophecies of the Gospels to the fact that riches once secreted in heaven were now to be found on earth. The most persuasive of these restatements was the secularization of Christ's promise that "many that are first shall be last; and the last shall be first," words that had done more than love to justify man's ways to man. Workers, "owners of mere labor power," condemned by their helplessness to suffer the insatiable extortions of capitalist masters, would accomplish a literal revolution, an overturning; the mired base of society's pyramid would be a platform toward the higher realms of freedom. The first step would be the "socialization of labor," which, along with centralization of production, would deepen the vulnerabilities of capitalism to approaching revolution.

Labor was socialized. The result was the modern economic bureaucracy. New historical possibilities had intervened. Without modern technology the sprawling structures of bureaucracy could not function. We would lack even the illusion of control. Nor could workers have been absorbed into the dominant economic structures until productive capacity had swelled to such a scale that only mass consumption could sustain it, until the rights of the few came to depend on the comfort of the many. In the late 1930s, it started to become apparent that to impoverish the masses was to strike at the dominant economic interests, that in the new economy, capitalism was incompatible with great wealth and power. So capitalism yielded.

An effort to define capitalism would be a historical exercise, like trying to define feudalism. It is a word developed to describe the evolution and structure of industrial economies in the mid-nineteenth century. It cannot be applied to the American economy of today without changing its meaning in fundamental ways. Indeed, the concept itself imprisons our thought, inducing us to cram new institutions into historical categories, and distracting us from the search for the source of our afflictions. Radical thought often seeks to preserve old enemies. Marx himself spent enormous energies in his opposition to religion at a time when its power to influence society had already faded. Modern Marxists attack private property as if that institution were the same as a century ago, and consequently make it more difficult to see that our oppressions derive from the management and autonomous function of property. Some even seem to think that if the government owned all property, it would belong to the people, although the entire history of the twentieth century denies this proposition. Even in America the government already owns a lot. Is it yours?

Once unions—socialized labor—were incorporated into the legal structure, the owners of "mere labor power" acquired a far more valuable property. They became owners of the labor resource itself. As with any concentration of economic assets, the result was to create economic power. Collectively, workers could deprive industry of access to labor, an asset much greater than the sum of their individual services. Through negotiations union leaders have a delegated power to share in determining the value of the labor resource —to set a price expressed in wages, benefits and conditions of employment. Workers have a claim to that value enforced by the law of contracts, a technique used to protect property from the very beginning of commercial society. Approached in this fashion, we can see that modern labor legislation—like the post-Civil War law of corporations—simply adds another dimension to the law of ownership.

The labor resource is not owned by workers as individuals. Part of it is in the hands of managers—the union leaders. Whenever widely dispersed property comes under central management, the result is bureaucracy. In a bureaucracy the managers are also owners, at least to the extent of their power to determine value. That is among the reasons that bureaucratic structures always have some interests distinct from those of its constituencies. Union bureaucracies, for example, must restrict themselves to goals consistent with their power, which is limited to the protections and rewards which can be taken from the present industrial structure. To the extent workers have needs which cannot be met in this way, unions cannot represent them. One can see that in pursuit of goals prescribed by its structure and function a union could be at odds with other needs of the workers. Should those other needs become dominant, the union would be compelled to act against the interests of the working class. We are about halfway toward this contradiction.

The conclusion that the socialization of labor created a new form of property—the labor resource—is further affirmed by the considerations which establish the value of labor. In a unionized industry there is no longer any way to fix the value of "mere labor power." Should an army of unemployed offer themselves at half pay they will not be employed, nor will existing wages be reduced (absent serious economic decline). The market mechanism for labor has gone the way of the whip, the chain and feudal dues, although it lingers in a few remaining pockets of capitalism. It has been replaced by the division of production.

The "law" of supply and demand does not fix the value of socialized labor. That law was a working rule of an economic structure which dispersed the property of workers and concentrated the property of capitalists. (Just as today the same phrase is used to impart a rational tone to the fact that the economic power of consumers is dispersed and that of producers is concentrated. If consumption should be socialized then prices and quality will be determined by capacity and not demand.) Instead, wage demands and settlements are based on corporate earnings, the general price structure—itself largely established by the economic bureaucracy—and by the sensed power of the corporation to pass the increase along in higher prices. This last is possible in both good times and bad, but not very bad, which is among the reasons inflation can accompany recession, but perhaps not depression. This basis for settlement is accepted by all parties, although they may differ on amount. Imagine a major industry rejecting a wage increase during a time of record earnings on the grounds that plenty of people were willing to work for less! Such standards demonstrate that unions are exchanging the labor resource for a share of the business, as do suppliers of equity capital. (Or, in contradiction to Marx's description of industrial relationships, labor *does* have "use value" to the worker.)

At times it is asserted that economic justice would be better served if wage increases were linked to productivity. The idea seems to fill a certain spiritual need. It is an ideological atavism, stirring memories of capitalist ancestors who paid men what they were worth—"a day's work for a day's pay." Such a standard has rarely been applied, although it was insinuated into discussions of recent proposals for economic controls. It is a pretechnological idea. It does not require that increased productivity result from increased worker effort or skill rather than from new technology, methods or investment. If there is no substantial change in the number of workers, increased productivity is virtually the same as increased production, and if prices are fairly stable, more production means higher earnings. The "productivity" standard, therefore, returns us to a division of production by a different name. Indeed, under normal conditions that standard is a device, a bureaucratic servomechanism, for maintaining the existing division. In the unlikely event of economic conditions which produce greater earnings without higher productivity, the standard would be jettisoned for it would then clash with the realities of economic power, with the structure of ownership. Theoretically, a productivity standard might encourage technological innovation, at least innovation of the kind which did not eliminate jobs, since some portion of the benefits would go to union members. But any such impact would probably be trivial; and in any event, economic bureaucracies are not very interested in technological innovation.*

Socialization has created an economic class distinct from both the working and middle class of the mid-nineteenth century. Since

* Automation is a special case. Extensive automation would require a change in the terms of division, and ultimately in the mechanism, of distribution through wages which is fundamental to the economic process—a reconstruction whose uncertainties strengthen resistance by all elements of the bureaucracy.

the character and interests of a class consist in the property it owns, the ownership of the labor resource, rather than mere labor power, has created a different set of interests. Foremost among them is the necessity to protect and sustain the economic bureaucracies on which the value of the labor resource depends. As these large industries flourish, grow and increase their earnings, the property of socialized labor, its claim to value, also burgeons. Should the industry decline or fall, the property and its attribute of power will also diminish. Individual workers may find new jobs, but the union, the collective bureaucracy, would be stripped of its property and reduced toward mere labor power. Unions are, therefore, and must be, a functioning component of the economic bureaucracy. To act in opposition would be to seek self-destruction.

In *The Power Elite*, C. Wright Mills, observing that unions seemed increasingly disinterested in the formulation of progressive social policy, explained that unions had become less involved in social movements once they were dependent on governmental power. Union "dependence" on government, however, is like that of corporations, i.e., they are legitimized, recognized by the legal structure. This gives them more power, not less, but that power is a consequence of their incorporation into the ruling economic structure. The behavior of unions has changed because their interests have changed, not because they are the objects of coercion.

Of course, union leaders dream different dreams than company presidents, shareholders and pension fund managers. They do not spend long hours studying to improve company earnings. Each component in the modern process of production—managers, shareholders, unions and creditors—differ from all the others in claim and estate. But all are linked by the immanent interest of the corporation itself—to function, grow and earn. *The nature of their power and property requires each of them—including unions—to act consistently with the purpose, the inbuilt tropisms, of the economic bureaucracy.* This is true regardless of what particular individuals think they are doing or what they want to do.

We can never hope to analyze the social process if we contemplate the interior and personal qualities of the agents of social power—are they "good" men, does a union leader really believe in socialism, is a company president a contributor to liberal causes? In the exercise of social power an individual's purpose is defined by his action, not by the contours of an inward will or illusion. In particular, the moral content of any exercise of social power is not related to the inner virtues of the agent, although the difference between the two helps to delineate alienation. The personalization of judgment is itself an aspect of the ideology and consciousness which support present economic relationships. So, as one would expect, there is a growing inclination to correlate social behavior, especially political behavior, with the personal attributes of those in authority. In so doing, the observer severs the ties between social process and individual actions.

Some union leaders are leaders of progressive thought and do not hesitate to ally themselves against large corporations on public issues. But the union itself is a creature of economics and not belief. Its attitudes and actions are determined by its structure and function. Should there be a fundamental challenge to the corporate structure, individual union leaders would have to choose. The union would have no choice.

There are always adversary elements in the relation between union and management, as there are between all major constituents of the economic bureaucracy. These differences can be accommodated without impairing the common purpose. For that purpose is the source of value for all. Thus, unions do not push wage demands to the point where profits would be almost eliminated. In earlier economic theory, the owner of a corporation would prefer even a small profit to closing down the company; just as the "monopolist" of the labor resource would push his advantage to the maximum. Today, however, so rigorous a settlement would menace the now and future strength of the company and consequently undermine the property of the union. This is so clear that any such demands would be perceived as a bluff or correctable error. In addition, unions are not dealing with owners but with managers whose more precarious interests are nourished by earnings and growth, not the desire for return on investment, and who might, therefore, sink the ship before allowing it to be plundered.† Once in a while nostalgic passions get out of hand, and one group or the other, its judgment clouded by fury and memory, threatens to haul down the pillars. When that happens in a major industry, the

† This is a hypothesis of analysis, a possibility, but one not likely to occur.

government can be counted upon to intervene. For the interest of government is also linked to the well-being of the bureaucracy.

The social power of unions like that of the economic bureaucracy is based on the concentration of corporate assets. There are about eighty million American workers. About twenty million, little more than 25 per cent, belong to unions. That membership, however, is heavily and strategically concentrated among the production workers in major industries. Since the value of the labor resource depends upon the assets and earnings of the company, the property of socialized labor—and its consequent economic power—is hugely disproportionate to the number of workers involved. In fact, there is no rational or calculable relation. (So long as the labor resource is essential, i.e., absent extensive automation.) If unions have lost some of their zeal to enlist the unorganized, it is for reasons like those which keep General Motors from buying up textile mills or garages. Union power, therefore, is not only dependent on the economic bureaucracy, but it is sustained by the same concentration of assets which creates that bureaucracy. Those identities are so extensive that unions must be regarded as constituents of economic bureaucracy, compelled by function and nature to resist all efforts to reduce its domination.

Union structure shows a relationship to the concentration of assets more openly than do corporate charters. Workers in many major industries are organized into a single union, with similar contractual rights regardless of the company they work for. When negotiations begin it is taken for granted that the first major settlement will be the model for all the rest. Functionally, one company is dealing with one union.

The polarity between merciless capitalist and oppressed workers has found a resolution truer to the dialectic than Marx's own—fusion into a single reality. The worker no longer stands opposed to capital and the process of production with "nothing to lose but his chains." He has been incorporated into that process, made part of a system which he cannot control, whose purposes and values must, therefore, dominate his life. His class interests, beyond labor power, compel him to accept and serve the relations of production which obstruct his own possibilities of freedom. Having overtaken the realm of necessity, no longer compelled to labor for material existence alone, he is denied the fruits of that achievement

—the enlargement of his humanity—by the process he continually reconstructs. The afflictions of modern life—the events and forces we have described—are steadily diffused into his daily activities and relationships. He is bound to the systems and structures which erode the possibilities of his own existence.

Marx's worker transferred a portion of his humanity to the goods he produced. His own labor stood "opposed to him as an autonomous power." Still, the source of his exploitation was not inanimate, but the ruling class, the capitalist employer. This relationship was not totally one of alienation, i.e., it was not completely the creation of the worker. However oppressed, he retained some autonomy, even if it could only find expression in the freedom to defy, strike and destroy. That is the difference between alienation and slavery—one the inward division of the self, the other an outward bond. Today's worker is not alienated to goods but to the process of production. The broken power of the capitalist was transferred—not to the worker—but to the system which absorbed both capitalist and worker, deepening alienation, extending the domination of an impersonal mechanism with its own methods, values and purposes. This has created a far more formidable adversary than ruling classes or individual tyrants. For rebellion is made to seem an act of self-mutilation. Barriers to freedom present themselves as dikes against reaction, as protection against a return to material misery, persuading men to maintain obstacles to the fulfillment of their own humanity.

CHAPTER 6

The Spirit of Transaction Past—from excavation to commodity
The Spirit of Transaction Present—from desire to possession
The Spirit of Transaction Future—from provocation to aban-
donment

Awareness and resistance are more likely to begin—if they do begin
—among unsocialized labor; the more than sixty million workers,
over 75 per cent of the national work force, who are not organized
into unions. The great majority of unsocialized workers do not
make anything; they do not shape wood or metal or plastic. Instead, they man the bureaucracy. They make the system run.
They are to the "private" economy what more than two and one-
half million employees are to the federal government, what most
members of the military are to the combatant few.

If production as the transformation of resources into commodities were still the key to the creation of wealth, this distribution of
the work force would seem some monstrous disproportion, irrational
waste on a titanic scale. But the vital force, the anima, of modern
wealth is the sorcering spirit of transaction—accomplishing through
the energy of motion what millennia of mining, craft and manufacture could not achieve. Unconfined by limited productive capacity or natural resources, wealth accumulates with the increased
motion of money, goods, people, desires, knowledge.*

* Productive capacity can be temporarily inadequate to rises in demand, usually
as a result of managerial misjudgments. But it can be expanded.

Transaction rules production, is incarnate among the power-masking vapidities of distribution, sales, advertising, cost accounting, communication and scientific management. The great automobile bureaucracies, for example, are able to dominate and exclude not because of their production plants but because of a nation-mantling web of distribution, sales and maintenance, which any domestic challenger would find almost impossible to duplicate or defy. The dealer and not the foreman is the principal guarantor of economic power.

Although most unsocialized workers belong to the middle class, they cannot be fitted into a single category of interest and ownership. They are not members of a single Marxist class. At the economic bottom are the remnants of the traditional working class, the owners of mere labor power: migrant workers, common laborers, the uneducated young and those in occupations which require neither training nor experience. At the top are large numbers of highly skilled technicians, engineers, managers and professionals. In the middle are millions of clerical and service workers, unorganized production workers and those who practice a myriad of crafts and skills.

Unsocialized workers do not own the labor resource. The bottom fraction have "mere labor power"; while the rest own that and something more; not only muscle and energy, but also some increment of talent, knowledge or dexterity. That increment can be the capacity to synthesize a new plastic or the more moderate intelligence needed to find the appropriate file folder. Through exchange they acquire a claim to the value of their property, and that value is a measure of their economic worth.

As befits their numbers and diversity, unsocialized workers establish their claim to value in many ways. The owners of mere labor power receive, as always, as little as possible—enough for survival and for compliance, where applicable, with minimum wage laws. Of the 5.2 million family heads classified as poor by the government, almost 1.2 million are over sixty-five. More than 75 per cent of the rest worked last year. As it was in Marx's time, work is no escape from poverty if you have nothing to sell but yourself.

The upper levels of unsocialized labor are occupied by a rather large minority who establish their claim to value by exchanging skills which are not easy to replace. The man who can coin phrases: the "Pepsi Generation" or the "Great Society"; the designer of car fenders; the contriver of computer circuits; the possessor of the kind of energy and calculation needed to establish or run a successful small business, e.g., the car dealer and the appliance merchant. Some are paid directly; others live on their own calculation of profit and loss in "independent" enterprises, many of which exist because and for the bureaucracy; while still others manage to extract some portion of what is left of a free economy. Members of the last group serve as tokens of illusion, new converts to a receding faith, permitting the naive and cynical to join in denying the departure of piety.

Although the possessors of desired skills—the top rank of unsocialized labor—are compensated for capacities beyond mere labor power, their value is not established by demand alone. Admittedly market accommodations dominate prices for many talents which are useful and not plethoric. However, the transaction economy and its prevailing bureaucracies cannot extort every transient advantage of the market. Production is an event, but process is a flow. The interruption of this process would be far more devastating than waste or temporary losses. To avoid interruption, ingredients essential to the creation of wealth must be available. It is economic to keep them on hand, despite the risk that changing or receding needs may render the investment worthless. Availability has a value of its own. Among the reasons that "war is waste" is the need to respond to possibilities which will never materialize—prepare for the unconceived attack, fling bombs toward the contingent soil. Although major corporations, in relationship to each other, make more love than war—their future still contains uncertain elements. Some wasteful preparation is necessary to protect the process, and as economic bureaucracies extend their planning over increasing time spans, the amount of intrinsic waste grows.

Many individuals prevail upon these necessities of process in order to increase their value, commanding a price based on incentive as well as the market. For example, abilities which require many years of training or education must be compensated at a scale which will tempt others to years of profitless preparation. A person who has already spent a decade at college, graduate school and business school learning the most sophisticated techniques of system analysis, cost accounting and other propitiatory arts will work for less if he must. He has little choice. But the auguring young would seek other trails to course. Commissions or markups must also be high enough to stimulate an energetic individual to sell that extra appliance and to fructify his dealership in good times and bad. A dealer, for example, must be restrained from relaxing during an especially good year in the belief that a few more commissions aren't necessary or worth it.

A high-price structure alone won't enforce such controls. A structure of values, an ethos, is also necessary. We have one—not the once potent, now whimsical, Protestant Work Ethic, but one of Success+Consumption=Gratification—a secular Good-Things-of-Life Ethic.

The worker may regard such compensation as a return on his investment in time, money or toil, but that requires the absurd assumption that the corporation is acting out of generosity or a sense of Greek proportion. To some extent he is being paid to be an emblem, a stimulus to the creation of still-disembodied skills. This increases his loyalty and submission to the process of production. For his claim to value is not only based on personal talents, but on the impersonal needs of institutions. He owns not only his skills but a fraction of the system. In this way a portion of his existence is incorporated into the economic structure.

Many also benefit from the scales of compensation established, in part, to help maintain order and authority in the bureaucratic hierarchy. No matter how excessive the supply, engineers will not be paid less than assembly line workers. This addition to value is also a creation of economic process, and increases the extent of merger into the economic bureaucracy.

Others in this skilled subgroup protect their value through association—joining in an informal and wordless conspiracy, among themselves and with their clients or employers, to keep prices up. For example, the high wages paid to workers by advertising agencies are themselves evidence that unusual skills are being rewarded. Compensation is proof of creativity. These payments help justify the fees which enable agency heads to get rich. Since serious price competition might endanger this structure, major agencies ordinarily restrict their competition to product. They do this by standardizing fees for those services which involve the largest cash flow. Most advertising money goes to buy media time or space. The agency receives a fixed percentage of this cost regardless of the quality, importance or even the presence of that creative contribution which is their major product. While most individual advertising men follow the path from martinis to milk, the advertising trade thus evades the rigors of the market place.

Through associations, combinations and conspiracies those with certain competences can secure some benefits of socialization. Income-enhancing associations are especially characteristic of skills whose product cannot be measured, weighed, seen or calculated; whose existence is itself often a matter of faith. Varying combinations of arbitrarily high wages, standard fees, time payments and "professional" limitation of supply are found among large law firms, psychiatrists, management consultants, tenured professors, research firms, television networks and doctors.

The most common method of eliminating price competition—i.e., of keeping prices high—is basing charges on time. Corporation lawyers, psychiatrists, consultants and television networks charge by the hour. Others charge fixed fees unrelated to actual performance. And within the relevant market area association members charge about the same. Lawyers in Topeka charge less than those on Wall Street, but Standard Oil doesn't send its legal business to Topeka. Members of the medical profession, the effective managers of a business which produces about seventy billion dollars in health services annually, protect their prices with a wide variety of devices —from fixed fees and arbitary standards of competence to deliberate restriction of entry into the profession.

Many of these associations such as advertising agencies, securities brokers and large law firms compete vigorously, even frantically, to persuade clients of their superior product. Product competition may be risky, it may corrode the organs, but it is not free enterprise. One of the purposes of market competition was to reallocate resources. When the price of a service fell—assuming demand was relatively constant†—investment or consumption dollars were liberated to go

† Such inelasticity depends on the nature of the product. If prices fall one might buy more advertising but probably would not see more doctors. (Although more people would see doctors if they were available.) The demand for the services offered by these associations is restrained by need as well as cost—in varying proportions. And the calculation is complicated by the fact that the need for many of these services is intangible, i.e., bears no calculable relation to productivity or earning.

elsewhere. Restricting competition to product tends to stabilize the existing allocation of resources. It helps ensure that about the same proportion of capital or earnings will be spent for the same products. Since the economic bureaucracies which purchase these services are under no great pressure to cut costs—so long as they pay equivalent rates—there is little objection to such price fixing.

One of President Kennedy's most effective weapons against the rise in steel prices was the Defense Department's threat to buy only from companies which kept prices down. The President's act was faithful to the spirit and ideology of free enterprise, yet corporate conference rooms disgorged alarms and maledictions. This ruthless display of old-time capitalism by the nation's biggest industry, defense, had transgressed the modern code of economic conduct. Economic bureaucracies in fields such as automobiles, communications, etc. have a similar, if somewhat less extensive, power. They could often compel lower prices—reducing costs, penalizing the inefficient and bankrupting the losers. However, the bureaucratic structure which they dominate and compose depends upon the absence of serious price competition. Like all social ideologies, this imperative manifests itself as economic "reality" or even "necessity"; e.g., there is no reason to take such action, because lower costs would require lower prices, higher wages or increased dividends. Moreover, if the dominant company reduced costs, all the others must follow and no one would win. This reasoning is fundamentally, but not completely, tautological: We must act like noncompetitive bureaucracies because we are non-competitive bureaucracies (and wish to so remain). We do what we do because of what we are. In truth, they are what they are because of what they do.

Corporate purchasers often have no more idea what a service is "worth" than does an individual when he goes to a doctor. If there is no way to value a product, one is tempted to assume it is worth what it costs. One of the more impressive triumphs of economic mysticism has been to create a belief in the value of value; price as a thing in itself. But there is also an indigenous explanation for the capacity to demand high and standardized compensation. It gratifies the congenital bureaucratic disposition to standardize the process of decision. The bureaucratic utopia would be a world in which there was no decision at all, where every set of facts would be matched to a logically inevitable response. This promised land is still far away, but the faithful continue their struggle to eliminate variables, and thereby reduce the disquiets of personal judgment.

A worker is expected to sell his skills. When skills are partly idiosyncratic, i.e., where they depend to a significant extent upon personal talents as well as knowledge of a craft, it is economic to base compensation both on demand and the worker's contribution to the creation of wealth. (The more idiosyncratic a skill, the less demand matters. Finally there is no market for skills that are unique—a fact which can make a pauper of a poet or painter into a millionaire.) Through methods like those which we have been examining, many skilled workers are able to establish a value which is not totally dependent on the combination of demand and economic contribution. They extract additional value from the ideology and structure of the economic bureaucracy itself. They are thus indebted, not just to product—theirs and that of their employer—but to the existing process of production, to its need for availability, aversion to price competition, reliance upon transaction, etc. To the extent their value is a creation of the system rather than of its product, its created wealth, they are part of that system; further examples of the economic bureaucracy's life-sustaining power to absorb those who make it function.

One should not be surprised that so many of the highly skilled desire and create the conditions of their own alienation. The values and methods of the dominant bureaucracies are pitilessly diffused through the entire economic structure. Many of the skilled associations are themselves mini-bureaucracies. The product of their labor is usually immaterial and, unlike traditional commodities, often has no potential value or even existence apart from present economic relationships. Since an incremental value, and thus the economic worth, of many highly skilled and educated workers depends upon existing patterns of production, they can be added to our growing list of those who have alienated themselves to the economic process. And the topmost fraction of this group contains the establishment—those whose value, worth, perception of power and identity have been so absorbed that they cannot distinguish their own existence from that of the social process. For some, preservation of the present becomes a matter of psychic life or death; the most fortunate of men they are also among the most alienated.

The identity between most skilled workers and the ascendant economic process is neither complete nor stable. Not too long ago the owner of a significant publishing complex fired the editor of *Harper's Magazine* and many of its writers. These men were defenseless. They lacked the basic protection against arbitrary decision by management which is the common possession of every factory worker in Detroit. They could not even compel the owner to make a case, to articulate a reasonable cause. Their response was to protest and leave. It does not seem that they had ever considered the possibility of forming an organization which, if confronted by such management action, could call a strike and seek to persuade established unions to honor their picket line. This surely means that they accepted the proprietor's power as given. They were willing to challenge the use of ownership, but not ownership itself. And so they lost. Yet, as the history of union labor proves, such powers are not inevitable attributes of the control of capital. They depend on the acquiescence of the powerless; a submission enforced by ruling economic relationships. In the case of much highly skilled labor that acquiescence is gained partly through ideological deception—which makes the idea of socialization appear hostile to the singularity of their occupation and ability.

Skills which are highly idiosyncratic and whose use decisively influences the final product cannot receive protection identical to that given the average factory worker. But there is no reason inherent in the nature of such skills why the manager of a publishing house or research laboratory should not be held to standards; permitted, for example, to discharge employees only for specific and demonstrated reasons and required to pay termination benefits. Indeed, it would seem logical for skilled employees of businesses where individual talent is critical to demand a share in management decisions. However, such rights cannot be extracted from a structure which premises power upon ownership. For "right" is just another word for power; what cannot be enforced or compelled is not a right but a gift—or a delusion. One must either change the premise (to, let us say, authority shall be based on contribution to the product) or, through socialization, become an owner. The second course is reform, the first, revolution. The second is easier and, on a large enough scale, might lead to the first. Then again it might create just another union. It is easier to follow the path of revolution than to find it.

Either of these premises would represent an adjustment in the distribution of power to conform to changes in economic reality which have already occurred. By concentrating capital and providing investment, the traditional capitalist performed a function which was essential to the development of an industrial economy.‡ Labor was essential, but it was available; it did not have to be created (although capital did create the working class). Since the activities of the capitalist were the initiating impulse of industrial growth, his power was related to his economic significance—even though he overstated and abused that power. But in many enterprises the relative importance of capital has diminished. Let us return to the *Harper's* example. The success or failure of that magazine depends almost completely upon its quality and appeal. If enough people or the right kind of people want to read it, and if advertising executives incline toward it, then investors will proliferate. Without that, the most generous investors cannot make the magazine succeed. Although capital is necessary to initiate such an enterprise, skill is the foundation of its economic growth. The same is true, to varying extents, in many specialized enterprises. Yet, in most cases, the distribution of power remains consistent with obsolete economic realities.

The position of many in the highest category of socialized labor is often the most vulnerable to changing conditions. It is difficult to halve the salaries of an aerospace engineer, computer specialist or magazine editor. But changing patterns of production and consumption, new desires and priorities, can eliminate the need for their skills entirely. Others find that economic stagnation or decline transforms the necessary into the expendable; most readily those whose contribution to the creation of wealth is immaterial and conjectural. These highly skilled and rewarded individuals are more at the mercy of traditional market forces than an assembly-line worker or a truck driver. They are part of the system, but they are not the system. They have neither the protection of socialization,

‡ This is a historical and not a necessary truth. Socialism provides an alternative method of concentration. However, it is doubtful that the conditions which make socialism feasible existed during the early industrial period.

nor a share in the power of decision. Corporate judgment, desire or whim can topple them without consultation or compensation. At such times, the security of bureaucracy is for them seen to be an illusion; as is the expectation of some that their special contributions or relationship to the bureaucratic hierarchy has entitled them, if not to power, to the right to limit its exercise. But awards, cocktail parties and friendly dinners are not ownership, and, therefore, confer no economic power.

CHAPTER 7

Probably a majority of all American workers—certainly the most
numerous single group—occupy the middle range of unsocialized
labor. They own more than mere labor power, or seem to, but their
property is not adequate to place them among the laboring elite,
the seneschals of bureaucracy. They are file clerks and embalmers,
secretaries and carnival operators. They move property, sell property, protect property and repair property. They keep accounts,
inspect accounts and try to collect accounts. They transport food
from factory to supermarket carts, diversion from videotapes to
vacuum tube, and credit from computers to mailbox. They draft
memos, type memos, read memos, post memos, duplicate memos
and file memos. They carry information to children and water to
fires. They survey streets, build streets, plow streets and arrest
those who speed on streets. Few are involved in production; i.e.,
they do not make things, palpable commodities, from material resources. But they make the machine run, and as transaction rules
production they are the unromantic fiber of our wealth. Destroy
factories and farms, and new ones would spring up on command.
But obliterate the system and knowledge of the system, wipe out
clerks and records, roads and manuals, and the giants of mining and
production would wither and dissolve. The plenitude of this middle group is both proof and consequence of our change to a transaction economy. When Franklin Roosevelt was elected to the New

York State Senate, in 1910, about 60 per cent of our work force consisted of common laborers. Today, less than four million (about 5 per cent) of our eighty million workers are classified as "non-farm laborers"; the change in language reinforcing the disclosure.

Lacking the incremental property of the socialized and highly skilled, members of this group are more exposed to the traditional hazards and uncertainties of the market. They are the first to be divested by inflation and the last redeemed by prosperity. They pay more taxes for fewer benefits. Whereas the poor have their prophets and the rich their chroniclers, they are enshrined in the annals of the registry of motor vehicles. Recently their existence has been acknowledged in the ambiguous term "middle America"— the filling in the continental sandwich.

These workers establish their value largely on the basis of need and scarcity. They own only labor power and skills. Since workers in such a reduced position are the most vulnerable to exploitation they tend to occupy the lower range of compensation. Although statisticians do not classify workers by the criteria we are using, they provide evidence for this tendency with figures showing that average hourly and weekly wages in the "industry groups" of retail trade, finance, insurance, real estate and services are far below those received by workers in manufacturing, mining and contract construction. The average weekly wage for mining, construction and transportation workers is almost double the pay of those who toil at retail trade or labor to provide us with services, both vital and redundant. Clerks and teachers, salespeople and unsocialized production workers belong to the class with the lowest value. (With the exception of the remnants of an impoverished under class whom we omit from this exploration of relative vulnerability to economic uncertainty and change. Most of those at the bottom are relatively secure in their poverty. Their relationship to shifting economic conditions is like that of prisoners to a changing of the guard.)

The income received by this middle group is not explicitly based upon their social or economic importance, their productivity or their contribution to the creation of wealth. Their economic value is what they can receive in exchange for their property, as with others it is largely based on ownership. Since they tend to own less

THE AMERICAN CONDITION 241

than other groups, they get less. Even when, as is often the case, individuals in this group are better paid than socialized workers—when, for example, their skills are in short supply or special demand —they remain members of this class. For ownership and not income level determines their relation to the process of production.

Given our general level of literacy and education, one might have expected the income of many in this group to have been depressed far below current levels. In a market economy those who own skills which are in profuse, even extravagant, supply must expect to be crushed toward subsistence. But our market contains a multitude of mechanisms and beliefs which enhances the value of all but the subjacent and the outcast. Social welfare legislation, for example, helps establish an income floor for many; either directly as with minimum wage laws or indirectly through welfare, unemployment compensation, surplus foods, etc. This second group of laws helps blunt the incentive to work for starvation or subsistence wages. The result is not simply to nourish the indolent, but to shield the diligent. If large numbers were stimulated or compelled to work for the equivalent of a dole, the value (and thus the income) of many unsocialized workers would be reduced.

In those areas of the country where legislative floors are relatively high, both median and average incomes are also higher. To some extent these areas pay more because they are richer, but they are also richer because they pay more. A substantial guaranteed annual income would, for example, undoubtedly raise both median and average wages in parts of the country where income levels are lowest. That is why many of the most obdurate opponents of increases in welfare, minimum wage, unemployment compensation, etc. come from states where important segments of the economy profit from relatively inexpensive labor, even though those states also contain the largest proportion of the poor.

The claim to value of the unsocialized is also strengthened by the compensation which socialized labor is able to extract. Market conditions might permit a company to cut the salaries of office workers while agreeing to union demands for higher wages. To do so, or to maintain too great a gap between the income of the organized and unorganized, would increase worker discontent and inefficiency. Such considerations can be more important with workers of this class than with traditional labor. A group of sullen file clerks can more easily impair function than a gang of resentful ditchdiggers. And somewhere in the secluded tower of the corporate superego must reside the admonition that such a use of economic power would probably precipitate the socialization of aggrieved workers. In fact, socialization is spreading, although slowly, to groups which have not traditionally thought of themselves as the stuff of organized labor. The tendency seems most advanced among those—such as teachers, retail clerks, government employees, etc.— who are not part of an enterprise which also relies on union labor. They lack the added protection of income standards established by the power of socialization.

These explanations alone cannot explain the value—artificially high by market standards—which is received by much of unsocialized labor. The considerations just mentioned would be irrational in a market economy. They must be supported by the premises of a different structure. Marx's analysis of the tendency, the economic compulsion, to force wages to the lowest possible level is unexceptionable. The capitalist entrepreneur who pays less for his resources strengthens his competitive position and perhaps his earnings. (Although the fiercest struggles of American capitalism were for power as well as for wealth.) Many small enterprises with access to a surplus of unorganized labor still behave this way. The wood mill in Kingfield starts men at the state minimum wage— $2.00 an hour—and keeps them there for a long time. Without this legal floor the hourly rate would fall even lower. In some restaurants waitresses are required to turn in their tips on the theory that the minimum wage amounts to gross overcompensation.

The elimination of the competitive struggles and hazards which once imparted righteous fervor to wage exploitation is among the principal functions of the modern bureaucratic economy. Companies still struggle for position, but the ground of conflict is product and not price. Even then, the rules of conflict ordinarily consist of stylized amenities. The playing fields of bureaucracy were won on the battlefields of capitalism. Underneath Guernica was Christina's world.

Among the major economic bureaucracies cost is more important than demand as a basis for price. When demand slackens, the principal response is not to lower prices or costs, but to reduce production and investment. If costs seem excessive there is more likely to be an effort to improve internal efficiency and eliminate redundant personnel than to force down the price of human or material resources. Slackening demand may even bring on a price increase. The only way to maintain earnings while selling less is to charge more.

Since costs are the principal internal standard for price levels, there is little temptation to lower wage costs. Our bureaucratic economy is under far less pressure to reduce wages—to extort toil and to exploit workers—than was free enterprise. This diminished pressure both protects the value of unsocialized workers and provides a protective framework for the other relationships which enhance that value. Above all, a bureaucracy strives for equable and continued functioning. Decent and relatively secure wages for unsocialized labor contribute to that goal. Although unsocialized workers are less concentrated in major industries than the unionized, their value is decisively influenced by the patterns, values and practices of the institutions which dominate the entire economic structure.

Transcending the behavior of particular enterprises is the fact that a successful effort to reduce wages to market value would damage the entire economy. The consequent drop in consumption would dislocate present patterns of production. In theory, reduced costs would end up in someone else's pocket. However, the wealth and future prospects of our economy depend upon increasing mass consumption. The "dislocation" caused by the reduced purchasing power of any large group would precipitate a decline in production. One of the reasons for recent economic slowdowns has been a decrease in the number of those brought into the consumption economy. Until recently our postwar growth has been accompanied by a rapid increase, not only of disposable income, but in the number of those with money to spend. As that increase is arrested, expansion suffers.

It is difficult to describe with any precision the links between the interests of the economy as a whole and the actions of particular enterprises. Why should our dependence on mass consumption—on widely dispersed purchasing power—restrain any particular enterprise from trying to reduce wages? The question unveils a labyrinth. Later we will examine the ways in which "economic realities," the "relations of production," the distribution of "economic power" influence individual and group behavior, ideology and values; a mechanism of influence constituted by the tangled circuits of an entire society. The existence of these relationships forces us to assume that the dominant economic institutions in an economy based upon consumption will not exert themselves to reduce or narrow purchasing power. This does not mean they will act in the general economic welfare, only that they tend to support the economic relations which made them dominant and on which their continued power seems to depend. Those relations may hold back growth, despoil society, reduce freedom and add to oppression —and they do all of these—but they don't encourage lower wages for the employed.

CHAPTER 8

Marx described alienated labor as that which was "external to the worker . . . he does not fulfill himself in his work but denies himself. . . . His work . . . is not the satisfaction of a need, but only a means for satisfying other needs . . . it is not his work but work for someone else . . . in work he does not belong to himself but to another person." This worker can be found in every shop and office of the land, but resistant ambiguities now shroud the identity of his owner. It took one hundred and twenty-five years of history to create men who could be possessed and yet unowned. "The worker," Marx went on, "puts his life into the object [his product] and his life then belongs no longer to him but to the object. . . . The *alienation* of the worker in his product means not only that his labour becomes an object, takes on its own existence, but that it exists outside him, independently, and alien to him, and that it stands opposed to him as an alien power." In Marx's analysis the kind of work a man performs, what he does with his energies, is determined by others, ordinarily by those who control the instruments of production. The product of labor is also theirs. The owners, the capitalists, own what they do because they have the power to coerce this kind of work, to demand alienated labor. Alienation is thus the inward presentment of oppression, the continuing reinforcement of exploitation. The power to extort the vitality of others must precede private property. Private property is, therefore, a consequence of alienation. This précis of Marx's analytical out-cries foreshadows our own afflictions and opens the possibility—now known to be true—that his healing measure, the abolition of private property, does not end alienation. The twentieth century has taught that economic power can fulfill itself in many ways; private prop-erty was not the seed of that power, but a changeling.

Socialized labor and some of the highly skilled have acquired a fraction of the productive process which enhances their value.* But the crowded ranks of unsocialized labor exchange only them-selves and their skills; the product of their toil contains them but is not theirs. That product is not usually a commodity, a thing. In-stead they are involved in transaction. They expend irrecoverable vitality and years—the substance of human life—on a process they cannot see, touch or understand. They labor, worry and suffer in the continual creation of a system they do not possess or control, but which shapes and limits the possibilities of their own existence. Although "in work he does not belong to himself," neither does such a worker belong to another person.

Ownership of the modern economic bureaucracy, as we have seen is dispersed and incomplete. Alienated labor is not owned by a single man or even a single class. To a very large extent, it is owned by a system, a process, which rules everyone and belongs to no one. The condition defies the satisfying simplicities of nineteenth-cen-tury radicalism—an under class dissolved into primitive misery and degradation confronting the parasites of power, the owners, whose rule was swollen with the life's blood of toiling masses.

Although there is no precedent for this modern condition, there is an analogue. From the Enlightenment onward, radical thinkers regarded religion as a paradigm of alienation. Man created gods, a moral code and a faith, to which he then submitted, forfeiting his claim to earthly justice. Men transferred some portion of control over their social lives to the order which they had constructed. Popes and priests were not the only recipients, the sole owners of this alienated existence; not in the sense in which an early capital-ist owned the work of his laborers. They were the managers and partly the prisoners of an institutional structure founded on an

---

* It would seem to follow that to this extent the product of their labor belongs to them. Except that which they "own" has no existence independent of the process which contains it.

ideology, and more than an ideology—a world view, a conviction of eternal process incarnate in the nature of things. One could kill the Pope, but the Church and its faith were invulnerable until history dissipated the material order which was its support and shield.

We have transferred some portion of authority over existence to a secular process; a prodigious complex of operations, which is all the stronger for its relative independence of control or ownership. These analytical abstractions and the process they relate are constituted of real people, particular acts and actual relationships. But because men guard their own prisons, it does not mean they are free to go.

The fact that the largest group of unsocialized workers is not forced into poverty helps to sustain their alienation and the power of the economic system. A moderate income is preferable to material misery. The poor are not free, but the non-poor have more to lose than chains. Their vulnerable economic position, their insecurities and fear of decline, influences them toward support instead of resistance. They lack the confidence of owners, the experience of the affluent, the desperation of the impoverished. Inevitably, they fear that fundamental change will dislodge their precarious gains, level the mild amenities of their lives. They are made reluctant to join any struggle to recapture their alienated existence and to halt the manifold devastations of social life. Radical change recalls to them the sardonic amusement of the union song at hearing an employee proclaim his good faith—"There'll be pie in the sky by and by."

How very powerful is an oppressive structure which can enlist the devotion of those whose freedom it divests. But devotion is not love, nor is it formed of "measureless content" and sensed fulfillment. The discontents of this group are acute. The restraints on freedom which we have described are also the facts of their lives. Indeed, they are more straitly confined than many of the more affluent. As they also share the general sense of larger possibility—the latent capacity for increased freedom—they thus contain the premises of a revolutionary awareness. Nor are they the victims of mass indoctrination, some brilliantly monstrous transformation of consciousness imposed by electronic incantation. No such science-fiction nightmares are needed to explain attitudes which are the logical consequence of economic position, of relationship to the productive forces and the social process.

Although the value of most unsocialized workers is enhanced beyond market value, that incremental enrichment is not a consequence of their ownership or power; as, by contrast, the value of organized labor is based upon ownership of the labor resource. They are the incidental beneficiaries of power which reposes elsewhere. Since that benefit is conferred by considerations of process wholly external to the autonomous elements of their existence, they are defenseless against changes which might diminish their value. Thus, even though large distances of income and social beliefs separate the lower ranks of unsocialized labor from the highly skilled, they share insecurities founded on their common exclusion from the process of production.

This vulnerability prefigures an immature flaw, an untended fragility, in the economic structure. That structure sustains its power and momentum, not simply by conferring wealth and liberties upon the inhabitants, but by incorporating important concentrations of current and contingent discontent. Those who garrison productive forces are permitted to derive their claim to value (an attribute of the concept "ownership") from the nature of our present economic system. They are worth what they are because it is what it is, and because they are among its constituents. Through this dependent identity individuals are induced to believe or fear that their integrity and being are at issue when the system is menaced. This is true for all workers, but those excluded from the process of production are also involved in a relationship reminiscent of traditional capitalism; i.e., as workers ruled by ownership which they do not share, yet whose content, as value, they labor to create. To this group, categories such as "capital" or "exchange value" appear as forces which still dominate the process of production. These shepherding spirits answer to legendary names—enterprise and ownership incarnate as Ideology, Belief, Passion, Disposition. Yet since the dispersion of ownership has reduced the importance of ownership, humbled its economic power, the forces of this alienation are generaled by phantasms. These apparitions cloud the true source of social power, disguise the fact that the labor of the excluded places them in opposition to those who share in the process—to their fellow workers—and to the process itself. In this way the ranks of unsocialized labor are denied awareness that exclusion is no longer a necessity of dominant economic relations, but results from the failure of those relations to complete themselves. They are alienated, in part, to illusions, nourished in the retrogressive mind after the historical conditions which bore them have withered. The ideas which persuade men to submission are nurtured by material realities, but in this case it is also the idea which, in part, creates the appearance of sustaining realities. That inversion is a seed of instability.

By failing fully to incorporate many unsocialized workers, by denying them ownership, the economic structure leaves a sense of vulnerability and intensifies the awareness of impotence, which weakens their identification with existing processes and furthers the possibility that they will direct their discontents against the causes and not merely the division of results.

But not by much.

CHAPTER 9

Ownership is a legal relationship, but it is haloed with ambiguous glints from the inward recesses of culture and society. "Nobody owns me"; "The Winter family owns that town"; translates a term of property into an assertion of human autonomy or submission, impotence or social control. The etymon of "own" means to master as well as to possess. When John Jay—revolutionary patriot and first Chief Justice—insisted that "the people who own the country ought to govern it" he was stating a fact as an imperative.

By eroding the power of individuals over property, the division of ownership made possible the institutional independence essential to bureaucracy. With ownership so divided and power reduced, the corporation could only function under the supervision of managers.

Managers are not owners, but they are part owners; i.e., they possess some fraction of an important attribute of ownership—the power to use and to direct the use of property. That power itself has been diminished by its severance from the other attributes of ownership. Managers may want to get rich, and many do, but they cannot devote all the resources of the corporation to their own aggrandizement. The corporation cannot be the instrument of their personal desires. Rather, they are rewarded for their service to the corporation. It is characteristic of a bureaucracy, being unowned, that its purposes and function rule the labor of all who work therein.

The power elite which C. Wright Mills described is largely, but not totally, a managerial elite; since grown more pervasive, intimate and powerful. The term "managerial class" is not a metaphor, but a category derived from the analytical principles of class description. The interests and consequent conduct of its members are largely determined by their ownership and the relation of that ownership to the process of production. The behavior and purposes of managers can change only when new economic interests and relationships displace or destroy those which now exist. The manager, by name or station, is largely a symbol for the organization itself. Henry Ford built automobiles; Rockefeller controlled oil; Carnegie made steel. But General Motors produces cars; steel comes from Bethlehem; and Standard of New Jersey drills, pumps and exploits compressed carbon, consumers and countries. Since the acts of managers in the economic bureaucracies are limited and directed by the structure and purpose of the organization, through observation of the managerial class we are admitted to the nature, the functional imperatives, of the modern economic bureaucracy. By depicting the ministers, we describe the tutelary authority of the institution they serve; which, indeed, in varying degrees, we all serve.

A ROMANCE

Last week the following newspaper column appeared in newspapers from coast to coast. Since its appearance, according to Mr. Anders, the telephone hasn't started ringing.

CAROUSEL USA—by John Anders

Unknown to the telephoning public, the recent retirement of Robert Baron, former president of AT&T, was not, in fact, due to ill health. He was unanimously ejected by the board of directors following a meeting at which he made several proposals for revitalizing the admittedly sluggish giant. A hitherto secret memo of this hitherto secret meeting has, as always, come into our hands. Although the document carries the highest classification of "unlisted," the public has a right to know the substance of Robert Baron's proposal.

Mr. Baron opened the eventful meeting with a brief statement. "Gentlemen," he announced, "we have two problems. We are too big and we aren't making enough money. There is only one solution. I propose we relinquish our monopoly position and turn over about 60 per cent of our territory to independent phone companies. This will enable us to concentrate our resources and talent in areas of greatest potential profit; permitting us to streamline our operation, cut out fat and improve efficiency. As an incidental benefit people everywhere will get better service, which will, I might add, improve the image of the telephone and permit a reduction in the public relations budget. In addition, this cutback will enable us to sell twenty-five to thirty billion dollars of our forty billion dollars in assets, largely to the companies assuming our excess operations. Through prudent investment our return on this money should exceed our current net profits on the entire forty billion. To sum up, if we adopt my proposals we can be more manageable, more efficient, have better service and make more money. How about that?"

Unfortunately, Mr. Baron has not been available to confirm this account since the disappearance of the company plane which, according to AT&T officials, was taking him to a well-earned vacation in Uganda. Nevertheless, the authenticity of the memo is beyond question.

It is bureaucracy, not economics, that makes Mr. Baron the Man of La Mancha instead of the man of the hour. His speech is the exertion of a mind unexpectedly regressed to the Age of Ownership. The consolidations, the trusts, of the industrial age were moved by a rational and comprehensible economic purpose: to establish the economic power needed to extort every possible cent of profit from buyers and from the toil of workers, and in the process, but not incidentally, to enrich the entrepreneurs. This romantically primitive conduct stands in about the same relation to the spirit of modern enterprise as does Jesse James to the Mafia.

Many earlier capitalists cherished individual desires for conquest and empire, but economically the elimination of competition was a means toward wealth and profit. To the economic bureaucracy, however, expansion and consolidation are an end in themselves. Competition is eliminated more to reduce uncertainties and risk than to maximize return.*

Since the modern managerial class has been created by the division of ownership, it can be found wherever an enterprise is "owned" by a lot of people, as in much of the United States, or by all of the people, as in Washington, D.C., and the Soviet Union. Managers are just employees—literally—but also as a man whose farm covers an oil field is just another landowner. A few own a substantial part of the enterprise they manage. But this is a dwindling group, and of little importance within the economic bureaucracies whose values and codes of conduct rule most of American business.

Managers do own skills: management skill, the ability to help the corporation function, and the skill, becoming increasingly important and distinct, to rise within the bureaucratic hierarchy. Like other workers they exchange those skills for income. Unlike most other workers, they also exchange those skills for a strategic position within the corporation, for a limited power whose ownership adds to their value. That power enables them to command compensation unrelated to the value of their skills or to their productivity; always within limits, of course, since even the highest manager of the largest corporation is neither king nor owner, but the chairman of a collective leadership. There are precedents and scales to be considered; nor can the manager be permitted to damage the corporation, either by infringing its capital or plunging it into serious battle. Within those constraints, however, a man can get very rich.

The executive is able to command excess compensation even though he is a "mere employee" because the corporation is unowned. He is only accountable to other employees, most of those who are in a position to object have their own interest in maintaining high levels of compensation, and only large rewards will attract desired talent to the uncertain, career-long struggle for position. A gifted corporation president might well make more money in a very different economic structure. He may receive even less than the value of his contribution. But what he *does* receive,

* Return on investment, not earnings. Earnings are a crucial indicator of bureaucratic health and growth.

his value, is established through his relationship to a particular type of organization.

One could try to justify the great fortunes accumulated by the robber barons of nostalgic memory by explaining that they created economic wealth through imagination, invention, will or villainy of the highest voltage. Today, managers are compensated for being at the controls. They are allowed to command the power which they do not own in their own interest, as long as they don't take too much—touch the principal or impair the machine. The compensations of managers are not, however, just an exercise of power. They are responsible for the most important bureaucratic purpose—the continuity of function. This being so, it is logical to reward the guardian more than the prophet.

Managers are the wealthiest and most powerful of workers, and the most totally dependent upon the existing structure of enterprise. Management skills, even at the higher levels, are not awesomely complex, technical or difficult. The necessary natural endowment is far more widely distributed than the talent to be a robber baron, a nuclear physicist or a successful magazine editor. The value of managerial talent is thus less intrinsic, less based upon a personal capacity to create, seize or command a segment of the wealth-producing apparatus, and more dependent upon its suitability, its correspondence, to the functional needs of established enterprise. And the other face of managerial skill, the capacity to rise within the bureaucracy, acquires its value, almost by definition, from the existence of the organization.

C. Wright Mills was the first to remark upon the accelerating tendency in the postwar period to choose executives from within the corporation. That trend may be continuing, but it is less significant now than when Mills wrote. In a transaction economy, the capacity to manage a large organization is less closely linked to a particular range of products. An individual who can market soap can probably market cigarettes or chain saws, just as an Under-Secretary of State can be readily appointed Secretary of Health, Education and Welfare, become chief of the Defense Department, and later be named Attorney General. Undoubtedly, most top executives still come from within the corporation, but hiring outsiders is no longer evidence of a desire for a fresh outlook.

In a recent magazine, an "executive recruiter" advises those hoping for recruitment: "If you're in Procter & Gamble and each of the four group managers has brand experience in Duz and none with Jif Peanut Butter, consider it a hint. That doesn't mean you can't make it from Jif, but it will enlarge your chances if you can get Duz brand experience." The point is not satirical. No one who has spent time in government and politics can ridicule the paths taken by the ambitions of others. But such knowledge, and the ability to act upon it, does not add to productivity, to the creation of wealth. It is valuable only because there is a bureaucratic structure, which rewards it. The skill to climb executive heights, as distinct from managerial ability, is often impressive in its imaginative vitality, but it is an inward skill, turned toward mastery of the corporate structure, rather than toward enlarging or maximizing the economic contribution and return of the productive apparatus. There is some relationship. Performance is a criterion for promotion. But as general economic competition dwindles and responsibility within corporations becomes more diffuse, the difficulty of judging performance by external standards such as profits and earnings makes internal standards even more important.

My own awareness of this managerial skill began while in government. At first I was puzzled at the success of men who were so often mistaken on important matters of policy and administration. No clearly demonstrated error of judgment seemed to impair the position of the Rusks, McNamaras, Taylors, etc., or to diminish the esteem of their fellow chieftains. At the same time, many individuals who had demonstrated superior judgment fell into disfavor or were clearly destined to languish in subordinate positions. What, at the time seemed a paradox, was only the even-handed enforcement of bureaucratic necessity. Mastery of the infinite and subtle skills of internal organization and "interpersonal" relations were more important to success than performance in relation to external purpose. Secretary Rusk was quite explicit on this point when, relaxing over a late afternoon scotch, he explained to a young associate that "the important thing to remember in Washington is not to fight the bureaucracy but to get it to work for you." President Johnson, supreme in his understanding of the government machine, after inundating an aide with flattery, added, "But all that doesn't help unless you'll just remember never to speak first at a meeting and always count ten to yourself before saying anything."

I regard some of my own feelings in the early days of the Kennedy administration as an illustration of the compulsions of bureaucratic momentum. I shared the absurd belief—which was then general, but far from universal—that Castro's rule over Cuba was somehow inimical to our interests. The entire history of the cold war, its positions and assumptions, converged upon the "problem of Cuba." Government bureaucracies, like all others, can question and modify procedures and implementations far more readily than purpose. The result is to create an inner barrier to new facts, knowledge and argument. (Although it is also true that government can shift its purposes more easily than private bureaucracies, since public goals are the creations of social structure, while private relationships are the structure itself.)

Observing the rules of conduct within the bureaucracy, private or public, is essential not only to success, but to effectiveness. Those who feel the need of occasional succor from principle argue that unless the rules are observed, one will have no "impact" at all. But the process of successful participation precludes any challenge to basic values, structure or direction. The requirements for influential membership by themselves, *ex hypothesi*, prohibit the desire for basic shifts in purpose. Effectiveness itself is defined as the capacity to guide, perhaps improve, the established process. Individual will is exercised along these lines of structure or it is annulled by the process. Basic alterations in bureaucratic structure or purpose come from outside the structure, generated by changing relationships within the society.

Discussion of the desirability of "working within the system" is itself a reflection of bureaucratic ideology. The phrase itself, although not the problem, is relatively new to public discourse. It resonates of organization, procedures and codes of conduct. (Just as "turn on" is the legacy of David Sarnoff and Milton Berle, as if we were breeding an entire generation of image receivers.) The "system" being discussed is usually assimilated to existing institutions and established process. In politics, for example, the system is defined as the party system. Yet there is no reason to restrict the definition of political system to candidates, elections and lobbying. The bus boycott in Montgomery and the Selma march influenced social change more substantially than all the elections of the 1960s. They were within the political system as differently conceived. And to Jefferson the system of democracy included the right, even the obligation, to revolt.

When a process is assimilated to an institution, when the institution becomes the embodiment of a process, we are in the presence of the bureaucratic vision. Not long ago a newspaper carried a story about the retiring president of one of America's largest corporations, for years the dominant figure in his industry. Still energetically healthy, he was asked if he really wanted to retire. "I am," he replied, "fully in agreement with the company's retirement policies." And how could it be otherwise? Over decades his will had fused with the organization in whose service he had been granted the highest success. That organization, any large economic unit, is not a thing, not a collection of factories, equipment and money, but a process of production, a material field of transactions and economic relationships. The rules, customs and directions which prescribe functions—that seem only to define and limit the process—are the process in itself. Just as the laws governing the strength and direction of magnetic attraction *are* magnetism; or the rules, explicit and customary, which govern the rights and conduct of courts, lawyers and parties *are* the legal process.

Submission to a process, rather than things, is the consummation of alienation, requiring the forfeit not only of desires, labor and vitality, but of autonomy of behavior and even thought. In a manner now familiar, the manager whose ownership, whose claim to value, is established by the institutional process, and because of it, is rendered unable to defy or alter it in any fundamental way. To do so would require him to contradict his own existence and to diminish his own felt worth. He is inwardly compelled to continue and strengthen the process, to extend its reach, not reluctantly but out of the powerful convictions which have supplanted his potential for autonomous defiance. And should, inconceivably, that autonomy survive, even the highest manager would not have the power to make fundamental shifts. He is, after all, only a manager, an employee, and if his conduct seemed to threaten the organization, either through failure or rebellion, the others of his class, as directors or executives, would displace him. Their interests and identity are also at stake, and the structure of bureaucracy always provides a mechanism to check conduct which is dangerously inconsistent with the bureaucratic process—not only in American business, but everywhere bureaucracy rules, in the Pentagon as it was in Khrushchev's Politburo. Structures built by men have acquired an independent intention whose necessities are not those of human freedom. And the authority to check that force, to redirect the apparatus of production, does not exist.

CHAPTER 10

I have never walked down Fifth Avenue alone without thinking of money. I have never walked there with a companion
without talking of it. I fancy that every man there in order to
maintain the spirit of the place, should bear on his forehead a
label stating how many dollars he is worth, and that every label should be expected to assert a falsehood.

New York beginning with 60,000 sixty years since has now a
million souls—a million mouths, all of which eat a sufficiency
of bread, all of which speak *ore rotundo,* and almost all of
which can read. And this has come to its love of dollars.

North America by Anthony Trollope, 1862

Send your man (the Attorney General) to see my man and
I'm sure they can settle things.

J. P. Morgan to President Theodore
Roosevelt when the government initiated
anti-trust action against certain
Morgan interests

Where has all the money gone?

Song of the successors of J. P. Morgan

A discussion of ownership in the modern economy would not be complete without a brief look at money—the most legendary of all possessions. More than a possession, money is an aspect of technology. The most important technologies are systems or procedures which increase economic capacity, e.g., the principle of interchangeable parts, which was the basis of mass production. From this perspective, money is part of the technology of exchange. Indeed, it is the foundation of that technology and no advanced state, whatever its economic ideology, can exist without it. For example, not only is the function of money enlarged by the technologies of communication and transportation, but the utility of those technologies depends on the kind of representation and exchange of value made possible by money. The fact that modern techniques of credit and accounting make it possible to carry on a great deal of exchange without money simply means that, to some extent, money itself is being displaced by more advanced technologies (although they retain the principle of symbolic value and use the quantitative measures eatablished by money; just as airplane engines are rated in horsepower).

Money can shed its more neutral, symbolic state to become a commodity, a thing in itself. It is invested with possibilities of psychic fulfillment. Its acquisition can be established as well as a means to consumption, desired for its sensual and psychic emissions. A millionaire industrialist, about to acquire another company, was asked why he wanted more money. "That's the way they keep score," he replied.

Although money can be exchanged for goods, it is something more than any particular goods it can buy. Once one buys a table, he has a table. Before that purchase is made the money which it required represented not only a table, but all goods of equivalent value. Once necessities are met, money is also the power of choice, an attribute which is independent of the value of the particular goods for which money can be exchanged. This attribute of money is among the reasons for "excessive" savings, and why such savings tend to mount during periods of uncertainty and turbulence. It is not only that people wish to protect themselves against economic hazards, but they are less sure what they want, or what they will want tomorrow. They retain an option in the form of money, and an option is a traditional form of property. Insofar as it is an option, money is also a commodity.

If we examine the function of money within the economy as a technology of process, we can disregard some of the more sweeping and mystic descriptions of money as the essence of value, as the repository of man's alienated powers or, as Engels wrote, the possessor of a coruscating acid which dissolves social orders. Still, the most careful analysis cannot fully eliminate an element of mystery in the nature of money. In some of its more obscure manifestations, no one at all seems to understand it.

For many years more money has been going from the United States to foreign countries than coming back. This fact has been known, at various times, as "the balance of payments crisis," "the gold crisis," or, more grandiosely, "the world monetary crisis," even though the total disproportion has amounted to an insignificant fraction of our national wealth. At one point, economists and financiers convinced President Kennedy that our national economy was at the mercy of those European governments and banks with claims on our gold. Some specialists could describe how such a crisis might occur, how the machinery would work. No one could rationally explain why foreign claims on a few billion dollars' worth of gold should influence, much less damage, an economy producing seven or eight hundred billion dollars' worth of goods and services. Recently, we responded to pressures of this kind by demanding changes in the code of behavior governing the finance of advanced nations. Inevitably, financial leaders yielded. In the chambers of international finance, as at the tables of Las Vegas, money talks. Yet, after the bankers and ministers had found a solution which, they agreed, would open a "new epoch in world finance," the difficulties continued.

When a mere economic issue like this one becomes harder to clarify than quantum mechanics, one must begin to suspect that the problem itself has become endued with mysticism. When the few accepted experts turn out to be wrong, and in different ways at different times, one is entitled to the suspicion that they are more augurers than scientists. Nor is this surprising. Money is very real, but it also contains a phantasm. Fixed, arbitrary and rigid conventions are necessary if this element of the fantastical is to be contained. That is also why the rules can be altered, sometimes drastically, without affecting the economic realities; only the way in which men make transactions.

Because money is idea as well as commodity, both crassly tangible and a category of abstraction, it has become a metaphor for the urgencies of freedom and the forms of oppression. There is no major poet of the construction industry, no prophet of the programmer's psyche, no folklore of the internal combustion engine. But money has attracted the talent of Shakespeare, the psychoanalytic musings of Freud, the apocalyptic reveries of Norman O. Brown, and expositions from a million pulpits. The ambiguous proverbs of money are as much the stuff of child lore as "First star, first star," or the fairy's compensation for the fallen tooth: "Money isn't everything," or "Money is the root of all evil" or "Money can't buy happiness." It has evoked passion and imagination rarely stirred by the tangible constituents of wealth—factories and goods and crops—although land gave off similar resonances in earlier times. In large part this is because money was not only wealth, but the bearer of an ideology: the idea of value which subverted the medieval hierarchy. Value launched the trading ships, enclosed the common lands, built the factories and gave life to economic man. And money was the indispensable vessel of value. Hatred of the moneylender was also a defense of the corroding hierarchy. The futile folk sayings also evidence a half-conscious protest against the abstraction of man and his labor into numbers and signs, which is a consequence of the idea of value.

Money is a medium of exchange, a commodity, an aspect of technology, but it is also part of an ideology, a world view. It is the crystallization of wealth and all that wealth means, and it is also a statement about the nature of society and the human condition. And it is to the study of society what mathematics is to science: both an independent pursuit and an instrument for the anaylsis and expression of other phenomena.

A lot of money can incite to lust or anger. But money in prodigious quantities, by the billions and tens of billions, glazes the mind and swiftly wearies reflection, except among the enraptured few who have found their El Dorado in a fistful of figures. Yet capital ownership as set forth in these caliginous and tedious accounts is of greater economic consequence today than it was when titans of opulence were heroes of the capitalist romance.

The flow of transaction is also the flow of capital. The process functions because capital or credit is available at every stage. Each movement of goods, information, ideas and advertising assumes or requires payment. For example, goods can move quickly to dealers and distributors either because they have the necessary access to capital or because the manufacturer's reserves are large enough to permit the postponement of payment. Modern capital not only buys things—factories, land or railroads—but it energizes the circuits of the ceaseless, swift and multiplying interchange which is the principal source of modern wealth. It regulates and limits the speed and scale of transaction, the exploitation of new technology, the expansion of industry.

Because only those with large resources can eliminate the economic risk of occasional error, loss or rejection, concentrated capital is a condition of economic bureaucracy. General Electric, for example, can assume that 5 per cent of its washing machines will break down and be returned. The price of washing machines can be set to provide against this loss. This can be done only by companies large enough to apply statistical averages to their accounting. It is among the techniques which permit large economic bureaucracies to insure themselves against many of the risks one associated with free enterprise. The cost of such insurance is borne by the consumer.

The dominant economic bureaucracies are protected by the inability of potential competitors to match their capital resources —owned, invested or available. Most importantly, the capital structure, who controls capital and under what conditions, often decisively influences what we produce and how. Since, in a world where capital availability is limited, such determinations are exclusive, the capital structure also determines what shall *not* be produced and which productive relationships shall not be permitted.

During the panic of 1893, in order to stem the flow of gold to foreign countries, President Cleveland did not impose a tariff or surcharge nor did he summon world monetary authorities into emergency session. He negotiated a gold loan from the House of

Morgan. Yet at the height of their power the legendary titans of capital—Morgan and Rothschild, Rockefeller and Krupp—did not control enough capital to sustain the modern economy for a week. Nor have they been replaced by more wealthy individuals. As with other elements of the modern economy, the ownership of capital has been dispersed, fragmented and bureaucratized.

CHAPTER 11

I do not dislike your bank more than all banks, but ever since I read the history of the South Sea Bubble, I have been afraid of all banks.

President Andrew Jackson to the president of the Bank of the United States

Of the fifteen largest corporations in America, ten are financial institutions: several banks, an insurance company and a dealer in mortgages known as Fanny Mae (FNMA). Three of these—Bank of America, First National City Bank of New York and Chase Manhattan—have more assets than either Standard Oil or General Motors, being outranked only by that Cronus amid the Titans, AT&T. (Five foreign countries have a gross national product higher than the total assets of the phone company.) In conformity to the ruling design of American business, commercial banking is dominated by a handful of institutions. Of the more than thirteen thousand commercial banks with a total of more than 646 billion dollars, only ten banks have a quarter of all the assets, and the richest fifty have almost half. Nearly all these assets are available to credit-worthy governments, businesses, home buyers and individuals. It's a great deal of money. Yet if, for purposes of description, we divide the sources of investment capital into three groups:

commercial banks, individual purchasers of stocks and bonds and non-bank institutions, the banks are the smallest of all.

Most of the owners of these more than six hundred billion dollars, the depositors, are not consulted on investment policy; although they can withdraw their money and go elsewhere, i.e., to another bank with the same policy. But that has always been true. What separates today's graylings from yesterday's leviathans is the fact that commercial banks are owned by widely dispersed shareholders, which means, as we have seen, that they are not owned at all in the traditional sense. The financier, the tycoon, has become a functionary, subject to the restraints, cautions and fears of bureaucracy.

At the turn of the century, bankers—often conspiring with industrialists—assembled giant trusts, controlled markets and pursued ebullient visions of consolidation. J. P. Morgan thought to own all the transportation in New England and, together with Hill and Harriman, all the railroads in the country. As late as 1935, Franklin Roosevelt thought it politically valuable to seek and receive the support of the House of Morgan for his decision to go off the gold standard. Today it does not even enter the mind of a conservative Republican President to ask the Bank of America or Chase Manhattan to endorse similar actions.

Bankers no longer seek empire. They look for deposits and secure investments, and, increasingly, branch out into new activities which involve the management of money. Instead of coercing and directing large corporations, they run errands and perform services in hope of receiving corporate business. Their capital is largely available only to established, ongoing enterprise—to investments which are backed by tested collateral. As a result, commercial banks serve and reinforce the dominant patterns of economic life. Six hundred billion dollars in the hands of a single individual or group would be a source of immense power. Controlled by the bureaucratic managers of public corporations whose ownership is dispersed and non-existent, the same money is a helplessly acquiescent creature of the dominant economic bureaucracy. The commercial banks are richer than ever, but far less powerful.

The shift in economic power has necessarily led to a decline in political power. At one time the eastern financial establishment, familiarly known as "Wall Street," but which included some favored colleagues in Chicago and on the West Coast, controlled the Republican Party. From the time Jay Gould and Jim Fisk of New York virtually cornered the gold market with the help of high officials under President Grant, this group had exercised an important and usually decisive influence over the choice of Republican candidates. As the postwar economy reduced their economic role, political influence also declined. In retrospect it can be seen that Thomas Dewey was the last candidate of Wall Street, although the waning of power was temporarily masked when Eisenhower was enlisted to defeat Robert Taft. It soon became apparent, however, that the Eisenhower administration marked the ascendancy of western industrialists. In a famous television vignette of the 1952 Republican Convention, Senator Everett Dirksen, supporting Taft against Eisenhower, pointed to a smiling Dewey and pleaded with his fellow Republicans not to follow those who had led them to defeat. Dirksen's candidate lost, but his cause was on the way to victory. In the moment of seeming triumph the forces of eastern wealth had been defeated. Today, under a conservative Republican President, Wall Street is virtually excluded from the board of directors.

Banks have also lost power because they are not rich enough. A handful of banks or wealthy individuals cannot palliate the capital hungers of our voracious transaction economy. That economy runs on the affluence it has helped create. Since the entire economy is characterized by large institutions dependent upon dispersed wealth, it can only function through mechanisms which draw upon the income and resources of large numbers of individuals. Such mechanisms are one of the qualities which distinguish the postwar economy from capitalism.

By dominating the income devoted to consumption of basic products, large economic bureaucracies funnel mass spending to a relatively few institutions. Analogously, the federal government draws most of its individual income tax revenues from the same consuming middle class—65 per cent from those with incomes between five and fifty thousand dollars. There is no other way to raise the necessary amount of money. ($1.00×200 million people is a huge fortune; $100 from the same number exceeds the wealth of the pharaohs and the assets of Standard Oil of New Jersey.)

The capital structure faces similar necessities and has evolved its own methods for tapping the resources of multitudes. The most visible technique, sometimes known as "popular capitalism," is the direct sale of securities and credit market instruments. More than thirty million individuals own about 750 billion dollars' worth of stock and about 250 billion dollars in credit market instruments. The total of approximately a trillion dollars, is twice the assets of all the commercial banks in the country. As we have seen, this dispersion of investment has nullified the power of the investor.

Although individuals constitute the largest single source of capital, they are not the most secure source. Individual willingness to purchase stocks and bonds is influenced by psychic and economic conditions, and there is no certain assurance that they will provide adequate new money when it is needed. In recent years individual investors have been withdrawing from the stock market at the rate of about eight billion dollars annually.

It seems inevitable that the securities market as presently constituted will not be able to supply capital necessary to economic expansion. Were it not for the fact that through the medium of insurance companies and pension funds millions of individuals had been made investors without their knowledge or approval the structure might already have collapsed. I don't intend to hazard an analysis of the stock market, but surely its inadequacy is partially due to its narrowness. For example, not too long ago the market value of a large corporation dropped fifty-four million dollars in a single day. Yet out of more than seven million shares outstanding, less then eleven thousand changed hands. A few pessimistic individuals were able to reduce the personal assets of thousands of shareholders. One can argue that these dislocations will right themselves, or average out, over some hypothetical long term. But the worth of a security on any given day is determined by how much a handful of buyers will pay for it. Whenever any shareholder seeks to realize the value of his investment, what he receives will not be determined by long-term prospects but by immediate realities narrowly controlled.

The present market structure was conceived at a time when stock ownership itself was relatively confined. The inadequacy of that structure was obscured by postwar expansion. In the early stages of that expansion, securities offered a fairly high return on investment; they could be purchased as a source of income. In 1955, the yield on industrial common stocks was 6.3 per cent; on bonds, 2.67 per cent. Since stocks were more risky than bonds, they paid more. The market was then overtaken by the "great growth bubble." An individual bought in expectation of selling at a higher price. The "make your money grow" philosophy was sustained and stimulated by the fact that a lot of cash was seeking a home both within corporations and outside. There was a great deal of concentrated liquidity. Indeed, until recently much expansion could be financed from corporate treasuries. But experience has repudiated belief. Stocks are neither a guaranteed hedge against inflation nor a participation in economic growth.

Among the changes necessary to sustain the market will have to be a substantial rise in stock yield. Why should individuals risk losing money for a smaller return than they can receive from secure bonds or savings? (We can await with interest the first mismanagement suit against a pension fund or insurance company for its investment in common stocks.) If the stock market is to provide capital for industrial development and expansion, it will probably be necessary to develop some mechanism for pegging prices to corporate values.

There is another reason, more isomorphic than functional, to expect this kind of a change in the securities market. To some extent, Wall Street is among the few surviving strongholds of old-fashioned free enterprise. Individuals can accumulate large fortunes; skilled professionals, adept manipulators, confidence men and swindlers can be rewarded; and there is a great deal of larceny. In other words, the market clings to qualities of nineteenth-century business. This residual free enterprise is out of tune with the dominant attitudes and structure of economic bureaucracy. Among other things, that bureaucracy strives to eliminate the kind of short-term uncertainties which characterize the market. The growth of large institutional investors—mutual funds, pension funds, insurance companies, etc. —is a step in that direction and provides leverage for imposing further adaptation.

The third and fastest growing source of capital investment is

designed to eliminate many of these uncertainties by abolishing the
remnants of individual will. It draws its capital from individuals
who retain no control over its disposition, rarely know where it is
going or even that it is being invested at all. This triumph of anti-
alchemy, the transmutation of ownership into impotence, is managed through institutions known variously as "non-bank finance,"
"institutional investors" or "financial institutions." The category
includes, most importantly, insurance companies, pension funds,
mutual funds* and savings and loan associations.

The time is not too distant when this group of institutions (already in control of over nine hundred billion dollars—far more
than commercial banks) will compose the single largest source of
capital in America. When that time comes, their hard-earned triumph will appear as inevitability. For the statistical projections of
their growth visibilize the ideological moments of modern society.
They are a bureaucratic Arcadia—capitalism without the capitalist;
money, like industry, in the hands of managers responsible only to
other managers and, of course, to the money itself. The institutions of an older faith relied upon a device called "the tithe." Our
methods are more diverse, more ingenious and much more fruitful. The contributors of old sought insurance of heavenly forgiveness, while we, more modestly, seek protection against the economic
hazards of age, death or misfortune.

The institutions of non-bank finance do not function in hostile
or indifferent coexistence with other sources of capital. Banks manage pension funds as do insurance companies. Through these funds,
along with the accounts which they manage for individuals, banks
buy other banks; just as insurance companies can invest in each
other or in banks. Larceny on the grand scale by respected institutions is called a "betrayal of fiduciary responsibility." Capital overlap of this kind almost guarantees such breaches. For example,
banks have a variety of relationships with corporations. They loan
them money, seek deposits and offer financial advice. If they man-

* Owners of mutual fund shares are a partial exception since they have decided to
put their money into common stocks; although they are basically investing in the
skill and rhetoric of fund managers. They do not decide which stocks shall be purchased. And the big funds all own the same securities or securities of the same kind.
The only possible way funds can manage billions of dollars is by investing in the
dominant economic bureaucracies. They alone can absorb large sums with comparative safety, thus reducing the number of investment decisions to the humanly possible.

age pension funds or trust accounts, they are also buying stock. As bankers their first responsibility is to the corporation or to their own shareholders. As investors their first responsibility is to those whose money they are managing. As bankers they may have access to inside information which it would be unethical or illegal to use in buying stocks. In addition, as bankers they often have a powerful interest in helping a debtor corporation through a time of trouble, while as investors the wisest course might be to sell the stock in such a corporation even though the sale, or knowledge of the sale, could add to corporate difficulties. It is, of course, possible to prohibit bank employees who deal with corporations from discussions with their fellow employees who buy stocks. It is a frail barrier to temptation. This particular conflict of interests is only one of many which arise from the inevitable blurring of responsibility and interest within organizations which manage other people's money and, at the same time, are in business for themselves. The inducement to prefer the institution's own direct interest in cases of conflict is strengthened by the fact that those whose money is being managed often do not know where it is going and are usually ignorant of the managing company's other relationships. The possibilities for illicit gain are enormous and virtually undetectable.

Insurance companies and pension funds together represent a little less than one half of all non-bank finance. Insurance companies have more capital, but pension funds buy more securities. Their ownership of equity stock is about twice that of either insurance companies or mutual funds. (Savings and loan associations put the bulk of their money into mortgages.) The contributor of equity is more useful than the investor who loans his capital, especially as major corporations find it harder to finance expansion from their own cash or to sell new issues to individuals. Thus, the expansion of pension funds, now more rapid than that of any other capital source, is more important to the corporate structure than the figures reveal. This helps explain why government, business, finance and organized labor are unanimous in their passionate concern that workers provide for their later years; willing even to substitute coercive mechanisms for the individual's lack of wisdom and foresight.

There have been, for example, proposals of a "tax incentive" designed to encourage contributions to pension funds. Tax incentive is a public-relations phrase for a redistribution of the tax burden. The general public is being taxed to benefit the recipient of the incentive or, at least, to stimulate him to certain actions. It seems almost radically paternalistic of a conservative Administration to tax everyone in order to raise the pensions of workers. The enigma is dissolved by the fact that pension funds are the most important institutional source of equity capital. The "incentive" is a general tax imposed in order to provide reserves for capital investment. And given the necessary investment policies of pension fund managers, these increased reserves will continue to flow to the dominant economic bureaucracies. Even the microscopic patterns of government action conform to private social relationships of power and interest.

Though different in function and origin, both pension funds and insurance companies transfer or loan most of their money to private business. (Commercial banks, by contrast, have about 40 per cent of their money in government securities and home mortgages.) Both are riskless enterprises. The protection they give is determined by payment received—either directly or through statistical averages—which also prohibits loss and, in the case of insurance companies, guarantees a profit. Pension funds are not profit-making, but they usually come out ahead by imposing requirements for the receipt of benefits which cannot be satisfied by many who contribute. The risk is borne by the public, or that portion of the public which participates. As with consumer credit, the risk is being socialized, and some of the cost of socialization is imposed on those who are not beneficiaries. For example, corporate contributions to pension funds, like some forms of consumer credit, are part of the cost of doing business, incorporated in the prices which must be paid by the unemployed and poor who are not eligible for pensions or credit.

The institutions of non-bank finance add little to the productive power of society. They transfer capital from time present to time future, from the hands of many to the hands of a few. If automobile sales doubled, the economy would soar. If the demand for insurance policies or pension protection doubled, the direct impact would be trivial. (But not non-existent. Insurance companies, for example, themselves provide jobs and construct buildings. The availability of insurance stimulates the commercial flow necessary to a transaction economy.)

Insurance companies, pension funds and some other institutions of non-bank finance support the cost of their socially important services by levying on the participating public, and can increase those levies in order to meet their obligations and make a profit. Although their activities add to the general welfare, they do not create social wealth. No definition of private enterprise subsumes such institutions. They perform a function whose nature is largely public, an activity appropriate for government—with one exception that overpowers all objections: They are uniquely unable to draw upon the income of millions and make it available to the dominant economic bureaucracy. That ability is their major contribution to the economic process, and through its exercise they enter into the governing relationships of society. This is achieved by severing the owner of capital, the contributing individual, from all power over his money. In order to provide for his future with his income, he must yield up almost all the attributes of ownership.

The managers of these funds, themselves not owners, are constrained by the limited nature of their own power to direct their resources toward dominant and established enterprises. Without choice and usually without knowledge, the participating public is made to contribute toward the economic relationships which diminish freedom. The insecurities of modern society feed the desire for safety and for protection, which desire in turn stimulates the flow of resources toward structures implicated in those same insecurities. This apposition of individual insecurity and capital concentration is not an isolated fortuity, but an aspect of design, an example of the world-ruling configuration of coercion and social dissolution.

Since the economic process could not function without access to large amounts of capital, that structure is the most committed support of the system. It may also be the point of greatest vulnerability. Factories, entire industries are irrevocably dedicated to the economic activities they were designed and built to conduct. Money is an outlaw, without nation, attachments, home or purpose. An automobile assembly plant cannot construct parks, but money can build cars or plant trees. It obeys only one rule of conduct—

to go where the power is. Since capital fuels the process, and the process creates demand, then power over money is also the power to divert and change demand—to change desire and the objects of desire and, in so doing, to reconstruct the process. Or it could be, were its control in different hands, subject to different purposes.

CHAPTER 12

Social wealth is distinct from calculations of national product or income. Social wealth, as we have defined it, is increased by an addition to production or production capacity which, in the context of the economic structure as a whole,* enhances the well-being of the members of society; that is, when it serves as the material basis for freedom. Bureaucracy reduces the yield of our knowledge and resources—the constituents of economic capacity—far below their potential for the creation of social wealth. Actual product is much less than contingent product, although within the bureaucratic structure the actual is necessity, and the contingent is impossible. Our inability to transform existing capacity into social wealth begins with the bureaucratic economy's displacement of the market.

The economic "market," in varied forms, is a principal subject of the analysis and expectations of all economic literature. Once a society can produce more than is needed for physical survival, the division of labor makes exchange necessary in order to establish a value for goods beyond, or different than, their intrinsic utility to the producer. The process of exchange, the manner of establishing value and conducting commerce, is called the market. If the process is controlled largely by "private" individuals or institutions it is

* It is possible to add to well-being in ways which strengthen an oppressive social structure. Although such benefits are tangible, they are also delusive, strengthening the belief that imposed obstructions mark the limits of possibility.

customary to call it a "free market." If it is largely controlled by the state, it is called "collectivism" or "socialism." All markets are established through the legal order, by the laws which prescribe property rights, contractual obligations, the distribution of official authority, commercial conduct, etc. Such markets are "free" in the sense that a man is free to choose his own government as long as he votes for the Republican or Democratic presidential candidate. All forms of control over the modern market evolve toward bureaucracy. Within the historical experience of advanced industrial societies, collectivization of the market extends and accelerates that bureaucratization, and increases the possibilities for oppression through the formal fusion of political and economic power.

This is not necessarily true for more primitive economies. The important capital accumulations in undeveloped countries are usually few in number and are often uneconomic; that is, they are operated for the benefit of a handful of "owners," whose personal wealth and/or orientation toward foreign cultures dull any incentive to expand and modernize. In these countries, nationalization can bring about an instant increase in the social and productive value of economic institutions. Therefore, socialism is a much more appealing course for the poor and undeveloped than for advanced industrial nations. If progress is made, however, the congenital necessities of technological industrialism will either spawn the oppressions of a fused bureaucracy or bring about fundamental modification in the socialist structure.

There is a third type of economy called "communism" which seeks to eliminate the market altogether, or radically alter its function by abolishing the division of labor. Since this has never been tried in an industrial state it remains in the realm of humanistic metaphysics and can only be described by reference to untested and rather fragmentary theory. To Marx, the abolition of private property was a means toward the development of communist society and would not eliminate the need to establish value through exchange. Marx seems to say that in the early postrevolutionary stages of progress toward communism individuals would be rewarded proportionately to their labor, not just the amount of labor, but also its "intensity." Such a standard "tacitly recognizes unequal individual endowment, and thus natural privileges in respect of productive capacity. It is, therefore, in its content, a right of in-

equality, like every right." The need to establish such values requires a market mechanism, even if the market consists of a dicta-
tor, revolutionary committee or a Parliament. However, Marx
promises that "In a higher phase of communist society, when the
enslaving subordination of the individual to the division of labor
. . . has vanished . . . when the productive forces have also increased with the all-round development of the individual, and all
the springs of co-operative wealth flow more abundantly—only then
will it be possible to transcend the narrow outlook of bourgeois
right and only then will society be able to inscribe on its banners:
From each according to his abilities, to each according to his
needs."

This seems to imply elimination of value, exchange and thus of
the market. As prophecy it is beyond analysis. The necessary historical conditions have not appeared in any advanced industrial
nation. At least two changes, however, would seem to be necessary:
first, a productive power great enough to free individuals from
necessary labor, and second, the existence of a true community
with shared values, purpose and ideology. The foundation of
theoretical communism is not the abolition of private property,
but the establishment of community. More than a century later,
it appears doubtful that these two conditions can coexist.

Value and exchange—essence and existence of the market—
mediate the material world in many ways. In the functions which
concern us here, the market provides a forum for the expression of
economic needs and desires, and it allocates resources to the satisfaction of those claims. Competition and the desire for profit
stimulate the creation of enterprise, the dedication of resources to
demand, and force the producer toward the most efficient, i.e.,
economical, use of those resources in order to survive or to defeat
competition.

This description is of the market as a model. As we have seen,
actual value is established in other ways: for example, as a consequence of the individual's relation to economic institutions or
through the imposition of economic power. Outside the realm of
the ideal the function of the market is never exclusive. In an
exchange economy dominant relationships force departures from
the market which invariably strengthen those relationships. Inter-
ferences with the modern market are never accidental and rarely

liberating, as we shall see after a brief précis of market function within an exchange economy.

In one sense market value is purely a factual statement, a consequence of the operation of supply and demand in the unadorned sense of that law: The "Mona Lisa" is "priceless" or a Rembrandt sells for, and thus is worth, a million dollars. However, market value derives its historical and functional significance as a constituent of the economic process. The term implies that the values set by the market bear a fundamental relation to economic worth, i.e., the contribution of that which is being valued to the creation of wealth. Something is of value not merely because it is demanded, but because it, or the process which produces it, adds to the wealth of the society. Obviously, there is a potential conflict or disparity between market value and economic contribution. But the two should be in harmony for the bulk of economic transactions. If they are not, the result is increasing waste, inefficiency and injustice. In such cases the market operates, but it doesn't work.

Early economic theory was formed amid the historical currents which uncovered a comprehensive exposition of the universe in Newtonian mechanics and replaced the last two days of the creation with Darwinian evolution. This age of secular systems was the transition from divine order to contemporary disorder. In such a time it was natural to conceive the market as some mechanism of nature, its elements in logical equipoise. Interference by human agencies would only distort or pervert rational function. Time and corruption revealed that the market, like all economic institutions, was merely a social creation, bound and defined by custom and the legal structure, themselves sustained by the relationships of power and interest which emerged from early industrialism. The ideology of non-interference disguised the fact that everyone involved in the market was struggling each day to distort and master its operation in their own interest; that power and wealth bred power and wealth independently of existing economic logic, law or system. Advocacy of non-interference was analogous to the exemption from foreign obstruction claimed by the Soviet forces which resubjugated Czechoslovakia. The poor and impotent are rarely heard in defense of the freedom to be left alone.

Much of subsequent economic history, and almost all the history of economics, has been concerned with correcting the inefficiencies and injustices of the market misconceived as mechanism. The intellectual bearers of this quest have been liberalism and socialism converging toward bureaucracy. In 1937, Walter Lippmann pointed out that "there is no way of practicing the division of labor, and of harvesting the fruits of it, except in a social order which preserves and strives to protect the freedom of the market." By then, the onerous inadequacies of capitalism were disastrously apparent. In order to restore and improve the market, Lippmann said, "Liberalism must seek to change laws and greatly modify property and contract . . . The liberal attack on monopoly, unfair competition, and necessitous bargaining has as its guiding purpose the maintenance of that equal opportunity which the exchange economy presupposes . . . the method by which liberalism controls the economy is to police the market . . . to make the bargains represent the exchange of true equivalents rather than the victory of superior strength . . ." Thus, "liberalism is radical in relation to the social order but conservative in relation to the division of labor in the market economy. In the liberal philosophy the ideal regulator of the labor of mankind is the perfect market . . ."

Of course, "true equivalents" are a conclusion and not—as Lippmann uses the phrase—a standard. It can only mean the values which would be established by an ideal market as Lippmann conceives it. One could, as a theoretical exercise, begin with a non-economic standard for true equivalence and then devise the appropriate economic relationships as a utopian construct. Without standards which are independent of the market, we must live by the values which the market imposes.

Two years before this writing, the Schechter brothers—proprietors of the abattoir whose chickens, tracing the still unrevealed cabala of modernity, fed the young Norman Mailer and his Brooklyn neighbors—attacked and, with the help of the Supreme Court, overturned the most radical effort at a liberal reconstruction of the market—the National Recovery Act. This act made it possible for government to participate in industrial management. Once it had been annulled, regulation was the only alternative. The difference is substantial. Participation imposes responsibility for economic conduct and, in the case of government, a responsibility accountable, in however diluted a form, to the general public. Our economic history would have been much the same had the act remained in force. But at this point in history, it might be slightly easier to resolve our problems if government openly shared in managerial responsibility for polluting the environment or building unsafe and shoddy goods. The NRA was ahead of its time. It is of interest as a mechanism which, under different economic conditions, might permit the assertion of human needs adverse to the interests of dominant economic institutions.

Before the New Deal, our response to economic concentration had been an effort to fragment economic power through anti-trust laws. It was first thought all trusts should be illegal. Then it was decided that only bad trusts were illegal. This was called the "rule of reason," and came to mean that if a large corporation exercised its economic power in acceptable ways it would be left alone. As it turned out the rules of acceptable conduct were unrelated to the social and economic consequences of consolidation. Finally we dropped the whole thing, and today's economic giants are free to do just about anything they might want to do, as long as they consult their lawyers, and as long as they do not endanger other economic giants. (This was the mistake of conglomerates which failed to realize that when you threatened one company in a major industry—even though the company was not itself a giant—you threatened them all. The intrusion of what appeared to be a new form of organization was perceived as a threat to established patterns.)

In retrospect it can be seen that the anti-trust laws could not hinder the emerging economic bureaucracy. The ravaging, profit-maximizing monopoly of capitalist legend has no place in our mass-consumption, transaction economy, being inconsistent with the needs and structure of ruling institutions. Industry, for example, is also a consumer. It is the most important consumer of many commodities, especially of raw materials and transportation which were the frequent subject matter of earlier trusts. The automobile industry will not submit to the mercies of Standard Oil, as Standard used to be. The clash of economic power and the emergence of new economic forms have played a far larger part in the decline of historical monopoly than the theory or enforcement of anti-trust. By now, of course, that type of conduct no longer makes economic sense, even for a *de facto* monopoly like IBM.

Why rob a bank if you can tax all the depositors—regularly and for many years?

Once failure of the anti-trust approach became apparent, the effort to "perfect" the market turned toward the creation of a central government strong and resourceful enough to regulate and control powerful economic interests. This was the guiding faith of modern liberalism. We needed power to check power, public authority to prevent private abuses.† The essentially traditional and, therefore, the negative nature of this concept is reflected in lack of support for government economic planning, to say nothing of socialism. It was not foreseen that economic and political power, instead of checking one another, might become leagued in pursuits and structures often hostile to the power of the individual citizen. Yet that has been the fate of the final liberal effort to perfect the market.

† The idea is as old as the Constitution. However, the relationship between government and the non-governmental authority is of a different order than the relationship between public bodies. And even the Constitution's checks and balances among sources of official authority cannot survive disparities in real power created by changing social conditions.

CHAPTER 13

The economic bureaucracy obstructs and distorts the function of the market, not on behalf of individual marauders, but from internal necessities of structure—in the interests of its own continuity and expansion. Ownership, being divided, has contracted, leaving behind an institutional authority which adducts and fuses the interests and values of individual managers. As managerial success is increasingly judged by the internal standards of the institution—how well they serve its purposes, smooth its function, ensure its future—the external performance of the institution, its service to the market, to the allocation of resources and to the creation of wealth, recedes in importance. The difference is of degree. Countersigns from the past—such as profit or return on investment—are still required, and not wholly as formalities. Nevertheless, the change is fundamental. With a few degrees' change in temperature the onset of frost displaces the entire world of growth.

Visiting Milwaukee more than a century ago, Trollope personified the spirit of American enterprise in the fictional speculator Monroe P. Jones. The streets of Milwaukee are lined with "vast buildings . . . called blocks" which Jones and his friends have constructed. "That Monroe P. Jones will encounter ruin," Trollope explains, "is almost a matter of course; but then he is none the worse for being ruined. It hardly makes him unhappy. He is greedy of dollars with a terrible covetousness; but he is greedy in order that he may speculate more widely. He would sooner have built Jones' tenth block, with a prospect of completing a twentieth, then settle himself down for life as the owner of a Chatsworth or a Woburn . . . So Monroe P. Jones, with his million of dollars accomplished, advances on to a new frontier, goes to work again in a new city, and loses it all . . . Jones is undoubtedly the man for the West. It is that love of money to come, joined to a strong disregard of money made, which constitutes the true frontier mind . . . Monroe P. Jones would be a great man to all posterity, if only he had a poet to sing of his valour."

The spirit of Monroe P. Jones is as removed from modern corporate life as single combat between champions is from modern warfare. Monroe P. Jones was ruthless, greedy, exploitative and, ultimately, intolerable. But he represented and contained the energy of a free market. His resources of capital and skill sought out emerging demand. He went where the money was. The impulse of economic bureaucracy is to thwart shifts of demand, to avoid the hazards of competition, to value continuity and safe expansion over the chance for sudden riches. Instead of seeking new fields to conquer, it continually strives to increase the yield of the old.

To the extent the institution is master—owner or the occupant of a gap in ownership—its own survival and continuity are the first preoccupations. The interests of managers, unions and investors alike are dependent on the ongoing structure. That is why the first command is not "make money" but "do not menace or impair the company." The psychic counterpart is "avoid failure." The avoidance of failure is consistent with the desire for success, but they are not opposites. One cannot seek to avoid failure and achieve success with equal intensity, except in a riskless society, or in one ruled by an omnipotent and arbitrary tyrant. The fear of failure drains enterprise from the desire for the achievement.

Within the bureaucracy a single large or dramatic failure can drown a lifetime of solid achievement, and not only in the bureaucracies of business but among those of government and politics— in the State Department as it was in the campaign of George Romney. The failure of the Edsel is already half a legend; extraordinary only because it is unusual. In a free market such disasters would be commonplace. The Edsel partakes of the epic only because, for a mysterious moment, the vast machinery of bureaucratic protection—safeguard heaped upon safeguard—didn't work.

The secluded commands of bureaucratic structure are divulged through the acts and anxieties of its managerial surrogates. Managers are preoccupied with earnings. Rising revenues indicate that the organization is functioning and perhaps growing, that it is doing more of what it is designed to do—making and selling more cars, communications equipment, soap or food. Managers are less interested in profits than an owner might be. Indeed, that portion of revenue which is to be classed as profit is often, and freely, manipulated—overstated and understated—by the use of accounting techniques designed to serve the annual objectives of management. (In a recent year, twenty-five corporations with revenues of over a billion dollars each had less than nineteen million dollars in profits.) What profits there are go largely to the government as taxes or flow back into the corporation. Less than a third are paid out as dividends. And even that fraction serves an institutional purpose—supporting security prices and maintaining a capital market.

A reduced emphasis on profits is consistent with the structure we are describing. Profits do not go to the managers, whose compensation is fixed by others of their class within the corporation. And the external distribution of excess revenues would diminish the institution. So most revenue simply flows back to the economic bureaucracy which generated it. And who has a better right; or who, with power, has a conflicting interest? Profits are still important as an index of performance, a market support and as a source of capital; but profits as an end in themselves, as an incentive to action which will maximize the productive uses of resources, are receding into obsolescence.

Capital is under even less compulsion to seek profits—to obey market forces—than is industry. The revenues of our more monstrous banks are much smaller in proportion to their assets than are the revenues of industrial corporations. Pension funds and many other pools of managed capital do not have to make a profit at all. And even individual stockholders have been persuaded or compelled to accept a declining return on their investment in the hopes that rising prices will enable them to share in

bureaucratic expansion. Thus, the behavior and ambiance of investment capital are true to the purposes of economic bureaucracy. Nor could it be otherwise.

From St. Paul, a managerial text: "Even as I please all men in
all things, not seeking mine own profit, but the profit of many,
that they may be saved."

To a large extent the traditional profit motive has been replaced
by the craving for expansion. This is the logically inescapable
goal of the corporation as end in itself. It is a shared and linking
element in the interests of managers, workers, capital and the
organization. Not only a phenomenon of economic life, the
passion for size, reach and growth is the soul of all bureaucracy.

Within government the fiercest battles are waged, not over
principles and ideas, but for jurisdiction, for control of old and new
programs. Radically new pronouncements and policies are often
digested with equanimity, but at the slightest hint of a threat to
the existing structure, to the distribution of authority over traditional activities, the entire bureaucratic mechanism mobilizes
in defense. Almost invariably, the threat is defeated or simply
dissolves in fatigue, confusion and the inevitable diversion of
executive energies. "Please," wrote President Kennedy, "give me
the reasons why we can do this. I already know the reasons we
can't," in his third futile attempt to make a change in the State
Department which would alter the relationships of authority
within the existing hierarchy.

During the interminable White House program meetings preceding the annual State of the Union address, proposed shifts of
organizational authority provoked the highest intensities of debate
and required the most skillfully placating talent. This was true,
for example, of a simple proposal to unify the anti-pollution
programs then scattered through various departments of government. Such programs were only a small fraction of any department's activity, and their integration was self-evidently sound.
Yet the controversy consumed more internal energy than was
required to reach agreement on all the new programs for conservation and natural beauty. Admittedly, jobs were at stake,
but the number was trivial; most employees could expect a tranfer;

and the high level officials who conducted the struggle at the White House would not be threatened at all. Even though most of those who represented the affected departments were presidential appointees, their emplacement within the bureaucracy had effected a metamorphosis. They had become representatives, not of President or public, but of the organization. Their discharge of vitality into the structure had swiftly created a bond, a partial identity, between the bureaucracy's integrity and their own.

Just as economic bureaucracies have established a commanding intimacy with the sources of investment capital, government departments usually develop a reciprocity of interest with the congressional committees which control their funds and activities. These committees often protect the bureaucratic structure against the dislocating desires, policies or actions of the always transient Executive. In structure as in policy, government echoes the ruling private interests and relationships.

Economic bureaucracies pursue growth relatively unrestrained by those considerations of economic efficiency and profitability which the traditional market thought to enforce. The costs of operating the largest corporations—paperwork and computers, accountants and analysts, along with the loss of flexibility and enterprise imposed by size—far exceed the savings due to volume of production and transaction. Such bureaucracies are hugely inefficient. There are too many people, memos, buildings, machines, meetings. But the lavish excess of cost is trivial compared to the waste incurred through mounting incapacities of control which are masked by the modern technology of organization.

Managers with access to wires, cables and the jetstream have abolished geography. Computers and the companion development of techniques such as cost accounting, economic analysis, market research, etc. have made it possible to assemble a swelling empire under a central directorate. The manager no longer knows the business. He must depend on a stream of information from experts and subordinates. Personal direction is replaced by "standard procedures," ripening into a code of conduct or bureaucratic mores. It becomes necessary to judge performance by "objective measurement"; and those measurements soon become an end in themselves, abstractions, criteria to which reality must be conformed since reality always changes faster than rules.

It is not possible to maintain rigorous standards of efficiency or quality, clarity of control and responsibility, or internal discipline, within the diffused members of such sprawling colossi. In the age of Nader, automobile companies do not want to produce a million defective cars which must be recalled and fixed. The Joint Chiefs of Staff did not want to massacre the inhabitants of My Lai. The Secretary of the Interior probably does not want to kill off the remaining American eagles.

So-called "planned obsolescence" may be a deliberate device to increase consumption, but it is far more plausible to regard it as a consequence of the drive to increase earnings while avoiding serious competition. (For one company to put out a product which was substantially better and more durable would be as serious an offense as price cutting.) Even without this incentive, however, shoddy goods, careless manufacture and sloppy "quality control" are inevitable in structures so large that the product is separated from the personal concern of producers, workers and managers alike. Bureaucracy and quality are incompatible. For example, a truly rigorous system of quality control in a mega-business would assume the dimensions of a subordinate bureaucracy, acquiring the consequent deficiencies of that form, as well as the incapacities received through the umbilical.

The concepts of waste and economic inefficiency themselves are relics of an extinct economic process. They imply an unnecessary or excessive use of resources in the creation of wealth, from the standpoint of the economy as a whole.* Theoretically, market forces operate to reduce waste by penalizing the inefficient, thoughtless and profligate. But if your objective is growth and domination of the market then "uneconomic waste" may be perfectly appropriate, even necessary, to such ends. It is not waste at all, but the appropriation of wealth, the diversion of resources from one purpose to another, which is more closely related to the interests of ruling economic relationships. And those inefficiencies

---

* There is no such standpoint to the extent it implies some ideal economy against which a particular economy is to be evaluated. It is used here as shorthand for the most economic use of resources to create wealth, however wealth is defined by a particular economic structure.

which are a necessary consequence of scale are, in fact, efficiently adapted to institutional goals.

Bureaucratic growth is not the consequence of designless inertia or unrestrained metastasis. It is impelled by the primal concern of bureaucracy—the security and integrity of the structure. Size and reach alone can eliminate the competitive hazards which might threaten the organization. Reduction of competition, in turn, makes possible the wasteful diversions which can nourish further growth. Admittedly, there is a struggle for customers; for new markets and for a larger share of the old. But the old-fashioned weapons of destruction are proscribed: serious price cutting and the marketing of a substantially superior product. This rivalry is to market competition as Pentagon war games are to war. The successful are praised and their careers are often rewarded, but no one gets killed and the defeated forces remain whole.

It is unnecessary to document in any detail the virtual elimination of competition among the bureaucracies which dominate the American economy. The prices of capital and raw materials such as oil, metals and chemicals are standardized. The same is true, with the help of the government, of all major suppliers of transportation and communications. Even a swiftly careless examination of *Consumer Reports Annual Buying Guide* demonstrates how marginal are the differences—in either price or product— between the major consumer goods marketed by large industries. And every American knows about the automobile industry whose only problem is to internationalize bureaucratic mores in order to halt harassment from foreign manufacturers. This achievement is probably not far off, since the economic forces in other advanced countries are replicating the bureaucratic structures we have pioneered; evolving (if nationalistic unreason can be stilled) into transcendently transnational bureaucracies able to exterminate the malignancy of competition in every corner of the globe.

In the age of ownership, competition could only be eliminated through agreement, and the anti-trust laws were enacted to outlaw such companies. The relative autonomy of modern economic bureaucracies largely exempts them from the necessity of conspiracy. Since their behavior is consistent with the function imposed by structure, it is only necessary for managers to understand and follow the rules of that behavior in order to avoid the more virulent forms of competition. And that's how they got to be managers. In a determined and ferocious competitive struggle the bureaucracy has everything to lose and little to gain. It must take the chance of failure, even of possible destruction. It will surely be invaded by multiplying and disruptive uncertainties; and will probably experience at least a short-term drop in profits and revenues. Its manner of function and values are not consistent with the flexibility, personal control and rapid decision required for effective economic conflict; i.e., it is not structured for competition. And even if victorious, there is no assurance that salaries or dividends will rise, or even that stock values will increase. A successful competitor would probably enlarge both revenues and institutional size, but only at the cost of disrupting the entire economic environment and creating expectations and instabilities which would risk a recurrent and costly renewal of competition. Among the larger economic bureaucracies it is likely that competition would have no victor; that all would end up at about the same size, only poorer. And that makes no sense at all.

The economic priorities embalmed in the pursuit of growth and the reduction of competition strip the market of its capacity to allocate resources to changing needs. Competition and the maximization of profit are the instruments through which the market can seek out, stimulate and strive to fulfill new demands while approaching the most efficient and austere use of social resources. Once these instruments are blunted or supplanted there is no way for the market to enforce either the most efficient use of resources (the most product for the least investment) or the allotment of resources to the satisfaction of needs—more accurately, to the fulfillment of desire. Desire, and not necessity, is the quickening genius of an advanced economy. Matched to the possession of value it becomes economic demand.

The perfect market—resources responding to untrammeled choice—is an abstraction, an unrealizable ideal. The concept contains its own denial since it assumes the absence of that concentrated economic power which it must permit. Nor would a perfect market be a solvent for injustice and oppression, since it could not require that available choices enlarge social existence or ensure justice in the distribution of its product. Its function is to create wealth, and it is now clear that the wealth created by even a perfect market would not fulfill the historically present possibilities for freedom. Indeed, this description of market function, although accurate, is also misleading. It implies an opposition, a necessity for choice, between social product and other social desires. That implication is itself an imposition of market ideology. For the market which produces wealth also defines it. The nature of wealth, what it consists of, is limited by the structure of the market, by what can be exchanged. If a state university, for example, "gives" an education, the individual's acquisition of that education does not enter into any calculation of national wealth, such as GNP.† It is not a product or a capital investment, even if we demonstrate conclusively that we have added to our economic resources and our productive powers. It is not wealth because it is not a market exchange. Yet nearly anything people desire which is external to themselves can become wealth if the economic process contains a mechanism for translating that desire into an economic demand.

An increase of freedom requires a redefinition of wealth consistent with the more spacious possibilities of our present capacity. That is not simply a semantic task. Nor can it be accomplished by exhorting the populace to new "values." Actual wealth is identical to potential wealth as long as the economic relationships which create it continue to exist. Wealth can be given a new meaning only if we overturn the fundamental assumptions of market structure and the distribution of economic power which gives rise to those assumptions.

Nevertheless, even though the perfection of the market as presently defined will not meet our needs, the conventional theoretical market does provide a model which can help us uncover the extent to which the existing structure confines our physical capacity and limits or enslaves our desires.

The catechism of a market economy: "competition," "profit" and "growth" are not moral terms. They describe the elements of an economic process whose consequences are much more than moral. Within the market competition for profit rewards the efficient: those who make the most productive use of resources,

† Some elements of the educational process are counted; e.g., purchases of buildings and books. But the education itself has no value.

who get the most for their money. There is continual pressure to reduce costs and find more effective ways to operate. Inefficiency and waste, poor judgment and mismanagement are penalized; they cannot survive the struggle. The result is to liberate resources, draw them toward more productive use. To the institutions of a market economy, growth is not an end in itself, but a source of increased profits. And within the market resources are available for expansion only if that is their most profitable use, i.e., if they cannot make more money, produce more wealth somewhere else. Nor is market supply a passive respondent to desiring demand. The market can only function when those who control resources, entrepreneurs and investors, are continually stimulating and seeking out new demand, risking capital on the judgment that if they make new alternatives available people will respond. In the market as process, demand dominates both sides of transaction; "supply" is simply a category of demand. And demand, as we shall see, is an account of human condition and possibility masquerading as a category of economic analysis.

By arresting this process the economic bureaucracy immobilizes the resources of society: not only capital, but talent, invention, enterprise, risk, energy. The reduction of competition eliminates most of the penalty for waste and inefficiency through a uniform "industry-wide" structure of prices and wages. Once the remorseless judgments of the market have been lifted one can no longer distinguish wasteful from productive use. The uneconomic use of resources becomes a necessary ingredient of bureaucratic growth. In a recent year, one of America's largest and most active manufacturing corporations earned a return of 6.2 per cent on its capital investment, while an investor who purchases corporate bonds would have received a return of more than 8 per cent. In a market economy new investment would be used to expand existing structures only when that investment could not find a more profitable and, hopefully, more productive home elsewhere. No such mundane considerations obstruct the will to growth of our economic institutions. They contain no owner, no capitalist able to increase his fortunes by purchasing real estate or bonds rather than expanding the plant. And growth which is not recklessly indulged will nearly always bring about some increase in total revenues. This kind of expansion requires access to capital equally

THE AMERICAN CONDITION

liberated from the compulsion to seek out the most profitable and productive uses. That necessary resource is available from the fragmented, dispersed and, hence, bureaucratized capital sources we have examined. These sources are commanded by their own structure and ties of interest to nourish existing institutions, to continually renew their support of established patterns of production —the ascendant assumptions and relationships of our economy. Capital, socialized labor, managers and, less completely, other workers are not independent forces pursuing their own ends but components in a single process, fused into ongoing enterprise whose existence, function and spread are also their own.

CHAPTER 14

The immobilization of resources, the dedication of wealth to the purposes of economic bureaucracies, not only confines choice among existing alternatives, but it discourages the evolution of new possibilities, fresh objects of desire. It keeps us from wanting those products which might enhance our freedom. It controls not only supply but the pattern of demand, and through that control denies the conditions of human fulfillment.

In an oversimplified form sufficient for immediate purposes, the traditional description of demand maintains that capital must go where it can expect a return—decent or indecent. It must be loaned to those who combine solvency with collateral; invested largely in enterprises with a market. People or companies want certain products and are willing to pay for them. That fact makes the producing enterprise a sound and attractive investment. Thus, demand determines production, which attracts investment. Capital investment and production are acquiescent to demand.

But demand is no longer the pristine creature of its capitalist youth. We have already noted its waning influence over prices and costs. Neither can it seduce production with former ease. Fading powers in so intimate a union would lead any leader of St. Simon to anticipate a reversal of relationships—demand's submission to production. And since in economics, as in life, what should be, is, production has acquired an increasing power to dominate demand.

If this is so, and since access to capital resources is essential to large-scale production, to the process of transaction, then the capital structure shapes the patterns of demand and, thus, of social life.

A recent newspaper gave an admiring account of the creation of a new and very successful vaginal deodorant. A handful of advertising men, including the creative specialist, met to fashion a name and slogan for the projected product. The deodorant itself did not exist. But they were confident that, if successful, there would be no difficulty is creating and selling a product.

Slogan picked, the chemists concocted something, the flow of distribution began and earnings rose. Production or, more accurately, the process of production, the mechanism of transaction, created demand. Admittedly, this appealing conclusion is not logically inescapable. It is possible that the new deodorant simply tapped a present and potential demand, an unfulfilled yearning; although the extensive history and abundant literature of human intimacies yields little evidence that a significant problem awaited technological resolution. It is also possible that the new product simply diverted demand from competing fumigants; although total sales of this "growth item" are rising. However, neither fair qualifications nor the necessary ambiguity of proportions dispel the certainty that some demand was created.

In a not unrelated context, one can witness demand at the moment of creation, when, during a toy commercial, a child's face is touched by a wishful determination to possess a product whose existence was unknown to him a moment before. Surely no sensible or compassionate society would allow highly trained adults to devise advertising aimed at a child's mind. An adult can be fairly assumed to have developed some skepticism and the awareness that he must choose among competing needs and desires. The young child lacks these protections. He is governed by a love of play, and the purpose of children's commercials is to create a psychic equivalence between that love and the possession of things. Even when the parent responds that such things cost money and that expense is a limitation, the denial establishes another link between money and pleasure. One can, of course, instruct the child in the inanities of material possession, but moral abstractions do not effectively confute the excitement of his contemporaries as they play with the latest hot wheels racer on the screen. This kind of corruption has greater potential for psychic injury than exposure to sex or violence. However, it is a particularly effective technique for implanting the values of a commercial society earlier in life and with a more enduring impact than was possible before television.* The toy seller is preparing the child for a lifelong quest, the search for the alienated self.

Advertising is not the only way in which the media reinforce the structure of demand. That structure requires that desire for one thing, e.g., love or recreation or sensual experience, be translated into a desire for something else, e.g., sex manuals, campers or hi-fi sets. The mass media, in its non-advertising content, continually portrays, fortifies and creates these psychic equivalents. This is true not only of television, but of the magazine industry, which is now dominated by periodical guides to the enjoyment of products and by publications which thrive on the emotional link between sex and the toys of modern technology. This is not the result of a conscious conspiracy between the rulers of production and the media. Demand is more than desire. It is an economic exchange and, as such, is an expression of choice. The motives for that choice —desire or necessity, coercion or envy—constitute a description of contemporary values. The values which guide and limit choice are largely an imposition of social structure. And the mass media of society, in all they do, are a conduit for the dominant ideology.

The mass media are themselves political; that is, they necessarily reflect the basic arrangement of private interests and powers in America. The major institutions of communication, including the most powerful newspapers, are also large and complicated bureaucracies. Like all bureaucracies they are guided, not by individuals, but by a set of stable assumptions, an ideology, which no editor or publisher has the power to change. Mass media do not protect the status quo only because they are dependent on dominant economic power. They also act in obedience to the internal compulsions of their own structure.

Because this is true, the media have less influence on behavior

* Presymbolic visual experiences have the greatest emotional charge. Commercials are by far the most skillful visual presentations on television. Since children are less mindful of verbal content, they are often more fascinated and absorbed by commercials—even for adult products—than by the shows designed for their benefit.

than is often assumed. The appearance of influence comes from the fact that they are expressing ideas which are already dominant. Telling people what they already believe, no matter how many are listening, is not power. It is doubtful whether television, for example, urges us toward conformity with greater effect than the social structure of a small town in the days of Sinclair Lewis or even now. Admittedly, the growth of national media has encouraged a homogenization of values, but pervasiveness is not intensity. And even this influence simply mirrors the uniformities of consumption inflicted by an economy dominated by those who control the expensive machinery of national transaction—for hamburgers as well as chemicals.

Certainly television is a force for dissolution, revolutionary in the worst and most destructive sense. But its command over our hours is still rather slight, despite all the figures which prove how many hours each day electric current courses through the picture tube. Fortunately, nearly all television is very bad. Were some omnicompetent and ubiquitous genius able to provide a steady stream of truly amusing, absorbing and stimulating shows, we would soon be in the deepest, irretrievable trouble; drowned in passionless curiosity.

The merchandising structure which includes advertising, media, market research, distribution, popular culture and much more is production's most overt and debated agent for the control of demand. But the apparatus designed for the direct stimulation of desire is not the principal means of control. The authority of media and advertising are themselves supported by two conditions which provide a more effective and organic power over demand:

1. If you want to be bigger, you have to be big.
2. The less you need, the more you want.

Even though the output of a rather small plant could deodorize the orifices of the nation, we find that the large chemical companies such as Union Carbide and Du Pont are among the leading competitors for this growing market. Their advantage is not in the size of their factories, but in their access to the workers and structure of transaction—advertising men, marketing analysts and television time; salesmen, distributors and dealers. The nation-spanning relationships which are the foundation of their present economic domination, and which define the economic bureaucracy, also compose the process for creating new demand. Lesser enterprises can inject new products into the existing mechanism of transaction, but not easily—only at certain points and in limited ways.

The power of dominant companies is further consolidated by their ready access to the capital needed to employ that part of the demand-creating process which they do not own. The expense of nationwide advertising and distribution, for example, discourages all but the large and wealthy. Since large institutions will invariably work to reinforce the patterns of demand which already sustain them (i.e., they will not act inconsistently with their present source of earnings), the power to create the new is used to perpetuate the old.

The ability to shape demand is further augmented by the increasing vulnerability of demand itself. For the first time a majority can spend much of their income for goods not historically regarded as necessities. Food, clothing, shelter, warmth—the essentials of a bearable existence—have the first claim on income. Beyond this, individuals tend to move upward from subsistence toward comfort along similar lines—more and better food, a well-constructed house, an effective heating system, electric power, personal mobility, durable and varied clothing. It is unnecessary to draw any fixed line between necessities and luxuries to establish that the nature of choice changes as income begins to rise. To decide between meat three times a week and new winter clothes is different from trying to choose among a second car, a stereo system or a trip to Europe. In the realm beyond necessity, desires are more individual, less certain, more whimsical. However urgent they are felt to be, such desires are social and psychic rather than natural. They are rooted in present values and in the social and economic process which sustains those values. They can be more easily influenced or diverted. The spread of affluence has thus enhanced the power of the economic process to confine and create demand.

That power is most effectively exercised by limiting the availability of goods. There is little or no demand for a good which does not exist or is not for sale. In pre-Volkswagen days, Detroit could say, and did, that there was no demand for small cars. How could there be? Dealers' lots were not crowded with frustrated buyers rejecting four-door-finned sedans and clamoring for something small, cheap and compact. That demand was created, not simply discovered, by the appearance of foreign imports.

The control of demand provided by the limitation of products is a result of the virtual elimination of competition, not only among the dominant institutions, but from others who might seek to enter the market. The price of entry, the capital required to build a structure of transaction, is far too high. For the most part new giants are built on new technology (e.g., IBM, Xerox), and once successful, they become preclusive bureaucracies themselves. There are rarely any new and successful enterprises in chemicals, steel, oil, automobiles, etc.—except for companies content with a small and specialized role at the margin of major industry. There is an ancient Boston banality about the *Mayflower*-bred matron who, when asked where she got her hats, answered, "I have my hats." In most important sectors of the economy, we have our companies.

The struggle to achieve or prevent a decisive competitive advantage is the economic motive for significant innovation by established industries. Liberated from the compulsions of such conflict, the course of technology is governed by the institutional values—the functional imperatives—which dominate the modern economy.

Existing institutions are not likely to market or create new products in a way which might imperil the source or magnitude of their present earnings. The creation of new products is retarded by economic bureaucracies for whom change is always a threat—to profits, dominance and to established habits of function. New products are not often suppressed, but the stimulus and incentive to innovate has been drained of its animating vitality. This is among the reasons for our current technological stagnation and our sullen and lethargic response to foreign innovations. The single exception is the technological effort of the military and defense, the last truly competitive industrial giant.†

There are new products, a continual flood of new products, but

† For example, to the extent there is an "energy crisis," it is a result of the failure to pursue technological alternatives whose possibilities have been known for a quarter century.

most of them consist of new ways to do the same thing. One synthetic fabric replaces another; a new pesticide kills the same old bugs; this year's unbreakable plastic plate ousts the unbroken platter of last year. Through this constant titillation, desire is kept from fulfillment, discontent continually aroused. But the same array of wants and desires is maintained. Demand is confined to established channels. The breakthroughs which would permit individuals to do without cars or washing machines, gasoline or television sets are unlikely to come from the same bureaucracies whose functioning is linked to those very goods. Nor is it likely to come from elsewhere, since the resources needed to create, produce and market such products are only available to large, ongoing enterprises.

These methods of shaping demand, effective as they are, seem almost trivial beside the prodigious power of a bureaucracy so swollen and enfolding that it has become a social force, capable of modifying the conditions of life to enhance demand for its products. For all the portentous declarations about the volcanic speed of contemporary technological change, no one under seventy has experienced an economic event as devastating as that initiated when, in 1903, Henry Ford left the Detroit Automobile Company to strike out on his own. The ultimate consequence of that move is the most obvious and important example of bureaucracy as a social force. The automobile made it possible for individuals to live at greater distances from places of work, commerce and entertainment. It helped to loosen the binding realities of neighborhood and even of the city as residence. As population dispersed, the need for roads grew. The building of roads increased the utility of the motorcar. The flow mounted. The spread of urban areas placed amusement and recreation beyond the reach of those without a car. The increase in automobile ownership contributed to the deterioration of other forms of transportation, making the car even more essential. Is this what people wanted? The question is unanswerable. To say that people wanted cars, that production simply responded to demand, is to claim that individuals, alone and as members of society, also decided to devastate and reconstruct the quality and fabric of human existence. Of course, the consequences were not always clear, but some perceived the possibilities long before they were upon us, and during the last quarter century we have had enough knowledge to support a sensible judgment. But at no point were consequences examined or alternatives discussed. Neither the individual car buyer nor society as a whole ever made a choice. The economic structure provided no opportunity—no mechanism—for choice. History and the process simply imposed their impersonal will on the human beings who had made the history and created the process.

The same is true, to some lesser extent, of the other bureaucracies. When everyone has a telephone, everyone needs a telephone. Other means of communication atrophy until the telephone seems almost an extension of oneself, a part of language and not simply a way of transmitting speech.

The computer industry is the most recent example of bureaucracies as a social force. The potential capacity of computers, tinged with technological mystery, has induced businesses to "modernize" far beyond their needs. The halls of enterprise are crowded with idle memory banks, indolent calculators, unpunched tapes—all purchased because they were available, and partly because others were buying them. Yet, computerization leads to more computerization, because the machines become a form of communication, and they can only talk to one another. When one segment of the flow of transaction becomes computerized, it exerts pressure on the other links. Information is available in the language of electronics, and that fact must be taken advantage of until, finally, it exists only in that language. Finally, entire enterprises come into being simply because the computer exists. One thinks of the mushrooming central credit bureau aspiring to judgment over the economic worth of every citizen. Yet such bureaus exist simply because they can exist, not because they increase the flow of credit or reduce the risk. No one even thinks to make such a calculation. The computer industry has become a social force bent toward increasing the demand for its own product. And the social revolution it presages will make the age of the automobile seem like a nostalgic idyll of ease and freedom.

One could make a similar, less dramatic, more fragmentary analysis of other large industries. The point would be the same. The process of production also creates demand. The economic structure not only responds to wants, it awakens them; it limits and regulates choice, denies possibility. To the extent of that power, it establishes priorities of exchange—what we shall buy with our wealth and labor, our resources and skills. And it decides what we will purchase with our clean air, open land and wildlife, with neighborhood and community, simplicity and privacy—for these are also the subject matter of economic exchange. These imposed priorities reflect, sustain and reinforce the values of society and the structure of individual life which are eroding human freedom. It is an impressive power, not lessened by the fact that many who share in its exercise are not aware that they possess it.

CHAPTER 15

The economic market, either as model or in its present form, is an instrument for creating material value and distributing resources. We have seen how the institutions which dominate the market limit choice and possibility. But our choices, the values of society, are even more rigorously confined by the structure of the market itself—by the assumptions and methods of exchange which seem a necessity of economic process and have, through this appearance, come to dominate our lives and fuse with our inward consciousness.

When the modern market and its ideology were fashioned, private property was largely individual property. Even capitalist property, the result of later accumulations, was mostly owned by individuals. Value was established through negotiations and exchange between individuals, but not equal individuals, for increasing disproportions of bargaining power made it easier for some to impose value on others. If the disproportions are great enough, the only limit to the value which can be commanded is the property of the consumer and the strength of his need or desires. Thus, for a long period, it was possible to buy a person's vital energies, his active life, in return for an amount of food, clothing and shelter hardly adequate to sustain existence, i.e., for the equivalent of those goods in wages. In many places this power still exists, qualified by a few legal restraints such as the Thirteenth Amendment and minimum wage laws. (The same principle permits the sale of a Rembrandt for a million dollars. Next to the very poor, it is easier to impose value on the very rich, if there are enough of them. To the poor, money is the concrete substance of subsistence; to the very rich, it is almost complete abstraction. The rest of us find it difficult to make the distinction, and our inability to do so is the foundation of today's economy.)

Within the market based on these relationships to property, demand was primarily individual demand. This was true on both sides of exchange, supply and demand each being an exchange of that which is owned for that which is wanted. Social units, such as families or communities, could enter the market directly only to the extent their members had common values and participated in an accepted process of decision. Otherwise, they could not buy anything. They paid taxes instead.

We continue to use the term "private property" even though, as we have seen, property has been endowed with very different attributes. A thing is not property. It is transformed into property, takes on value through the legal structure, which is itself simply and always a formal recognition and sanction for existing economic relationships and organization. Nor is it useful to call property "private" because it is not owned or wholly controlled by government. That does not describe the relationship of owners and managers to property, or the extent to which a material economic unit has acquired autonomy. Yet those relationships, not legal title, determine function, which is why even government property can become a vested interest, seeking its own ends in defiance of the general well-being.

The modern market and its structure of demand necessarily reflect the changed aspect of property and property's relationship to human beings. For example, the economic bureaucracy and the labor union can exert demand which is collective rather than individual. That demand expresses the interest, not only of shareholders, managers and workers as human beings, but of the impersonal process to which they have become alienated, a process whose evolution has demolished the innocent belief that "collective" was virtually an equivalence for community. Many of the market changes we have already examined are the consequence of this contemporary "collectivization." As long as these relations subsist, we will be unable to transform the economic process. For the form of control, the location of power, blunts and seduces every intention to its own nourishment.

The largest components of economic demand have not been "collectivized"; among them the "personal consumption expenditures" which amount to about six hundred billion dollars a year, approximately two thirds of our national product. Within that category is contained the alienated sustenance of mankind. For "personal consumption," we expend that portion of our work—of our waking life and the sleep which reconstitutes us for tomorrow's labor—which does not yield fulfillment in use alone. For the most part, we make that exchange as individuals or as members of a family unit which is itself threatened by contemporary forces of dissolution. It is I, the universal I, who buys an automobile or television set, contraceptives to safeguard the moment and a Polaroid camera to record it. These are the "private" wants. Our ability to satisfy them is extolled as an incarnation and objective of freedom, although the category itself imprisons our possibilities.

The distinction between private and public wants is a description of market structure. It tells how something can be paid for, or whether it can be purchased at all. One never sees the "public" sitting at a school desk. It is not the "public" which speeds along a freeway or litters a national park. The individuals who own the cars also consume the road and the park to which it leads. "Public" is a category for those collective wants which cannot be translated into economic demand except, to a severely limited extent, by governments.

"Collective wants" are not simply those shared by large numbers of people, e.g., the desire of millions to own an automobile. They refer to those needs and desires whose satisfaction depends upon consumption by numbers of individuals. A park or school or library is produced for collective use; that production assumes, is created by, an expectation that many will share access and use. A market based on personal consumption provides no forum for these wants, no mechanism to translate them into economic demand. It is, of course, hypothetically possible for a group of individuals to combine in order to buy a park or school. But that possibility does not exist within a society where most human bonds have been shattered or seriously weakened; except on rare occasions of great provocation or in places yet to receive the full impact of contemporary culture. Social fragmentation reinforces control over economic demand.

For the most part, wants excluded from the market are denied satisfaction. Very few individuals have consciously chosen a new Polaroid camera instead of a better education for their children, plastic dishes in preference to more free time, a new office building for their city instead of health clinics or parks. Yet, all these are objects of production. They all require labor, skills, materials. But they become wealth only when they can be bought, when there is a market.

It is true, of course, that we have few "collectivities," or organic human groupings, through which collective wants can be expressed. And even if such communities existed, they would be too small to compel satisfaction of the more extensive wants. No neighborhood or community can buy or compel an end to pollution of the ocean, ineffective drugs or unnecessary labor. This requires a society with shared values, a common awareness of needs, so strongly and concretely felt that the same demand arises from thousands of uncoordinated centers, powerful enough to transform or redirect the economic process and enter into the dominant ideology. Demand of such force and the common awareness which it requires can only come from underlying changes in the distribution of social power. For the absence of collectivities, the erosion of human relationships and shared values, is not simply a fact or a condition which can be changed directly.

CHAPTER 16

THE CONQUEST OF PAGANISM

(1) All day long the right honorable lord of us all sits listening to bores and quacks. Anon a secretary rushes in with the news that some eminent movie actor has died. The President must seize a pen and write a telegram of condolence to the widow. He is repaid by receiving a telegram from King George on his birthday. It takes four days' hard work to concoct a speech without a sensible word in it. Next day a dam must be opened somewhere. Four Senators got drunk and try to neck a lady politician. . . . The President's automobile runs over a dog. It rains.

H. L. Mencken on the American presidency
in 1920

(2) The man who sits in that Oval Office is at the very center of the world. Where the action is, he waits in poignantly majestic isolation for the buck to stop—right there, in the steaming kitchen of our continental diner, where he reposes in solitude, all alone; just him and his powers, the awesome ones.

Eric Cronkite Brinkley Reston on
the American presidency in 1972

Not all consumption is fragmented. The economic bureaucracies exercise a collective demand for the components of production—raw materials, power, transportation, etc. They can restrain the economic power of those who supply these resources, conforming prices and general methods of conduct to their own needs and values. The steel industry, for example, can raise prices but not to the point where they might endanger the position of automobile companies. In general, the relationships between bureaucracies of supply and manufacture embody accepted patterns of economic behavior: their mutual dedication to existing function prevents economic pressures which might imperil survival, position or the common ethic which sustains them. This collectivization of demand, however, does reduce the control of those who supply major industries and increases their vulnerability to traditional market forces, especially to technological displacement (to the extent consumption of their products is collective rather than fragmented; oil companies, for example, sell to individuals as well as industry). Moreover, some components of transaction (such as communications, transportation, etc.) have not been fully bureaucratized, making it difficult to establish relationships based on mutual interest and accepted codes of conduct. (It is far easier to deal with the International Brotherhood of Teamsters than hundreds of trucking companies; it is the union that represents the industry in the councils of bureaucracy.)

These deficiencies in present economic relationships are, for the most part, compensated for by government regulations or subsidies which protect both supplier and consumer from the rigors of the market place, and which force or allow the regulated industry to behave as if it were part of the bureaucratic structure. General Motors sets automobile prices while the government sets airline fares. The objective of both General Motors and the government is to protect the health of the concerned industry in a manner consistent with the needs and continued function of dominant economic institutions. Through government ruling economic relations are extended to those institutions whose own structure does not ensure conformity with bureaucratic function.

But the most important exemption from the fragmentation of consumption is the political structure itself, which collectivizes demand on an immense scale. Purchases by government at all levels now account for about a fifth of our entire Gross National Product. This potential influence is magnified by regulations, tax codes, commissions and subsidies which touch every important element of economic life, and by government's formal power over the legal structure which creates the forms of ownership, and grants and limits the rewards of control over property.

"Facts" like these persuade us, in Michael Oakeshott's words, to look upon government as "a vast reservoir which inspires [us] to dream of what use might be made of it." In this context, that dream is of a remedy for defects in the economic structure, a vision of authority bestowed and taxes paid in order to satisfy the collective wants denied by the market place. This vision persists despite the fact that the conditions we have described, the denials of freedom and the barriers to human fulfillment, have persevered and increased alongside the ceaseless accretions of government. The commanding institutions of our economy have increased their ascendancy through every administration. Yet no experience or analysis, no frustration or visible event, seems able to dispel our faith that the remedy for our afflictions is concealed within the tumescent labyrinth called politics.

We persist in believing that the advent of some new leader, the coming of a wiser government, will reverse the process of modern life and take arms against the sources of oppression; that the fault is not in ourselves but in our political stars. An expectation so at odds with historical experience must be false.

CHAPTER 17

As a preliminary to discussion of government itself, an examination of the educational system may help illustrate the necessary conformity between public institutions and private relationships. Its illustrative force derives from the fact that within a different social structure education would be an important instrument to stimulate and cultivate the faculties of social man.

A decisive literature documents the failure of our educational system to stimulate imagination or the desire for knowledge. Yet the structure plods along seemingly impervious to the evidence of its inward devastations. That resistance is not the consequence of stubbornness or lack of vision. It reflects the inability of the educational structure to transcend the society which contains it. Education has conformed to the imperatives of the modern economic process, just as it served the earlier industrial economy it was created to sustain.

Horace Mann, more than any person, was the liberal father of free public education, whose virtues he extolled in his 1848 report as secretary of the Massachusetts State Board of Education: "Education . . . is a great equalizer of the conditions of men, the balance wheel of the social machinery . . . It does better than to disarm the poor of their hostility toward the rich: it prevents being poor . . . for the creation of wealth, then—for the existence of a wealthy people and a wealthy nation—intelligence is the grand condition . . . the greatest of all the arts in political economy is to change a consumer into a producer; and the next greatest is to increase the producing power, and this is to be directly obtained by increasing his intelligence. For mere delving an ignorant man is but little better than a swine, whom he so much resembles in his appetites, and surpasses in his power of mischief."

Not only an effective plea for education, this report is a significant addition to economic theory. Mass education was essential to the creation of an economy based on mass consumption.

It was well into the nineteenth century before free and compulsory education spread to most of the country. It was in the advance guard of the industrial revolution, carried along by the railroads and factories, finally taking firm root in the South only after the Civil War had destroyed the vitality of agrarian culture. The economic arguments for education could only have real force in an industrial economy. The victory of free and compulsory education accompanied the growth of economic relationships within which an educated populace would contribute to the creation of wealth.

A few proponents of popular education also claimed that an educated citizenry was necessary to the responsible exercise of democratic rights. But this argument was either ornamental or a euphemistic assurance that schools would prevent the spread of radical "foreign" ideas. The Founding Fathers, our first and last political theorists, had rarely mentioned any such relationship. And education was not included in the summary of American hopes, rights and principles contained in Jefferson's first Inaugural.

Our investment in education has paid off. It has been the "grand condition" . . . "for the existence of a wealthy people and a wealthy nation." As predicted, it transformed the "consumer into a producer," and, as an unforeseen benefit, helped to create a consumption so omnivorous that it has displaced production as the dominant factor in the creation of wealth. Those who advocated universal, free and compulsory education as a bulwark against radicalism were equally prophetic. Education has been one of society's most effective instruments for securing a general acceptance of established values and ideology. Except for a few intellectual enclaves, most indigenous American radicalism (from Shays' Rebellion to the early labor movement, southern populism and the black insurgency) has come from the least educated of our people. Even the support for liberal reforms and candidates has generally increased in inverse proportion to years of education. Those with less education are usually poorer, and their support for change has been more a result of economic status than their escape from education. However, the relative conservatism of our society has been enforced by an educational process that was deliberately conceived to harmonize with the social system. The qualities rewarded in school are those valued by the economic bureaucracy—from good fellowship to achievement in a competition conducted along rather narrow and standardized lines which reward diligence. Slow and steady wins the race. After a person has spent his entire youth in such a structure, it becomes progressively more difficult to imagine anything different, and finally the investment of years and energy becomes so large that it is very hard to want anything different. He has been prepared for the conditions of adult labor.

CHAPTER 18

Government is society's past. Although the political state may provide ambiguous clues to the direction of social evolution, it must, as the creation of civil society, conform to dominant private relationships and their supporting ideology. Its function is to reconcile the private interests established by society and to sustain the existing distribution of economic power. This ministering function is established by the nature of social life. It is a feature of social design. The relationships of the social order are the framework of political life and confine public institutions and the boldest of public men.

As a regulator of discordant forces within the existing order, government can be an agent of reform. It can never change the ideological assumptions and material relationships which are the foundation of that order. Such change occurs only if the relationships between private interests are altered or overturned from without.

Within a society there is no "public" interest; only individuals with common private interests. To assert, for example, that the public interest requires a plan of installment payments to contain a clear statement of the total amount of interest to be paid means that we prefer to protect those whose ignorance might lure them into debt, rather than reward the agility of an entrepreneur who might benefit from the deception. (Further analysis would reveal other possibilities; e.g., certain types of deception discourage commerce, or production is maximized when consumers are on the brink of bankruptcy, not over it.) No distinctive public interest exists even when it seems that everyone benefits, as, for example, when the government finances cancer research. It is ordinarily the more affluent who place cancer high among their concerns and wish to give priority to the search for a cure. Nor can the public interest be categorized as the interest of a majority. This is just the private interest of a large number of people. Nor would such a definition describe some traditional objects of political concern. The interest of one man in speaking his mind can be thought superior to the interest of almost everyone else in shutting him up. (He is also protected by the larger interest in denying any official institution the power to suppress certain private liberties.) The public interest is composed of those private relationships which can be enforced by public institutions.

Although government has a formal, i.e., legal, authority to make fundamental changes in some private relationships, that authority cannot be exercised, that is, it is not a historical reality. As the creation of private life, the form of government reflects private needs and powers at any moment in history. Government, therefore, is private life; that is, all the important elements of its existence are private; just as the atom *is* all of its particles and forces even though the relationships are obscure. Government could make fundamental changes in private relationships only by giving itself a new form, by becoming a different kind of government. One cannot, for example, imagine the Soviet Union restoring private property without an equally basic change in the Soviet state. It is true that political reforms often appear to modify private relationships. The state can create a new welfare system or prohibit industrial monopolies. In all cases, however, such reforms will be a response to changing private realities, designed to protect dominant private relationships against threatening new conditions.

In the postwar period the desegregation decision of the Supreme Court recognized changes in the black condition which had followed the advent of World War II. The "one man, one vote" decision was an adjustment to the established social reality of urbanization, arrived at after the cities had elected three Presidents; and the delay itself can be attributed to the fact that state legislatures had lost much of their power to influence the urban condition. The most prominent social movements of the 1960s—the civil rights movement and protest against the war—were not initiated by government. Public action was possible only when concerned private groups had acquired dimension and force which could not be ignored. Nor has public action gone beyond that necessary to dissipate any potential menace to the existing order. (Movements for social change lose political support as soon as they come into conflict with stronger private interests. That conflict may be real or it may be ideological as when dominant institutions enlist oppressed groups in their own defense.) More recent movements such as Women's Liberation, consumerism and ecology had their genesis in private life. They too have discovered a willingness to yield until, and only until, the sources of dominant social power appear to be threatened. Government undertakes to heal social afflictions only when they are problems of administration, that is, when solution is possible without upsetting the existing social process or, more particularly, the dominant private relationships of society. It cannot act effectively if the source of discontent is fundamental, residing in the design of society.

Over a period of time an accumulation of reforms may add up to basic change. In retrospect, however, we will find that the nature of government has also changed. The ingathering of power by central authority comprises the most important political change of modern times. For our entire first century men debated the right of a disgruntled state to detach itself from the union. Today, state governors accept their exclusion from matters of national policy which do not directly concern the conduct of state government, and travel to Washington to request some of the money taken from their citizens. Revenue sharing comes more than a century and a half after Jefferson proposed to distribute all excess federal revenues to the states; and in its present form "revenue sharing" is a device to reduce the resources available to state and city governments.

This basic change occurred without a modification of the elaborate constitutional prescription for a federal structure. It came as a consequence of changes in social relationships. Nearly every new assertion of central power during our first century involved territorial expansion, public works and the regulation of commerce.

Most of that "regulation" was to protect an increasingly national economy from local harassment. Private interests, which themselves transcended state borders, could best assert their dominance through a central authority. The growth of these revolutionizing pressures culminated in the Civil War. By creating the Union, the Civil War accomplished for the United States what Bismarck and Cavour had done by unifying Germany and Italy. The issue of union had always involved a clash between economic forces—a clash which could not be resolved until the advent of industrialism in the middle of the nineteenth century tipped the balance of private power against agrarian society and thus against the political forms which sustained that society. Once this had happened the political revolution known as "unification" and, later, as "centralization" was inevitable.

A political revolution recognizes new private relationships; but only a social revolution creates them. Over a period of time, changing conditions shift the distribution of social power. Threatened institutions and their inhabitants resist. And so does the state which they created.

If there is a great deal of flexibility in the political system, newly emerging private relationships will gradually re-create government. If there is a great deal of resistance, the opposing pressures between social realities and political structure will increase until there is a seismic release, a revolution. Louis XIV's reported assertion *"L'état, c'est moi"* meant that he was the only individual who counted. Had he been more of a social philosopher he might have said, *L'état, c'est nous,* thus including his associates in the French aristocracy. The revolution came, not because he was wrong, but because he was right; and since private power was in other hands, the state had to go. Neither the French Revolution nor the American increased the power of the middle class; they confirmed that power. And despite the egalitarian rhetoric of both these events no other outcome was possible. The powerless may help to make revolutions. They do not win them, except perhaps during those rare moments when all private power is destroyed or in disarray.

The ministerial function of politics is discharged by its practitioners; men whose lives have been directed to the acquisition and use of power, a pursuit so demanding that it tends to diminish all other sensual and intellectual ambitions. To acquire high political office usually requires a single-minded and highly competitive temperament joined to great physical stamina. Nor can many men spend their lives in politics without believing that the power they seek is real. Successful politicians generally have faith in their personal powers of action and in the significance of the public powers on which they expend their vitality. Consequently, they also believe that social ills will yield to wise conduct of the existing form of government. Men of action must believe that action has results. This makes them reformers, as the assumption of their action is the existing structure of the society as reflected in the political structure they have striven to master.

CHAPTER 19

Since politics can neither transcend nor oppose the civil society, political issues—although they may influence the welfare of individuals and groups—do not challenge the form of society. They are not a contest over important social power. Marx wrote that "the clearer and more vigorous political thought is, the less it is able to grasp the nature of social evils"; a caution especially to be heeded by Americans, the most political of people.

Yet, even when discontents are contracted to the modest dimensions of public discourse, if their source is fundamental something of that will be revealed. Basic sources of oppression are not revealed in the grand themes of political argument. They can sometimes be recognized in hints supplied by subtle changes in the manner of presentation and the character of public response. Problems of war and welfare, income distribution and civil liberties have been with us for a long time. Yet the conditions and conduct of contemporary debate are distinctive. That difference can help to point the way.

In 1887, a scientist named Hertz set up a machine for making electric sparks. Across the room was a thin iron wire which was bent into a circle whose ends did not quite meet. When Hertz turned on the machine and the sparks began to fly, a slight glow appeared in the tiny gap in the iron circle. The experiment was a

success. He had proven some fundamental theories of electro-
magnetism and, in the process, created the world's first radio signal.
Hertz also noticed, however, that when the light from the spark
machine shone on the iron circle the glow seemed to increase
slightly. The small difference did not disturb the exciting results.
It was ignored for years. Yet, when its causes were unraveled we
knew that many of man's theories about the structure of the material world had been wrong. That same difference—the so-called
photoelectric effect—helped to support an entirely new theory of
matter and, incidentally, provided the scientific basis for television
and the movies. Whether or not light struck the wire, the event
was just about the same and could be identically described for the
purpose of the experiment—i.e., the sparks created a glow between
the ends of the wire. But the glow sometimes changed a little, and
that small change altered our understanding of the universe.

In the last decade a succession of events has helped to illuminate
some sources of the modern condition. On June 8, 1964, after a
brief delay caused by the protest of Ambassador Leonard Unger,
President Johnson ordered an attack on communist anti-aircraft
installations in Laos, beginning the chain of offensive escalations
whose consequences were to change American politics. Only the
Civil War had a greater impact on American attitudes than the
war in Vietnam. (The much greater dislocations of World War I
were experienced primarily in Europe, coming later and indirectly
to America.) Riots in northern cities awoke the nation to the postwar transformation of racial problems. Black disabilities could no
longer be relieved by striking down elements of a southern network
of ordinances and customs designed to bar the black from the institutions of society. The principle of "Equal Justice Under Law"
was too narrow to nullify exclusion from the economic process or
to heal the consequences of that exclusion.

War and racial injustice are among America's most enduring
mortifications. But the terms of our response are a reflection of
contemporary conditions. Behind the question "Why are we in
Vietnam?" came the challenge "What kind of a society are we,
that we wage such a war?" Does the language of commitment and
security rationalize the pursuit of economic imperialism? Does
imperialism itself conceal an indigenous American violence? In the

past several years many articulate men have joined in these accusations, and an influential group of scholars has reinterpreted our history in accordance with these conclusions. The answer to this critique has been characterized more by a reaffirmation of faith than by rational argument. Indeed, on both sides argument is readily displaced by the assertion of moral absolutes, reflecting that self-doubt which has spread through the society.

Similarly, the struggle to eliminate disabilities imposed on blacks has been supplemented by censure of the entire society as racist, while fear and hostility invade the current white response to the desires, and even the existence, of the blacks. Yet only a few years ago an American President could proclaim, "We shall overcome" to almost universal applause.

There is, as another example, the frequent emphasis on the need for psychic conversion voiced as a complaint that people do not value those things which would increase the general well-being. Yet values and desire are not the creatures of persuasion, they are conformed to the imperatives of the material process. Similarly, our diminishing confidence in political solutions is an intuitive response to the fact that no such solutions exist. And problems that are beyond the reach of public life are fundamental. However, it is not public issues themselves, but the form and temper of contemporary division that point to important flaws in the social process.

Nor can the social implications of political events be confined by categories like "liberal," "radical" and "reactionary." They are political terms and do not describe the nature of social change. Political conservatives, for example, have been among the most militant advocates of the industrial and technological growth which has revolutionized American society. Industrial society gave content to the idea of "conservative" and "liberal," of "socialist," "humanist" and "fascist." All we can say of the relationship of industrial society to these terms is that it contained them. That tells us something about the nature of the society, but what it reveals cannot be expressed in political language. Even more immediate extrapolations are hazardous. To claim that the country is "going conservative" because it elects a conservative President is like saying the residents of a community are becoming alcoholics because they have voted to allow liquor. They may be responding to effective propaganda, or trying to get rid of gangsters who are thriving on illegal sales or hoping to attract a distillery in order to create new jobs. On the other hand they may all be incipient alcoholics. We must know a lot more than the results of the vote before we can decide.

When a social problem can be specified, e.g., substandard housing, and a concrete solution can be formulated, the difficulty does not result from a defect in basic assumptions or structure. But today's vagueness of complaint, the non-ideological and even purposeless qualities of the desire for change, along with our inability to devise new public policies for obvious disorders, all point to an underlying condition which is beyond the scope of the assumptions and techniques of the past. Discontent of this nature can produce a wide variety of responses and movements. For if the causes are fundamental, and therefore obscure, no particular set of solutions will seem rationally and morally compelling. In such a situation people may well choose among different kinds of change for reasons that have little to do with the nature of the problem. There is one dangerous exception derived from the fact that the choices are social and not individual. If the choice seems to be between chaos and the illusory certainties of order—if there is no rational alternative—social man invariably chooses order. And that is among the chief dangers of our present condition.

CHAPTER 20

The capacity to influence society is conferred and limited by living structures and relationships and not by formal and historical grants. The power of government, the social influence of politics, can be understood only by examining its actual relationship to private centers of power and interest, and to the confining circumstances, the historical realities, of modern life. *The true province of politics is the administration of existing interests—to remedy defects, mitigate abuses and to reconcile competing claims. The form of that reconciliation must be consistent with the relative power of the interests being asserted.*

Madison saw this as clearly as the conditions of his preindustrial time permitted. In the tenth *Federalist* paper he explained that society was divided into factions and that "the most common and durable source of factions has been the various and unequal distribution of property." Those factions were represented in the political process by the legislators themselves, and "the most numerous party, or, in other words, the most powerful faction must be expected to prevail . . . It is vain to say that enlightened statesmen will be able to adjust these clashing interests, and render them all subservient to the public good." He concluded that "the causes of faction cannot be removed, and that relief is only to be sought in the means of controlling its effects."

Madison's remedy was to apply Montesquieu's dictum "It is

necessary to have power check power." Constituencies would be large enough to permit a legislator to escape domination by any single interest, while the size and diversity of America would ensure factions so ample and various that none could obstruct the general good. The condition of Madison's America provided some support for the hope that interests might remain dispersed, and that political forms could help maintain natural discrepancies of desire. The advent of industrialism struck at the foundation of the Madisonian expectation. While the unparalleled fusion of interests within the modern economy has left little hope that power will check power, freeing government for more transcendent purposes. Rather it is the citizenry, the American community, the "public good," which has become fragmented and made incapable of effective assertion.

Decades before Marx, Madison had realized that political life is entrapped by the economic interests of society. Indeed, the leaders we associate with revolutionary change, men such as Jefferson, Jackson and Lincoln, did not create the social conditions over which they presided. Their achievement was the wise and forceful adaptation of politics to new relationships of power and interest. Such achievements deserve gratitude. For a political structure which embodies obsolete or displaced private relationships may resist new necessities. In such cases the political structure loses its claim to legitimacy; it is at odds with society itself. The consequence is decline, instability or even revolution. To respond to change, however, is not to initiate it. It sometimes appears that way, because the act of ratification is often the first public, historically dramatic, appearance of the subterranean alliances, negotiations and shifts of position which have created new arrangements of social power.

This relationship between politics and private society goes largely unremarked because it is fundamental. Nor do the practitioners of politics ordinarily view themselves as agents of private power. The Church was once allied to the interests of the feudal structure. Yet one cannot doubt the intensity of ecclesiastical convictions in matters of spiritual faith, nor in the righteousness of purpose of the earthly Church. The Grand Inquisitor could not have been conceived until it became possible to view the Church from without, through the consciousness of a new society.

Events occasionally give us a slight glimpse of the circuits which link politics with private power. Early in his presidential campaign, Senator George McGovern made a series of economic proposals which did not come under public scrutiny until, well after their publication, he was seen to be a substantial candidate. These proposals for change in the tax and welfare laws were not radical. They contained no threat to dominant institutions or to the economic process. No tax "reform," for example, can hope to damage the economic bureaucracy; all transfers of demand inevitably contribute to its growth. But some of McGovern's language seemed to imply a call to arms against economic power as such. I asked a wealthy friend of mine, an active and productive leader in the economic establishment, why he, a liberal Democrat, opposed McGovern's economic policies. "The programs don't worry me," he said. "I'd do even better." (Of course.) "But I'm afraid he might unleash class warfare." There was, in other words, the smell of danger.

Moreover, two of the proposals seemed, ever so slightly, to infringe upon principle. The first was a 100 per cent tax on estates over five hundred thousand dollars. The imposition of such a tax would not have the slightest effect on General Motors or Du Pont. But a 100 per cent tax is confiscation and the concept of confiscation clashes with principle. It implies political power independent of private relationships. The second proposal was a welfare program which seemed to say—but did not—that every American would receive one thousand dollars a year from general revenues. The tone of this proposal, the manner of its presentation, conveyed not just a desire to redistribute wealth but to modify the principle of distribution itself: the tenet that social reward, income, is to be allocated in return for value, however disproportionate the exchange might be. It is one thing to help the poor. But to attack the principle of distribution through exchange is to challenge the foundation of the economic process.

Once the McGovern proposals and their ambient rhetoric had entered the public consciousness, the only political possibility was amendment. The inheritance and welfare plans were dropped, and a modified economic program, wreathed in fulsome praise for the glories of free enterprise, was devised by most solid and respected economists. Undoubtedly, the second presentation was more faithful to McGovern's own convictions and to the possibilities of presidential action. Indeed, the whole episode was essentially a misunderstanding, combined with the fact that the proposals were not examined and disseminated until they had hardened. (In most campaigns such slips would be caught and recalled within a day.)

More significant than McGovern's adjustment is the fact that protest did not come from the rich and powerful alone, from investment bankers and industrial managers. It came from everywhere, from the society itself. Factory workers were repelled by the 100 per cent tax. A neighbor of mine, a forest ranger with an income of about six thousand a year, declared, "That fellow McGovern frightens me." The hint of basic change, like a scent of sulfur in the air, evoked unconceived apprehensions of chaos and descent. That this should be so is, of course, a necessary implication of our entire analysis.

CHAPTER 21

Government neither supplies those collective wants denied us by the economic structure, nor provides the conditions which would permit their expression. Demand materializes an act of will, a decision, and when we transfer value to government—as taxes or authority over property—those decisions are made by others.

Clearly, no government with jurisdiction over multitudes can satisfy collective wants or even identify them beyond the elemental requirements of social order. Some must pay to benefit others. The economic function of government is to transfer demand. The judgments which support those transfers are said to be made from the viewpoint of "society as a whole." The phrase conceals far more than it describes, for it can only refer to present society and the relationships which dominate it. The decisions of government are imprisoned in the web of claims and desires, values and perceived possibilities constituting a social structure which creates and re-creates its politics. Government as a countersociety, endowed with transcendent power, is a creation of mysticism, a secular analogy to the City of God. Through the ideological separation of private and public needs, the pressures of discontent are diverted from the economic structure, enticing us to address our pleas to those who lack the power to grant them, to mistake debate and official titles for choice and resources.

The guardians of government pursue different ambitions, respond to different claims and voices, than do industrial managers or union chiefs. They are part of a process in which a great variety of interests are bent to a common purpose: the integrity and growth of the institutions which rule the economic process. It is not necessary for every act of government to advance this purpose. All that is required is consistency or, at least, an unwillingness, an inability to obstruct or damage. Antagonism and conflict are contained within shared assumptions. Indeed, one of the principal functions of government is the prevention of mortal clashes between powerful private interests. When this is not possible, as during the 1850s, force and not politics decides the issue.

Nor can one judge the nature of conflict between government and economic institutions from the intensity of the advocates. Men on both sides believe in the ideology which forces them to perceive surface adjustment as a struggle over principle. And issues whose resolution will not disturb the structure of power may still decide the success and fortunes of particular individuals, companies and parties.

Recently the government "settled" an anti-trust suit against the International Telephone and Telegraph Company. The "settlement" was an agreement by the government to let ITT keep the company whose acquisition had caused the suit. Shortly thereafter the public was entertained by some memos which proudly linked the settlement with large contributions to the Republican Party. It became known that the president of ITT and his representatives had met with the most powerful and highest officials. The assistant Attorney General who dropped the case had swiftly moved to a judgeship. Stories from all sides were in irreconcilable conflict. And in the midst of all this, a man armed with a paper shredder had consumed several pounds of ITT files before an admiring audience of employees.

The story shows only that ITT's understanding of the relation between business and government is woefully out-of-date. When government action touches upon the interests of more sophisticated economic bureaucracies, they do not write inane memos or haunt the halls of the Justice Department. Their chief executive officers remain securely within their offices. Standard Oil, for example, virtually ran our foreign policy in Peru for two years. One could safely wager that there is no record of an explicit agreement between the State Department and Standard; not because the record was destroyed, but because formal expression was unnecessary. Both wanted the same thing, and each understood what the other wanted. A phone call, an expression of concern, a meeting between lawyers, and the thing is resolved. The lawsuit is never brought, or if a naively literal official is not restrained in time, a settlement is drafted which is fair to all, in the judgment of the representatives of both parties—i.e., the government lawyers who will someday return to their law firms and the company lawyers who will undoubtedly take their turn at public service.

The illusion of political power is intensified by the fact that ruling interests often struggle zealously against changes which ultimately strengthen their position; while the oppressed and their advocates in politics often pursue causes which also benefit their adversaries of the hour. The fiercely won struggle to organize labor brought specific rewards to workers, but, as we have seen, it later strengthened the dominant economic institutions by fusing the interests of socialized labor with the economic bureaucracy. The imperatives of the economic process are not identical with the ideological passions of its individual trustees. Indeed, the inability of ruling interests to understand and pursue their own interests is a more threatening and revolutionary fact than the discontent and outrage of the poor and powerless.

Over the last decade managers of industry and finance registered opposition to many of the political decisions that swelled the power of economic bureaucracy. So, too, the military chieftains violently opposed the McNamara reforms which increased their economic power; which, in fact, created the military-industrial complex. Even today many leaders of industry oppose programs to redistribute wealth and create jobs which would ultimately increase consumption of their products, their revenues and their size. Part of the reason for this apparent ignorance of interest is that an economic process as a dynamic system can only sustain itself by continuing adaptation to changing realities. And it can expand only when shifts in technology or in the dimensions of production extend its reach. But the individual manager perceives this strengthening change as uncertainty, and in the bureaucratic lexicon, uncertainty is a synonym for danger; while most of those at the top are also at the end of a long ascent, psychically wedded to the conditions of their past success.

Nevertheless, the needs of the process and its institutions are nearly always stronger than the exertions of the guardians. Whenever this is not so the process itself is in danger; ruling structures, however imposing and imperturbable their appearance, are in inward decline or disarray. In such a period (in the 1920s and '30s) the rulers of historic capitalism, able to impose their will, deepened the collapse which led toward economic bureaucracy. The titan of finance who pressed his wisdom on the Hoover administration only hastened his replacement by banking bureaucracies, mutual funds, insurance companies, pension funds and the mass conscription of capital. He could not have done this, however, unless the agents of decay were already close to the core.

To compile all the expressions of relationship between politics and civil society would require a detailed examination of the acts of government, the private consequences of political organization and the form of politics. The task would be complicated by the fact that since dominant interests are not the total society, unrelated claims are frequently allowed assertion. However, the factual outlines are convincing.

Most federal money, for example, goes just where private money goes—into the industrial bureaucracy. To a large extent, the middle class is taxed in order to sustain the rich—not rich individuals—but rich institutions. Not only does public spending lead to private revenue, but money goes to the same kind of companies for the same kind of products.

Using fiscal 1971 as our illustration, most federal spending went (a) directly to the institutions of economic bureaucracy, (b) to sustain the economic "infrastructure," i.e., to components of transaction, such as transportation, which are not owned by dominant institutions, or (c) to maintain an educational structure able to endow the population with skills of production, desires of consumption and the values needed to sustain both; a structure whose non-economic contributions to human possibility are limited to those consistent with the necessities of the economic process.

Not counting the trust funds* we spent about one hundred and fifty billion dollars in 1971. About ninety billion went to national defense, "international affairs" (mostly assistance programs tied to purchase of U.S. products), space and veterans benefits (the bonus, incentive and protection program of the military-industrial complex). Of the less than sixty billion dollars remaining, about twenty billion was divided between payment of interest and the financing of transportation to move goods or extend the horizons of the automobile. A little over five billion dollars went into agricultural programs, increasingly to large units, but also as recognition that even if farming is unprofitable people must eat. (In addition, without quotas and subsidies agriculture might well become bureaucratized and thus acquire a control over supply and prices which would infringe on all other consumption.) Education and manpower training received a little more than eight billion dollars; water resources and power, about three billion; while the costs of running the government were over four billion.

Even more significant than spending is the labyrinth of laws, agencies and commissions with formal authority to fashion and regulate much of our economic life. Thousands of studies con-

---

* The relatively new "unified" federal budget was conceived through a fortunate liaison between Keynesian technology and the natural political tendency toward obscurity in all matters of money. That budget combines, *inter alia*, payments from federal trust funds with other expenditures. Most of these funds are publicly operated insurance programs such as social security, unemployment compensation, hospital insurance, etc. These funds, as a class, generally take in more money each year than they pay out, although individual funds often have deficits. They were included so that economists could more easily discuss the consistency of all government economic activity with Keynesian theory, e.g., what was the "real" deficit. Before this it had been necessary to add up the figures.

In the interest of "totality" other transactions such as property sales, oil revenues, etc. were also included, making it possible to change the budget to accord with political exigencies by simple bookkeeping. This means there are two budgets: the "real" budget and the "President's budget," of which only the second is released to all the people. (The fact that private industries often manipulate earnings in the same fashion only exemplifies the universality of bureaucratic conduct.)

The new budget obscures and dissembles federal influence on the economic structure, on the society as a whole. The purpose of government spending is to transfer demand. Value is taken from individuals and companies who would otherwise have exchanged it for their own needs, and used instead to satisfy the wants expressed through politics. For the most part the trust funds do not do this. One pays now for some measure of protection against the uncertain future. A particular individual may not receive awards measured to his contribution, but the class of beneficiaries is the same as the class of contributors.

ducted over decades tell how this legal structure serves the interest of dominant economic forces. A decade ago, for example, experts and commissions indignantly proclaimed that regulatory agencies were more dedicated to the health of their regulated clients than to the "public good." Since then, nothing has changed.

In *The End of Liberalism*, Theodore Lowi demonstrates that current laws, programs and agencies support the existing relationships of private power—although that is not his phrase. Rather he refers to the chief beneficiaries of politics as "interest groups" (meaning organized interest) or as "privilege." He locates the cause of what he regards as an overwhelming defeat of "justice" in the failure of modern political thought, which he calls "interest group liberalism." Lowi points out that "even when the purpose of the program is the uplifting of the underprivileged, the administrative arrangement favored by interest group liberalism tends toward creation of new privilege instead." Nor are conservatives exempt from this tendency. "(T)he only difference between old school liberals and conservatives is that the former would destroy the market through public means and the latter through private means. . . . The most important difference between liberals and conservatives . . . is to be found in the interest groups they identify with." And even these differences tend to disappear in action. President Nixon, for example, imposed public controls on the market; while Democratic administrations inevitably make special and successful efforts to demonstrate their concern with the welfare of the economic bureaucracy. (This is true of political and not intellectual conservatism, which is at odds with the necessities, if not the formal creed, of major economic institutions.)

Lowi's examination is thorough and convincing. However, the conditions he describes, however, are not consequences of political failure. Terms like "special interest," "interest group" and "privilege" are simply pejoratives for the important and influential. All interests are "special," but only some are powerful. Nor are they powerful because they enjoy special and private access to the instruments of politics. Their strength rests on the tangible resources or strategic position which allow them to dominate the social process.

The relationships between government and the chief sources of social power are incomplete. By straining logic and language it might be possible to attribute all political behavior to specific interests. Political life is the creation of civil life, but the relationships which dominate society are not coextensive with society. A ponderous welfare bureaucracy, for example, is neither a construct nor necessity of dominant economic institutions. The word "creation" is not intended in its biblical sense—"So God created man in his own image"—but to designate primal authority—as in "all men are created equal."

In many aspects, government is itself a "special interest," i.e., it is invested with momentum and purpose largely independent of its popular constituency and even of its transient managers. For politics takes on the forms as well as the purposes of private society. The structure of official power tends to replicate that of private power. The conditions which have led to economic bureaucracy— material concentration and dispersion of authority—have their political counterparts.†

Central government has added more to its reach over the last few decades than during the previous century and a half of our history. In this respect, we are more distant from Herbert Hoover than he was from George Washington. The sovereignty withdrawn from states has gone to augment the immense, continual and unimpeded accumulation of authority within the central government, especially its executive branch. The result is an Executive vested with almost exclusive power to take substantial initiatives; a virtually unappealable veto over the actions of states and Congress, particularly in economic matters; and the almost sole management of government bureaucracies which infringe upon the economic process at every strategic point. Many of the traditional constitutional divisions continue a formal existence, but they have lost their power to restrain.

Every four years about seventy million voters elect a President and a presidential spare. They choose between two men designated

† In every significant respect the Defense Department is not a counterpart, but a true economic bureaucracy—an autonomous institution whose managers are confined by bureaucratic function. The legal structure does seem to give the public and other branches of government a great deal of authority over the Pentagon. Experience has shown this authority to be as illusory as that of shareholders in Du Pont or AT&T. Since the Defense Department has become part of the relationships which dominate the private economy, public control is precluded.

by political parties through a procedure which involves a small fraction of the electorate. Each of these two then selects the potential beneficiary of his mortality. When Lincoln spoke of "government by the people," he was not referring only to this right to vote for President. More compact constituencies selected officials and legislatures of town and state. Citizens separated into hundreds of districts chose the members of a Congress which was solely empowered to pass laws, dispose of public funds, even to impeach the President. These exercises of choice increased the authority of the citizen, not just because he was a bigger fraction of the total, but because smaller numbers within a limited territory made possible a familiarity, a play of claims, desires and cultural inclinations between citizens and their representatives. One can more easily persuade the local dealer to redress complaints than General Motors. Not only does he need the sale, but people talk.

We still elect all these officials and more. The application of direct popular sovereignty extends far beyond the original settlement. But the right to select officials is not authority over the functions of the government. The flight of political power to the federal executive has dispersed the citizenry's authority over the function of government. This fragmentation of influence diminishes the reality of control, by the individual voter and by the body of voters.

These parallels between the political structure and the economic bureaucracy are neither formless nor accidental. The modern transaction economy—increasingly exempt from traditional market restraints—requires a strong bureaucratized central authority to help make the accommodations between divergent interests which were once the function of the market. Political resolution must be coextensive with that of modern economic bureaucracy, whose authority cannot be hindered by the annoying diversities of state or city. Some agency must provide those components of transaction which cannot be owned or exclusively controlled by particular industries—e.g., transportation, communications, monetary structures, etc. Those elements of transaction which are important to a variety of enterprises and which are in private hands must be protected against economic collapse while, at the same time, be denied the power to restrict access or to impose undue burdens for their services (e.g., telephones, airlines). The political structure which performs these functions and which is also an influential part of the economic process must be shielded from the hazards of public fashion or the vagaries of misguided leaders.

Bureaucracy is the form of solution, as it is a source of the problem. Votes are the tokens of ownership, the inherited shares, in government by the people. Institutions, political as well as economic, which are "owned" by legions of shareholders are liberated to follow the inbuilt inclinations of their structure. Nor can the elected manager of the executive enterprise lead his institutions far from their accustomed rounds. There is an illusion of control. Orders can be issued, officials designated, and men fired. But the public bureaucracies have acquired a substantial independence of managerial control, not because of size and remoteness alone, but through a multitudinous web of relationships with interests beyond the White House and outside the government. Any effort seriously to remodel the major institutions of executive government strikes at centers of private power throughout the society. Almost every President who has made the effort has given it up. In government, structure is still policy, and that structure resembles, because it serves, the dominant forms of private life. Hegel wrote that "the world spirit is the spirit of the world as it explicates itself in human consciousness"; in this sense of "spirit," politics as bureaucracy is the palpable show of the spirit of the time.

Survival and growth are the first prescripts of the political bureaucracy. It is even freer to pursue these virtues, the bureaucratic essence, than its economic counterpart, since it is less restrained by requirements of performance and product. Government bureaucracies are, at the margin, subject to shifts in public sentiment or political direction, but most change comes, when it does, through accretion, transfers of authority within the executive, and in those activities of least concern to important economic interests. Evidence is as extensive as government itself. It is generally agreed, for example, that government housing programs are not adapted to urban problems. Nor is this a recent discovery. Yet, the housing bureaucracy has persisted and grown for a quarter of a century.

Through the bureaucratic process public protection of the economic structure can be made to appear an exercise of the virtues of deliberation, wisdom and restraint. For example, a manager who demonstrates his open-mindedness by seeking a multiplicity of

views and wisdoms, has also devised a mechanism to justify existing behavior, since there will almost certainly be no agreement on
important change. Even our most sincerely compassionate candidates for high office proclaim their intention to be "President of All
the People"—to improve the welfare of businessman and farmer,
rich and poor, banker and worker. If this means anything at all, it
is that no one is to be damaged or reduced in order to benefit another; that is, the existing distribution of social power and rewards
will be preserved.‡ The candidate himself is usually not lying about
his hopes. Like many others he believes there are no mortal and
irreconcilable differences of interest and desire; that all, equally,
would benefit from the elimination of exploitation, oppression and
injustice; that social conflict is the product of misunderstanding, a
failure of communication; that differences can be resolved by increasing the wealth and perfecting the techniques of the present
social structure. Thus is the urge and rhetoric of liberation transformed into the ally of oppression, not by cynicism or conspiracy,
but through dedication, belief and energy.

Were politics to become the repository for interests different in
nature from those which dominate private life, then politics would
be at war with society. This has happened at certain historical moments. When it does the only alternative to ravaging turmoil is the
total submission of the political structure. Democracy practically
eliminates this peril by making it necessary for elected officials to
continually re-establish their support within the society. Failure to
respond brings the peaceful deprivation of office. The procedure is a
public counterpart of the authority to check managerial transgres-
sions, contained in the structure of all bureaucracy.

Unless there are serious changes in the social structure, we can
expect the political evolution of recent decades to continue—the
dilution of popular control, remoteness and bureaucratization, accumulation of central authority and, increasingly, the integration of
government into the economic process. There will be exceptions

‡ Although income is not the equivalent of economic power, the fact that the distribution of income has not changed in a quarter of a century is a token of the resistant durability possessed by more fundamental distributions. In 1947, the poorest
20 per cent of all families received 5 per cent of the income and the richest 20 per
cent received 59 per cent. In 1973, those percentages are virtually unchanged. The
same is true for all intermediate groups.

and temporary retreats, but this is the direction of movement. Recent administrations, for example, moved from "guidelines" to forceful admonitions, to control over prices/wages. This transformation occurred when habits of decision compatible with economic expansion proved not to be appropriate or healthy during the relative stagnation which began in the late sixties. Yet managers were trapped by institutional inertia and by expectation—their own and those of other parts of the bureaucracy—especially the expectation of undiminished revenues and rising wages. Controls relieved these pressures, stabilizing the bureaucratic process within a slightly changed context. When demand began to increase, the controls were suspended, permitting enterprise full advantage of the opportunity for increased earning. Inflation during stagnation harms everyone, but inflation coupled with expansion damages only the general public (provided the inflation is not so great that it impedes the flow of commercial transaction).

The greatest weakness of bureaucracy is a tendency toward rigidity, an inability to adapt to changes in external conditions. The protection of government, its jurisdiction over the total economy, will be increasingly invoked to heal this deficiency—through controls, support of technology, direct subsidy to distressed enterprise and through economic planning conducted in government offices under the supervision of private institutions. Government will also accelerate its efforts to forestall disruptions caused by the fact that bureaucratic restraints still operate, for the most part, within national borders. The growing internationalization of capital and of bureaucratic mores will bring about a world market modeled largely on the American economic process. When President Kennedy, in 1962, called for "interdependence" between America and Europe, he was thinking primarily of legal structures and relations among governments; of common market, shared defense, treaties of trade and co-operation. That interdependence has become a fact, the consequence of private economic relations.

The process of assimilation is far advanced. The leader as hero becomes the leader as manager, yielding to the leader as chairman of the board. More people are bombarded with more information about politics in more ways than ever before. But the economic function of government, its multitudinous ties to the private economy go almost undiscussed. Such subjects do not match the drama of China summits or election clashes, nor do they command the passions stirred by racial conflicts or violent crime. Yet the tendentious and pedantic phrases—the decisions, orders and regulations which most ignore or never hear—report a continual assault on the magnitude of our existence.

Politics is not pure illusion. The politician, as candidate or official, is not an automaton whose acts are enjoined by a programmed calculation of private interests. Politics reflects the relationships of civil society because it is an aspect of that society, part of the social process. It is the creation of private relationships, but, as created it is also a reality, a force, which influences those relationships. Economic claims are asserted in specific ways and forms because of the political structure. For example, if there had been no elections in the fall of 1972, automobile companies would probably not have rolled back their price increases. They might not have been asked. Concessions are made to maintain social stability, "domestic tranquillity," which would not be required if politics were different. Such concessions are never basic. Power and function are not impaired. But they can make a difference to many people.

Moreover, social evolution is not subject to laws of biological necessity. The "relationship of production," the disposition of private interest and power, can be served and sustained in many ways and under many conditions. One can, within limits, be generous toward the poor or brutal, protect civil liberties or suppress them, without threatening bureaucratic ascendancy. Such choices can be enormously important, but they will not arrest the alienating process which is consuming human freedom. Indeed, this process has become so powerful that the varied cultures and politics of advanced nations are urged toward a symmetry unequaled in the modern age.

CHAPTER 22

Even as sources of oppression harden and extend their domination, the militant and thoughtful, the public spirited and ambitious are increasingly lured toward the promised rewards of politics. Politics absorbs the force of the moving remnant,* provides entertainment for the casual majority and seems to offer an antidote for sensed impotence to all. "Power to the people" becomes political power; participation in the social process is translated as "participation politics." Acolytes and addicts are offered ceremony and indulgence without remission through the daily reports of political acts and follies. And every four years the disbelief of millions is suspended while the course of the world seems to ride on the clash between champions, the finalist survivors of the grand elimination. Never has the nation been so politicized. Never have so many given so much attention to so few.

Incessant discontent and frustration and the continued absten-

* The moving remnant is that minority whose concerns extend beyond the im-mediate and personal—home, business, university, etc. This does not mean they are idealists. They simply relate their feelings or concerns, even their personal self-interest, to a larger social environment; e.g., a businessman concerned about inflation or the contradiction between controls and free enterprises, a journalist in search of cor-ruption, a conservative philosopher describing the decay of institutional traditions, the organizer of a Black Panther group. This is the group that influences society and can change it within the limits set by historical conditions—not by moral example or persuasion, but by uniting their concerns with social power. The forces that move society cannot be counted. They must be weighed. Power through numbers is the distinctive illusion of democratic politics.

tion of a new spirit of liberation are attributed to unpredictable misfortunes and fatalities, mistakes of leadership, the accidental convergence of unfavorable circumstances, incompetence or flaws in the political process. The solution, therefore, is to avoid mistakes, think more wisely and above all, to "perfect" the process—restructure Congress, open up the parties, eliminate secret contributions. But political "reforms" do not change the distribution of social power. Any political structure, however devised, will reflect the dominant realities of private life. Were the entire population, via cable television, to participate in drafting a new fundamental law, still, economic relations would remain essentially unchanged, although political powers of repression might be enlarged. This outcome would not be the consequence of mass ignorance, fear or narrowness, but of a false premise: the belief that politics can create power, when, in fact, it can only accommodate the competing claims of existing power.

The modern erosion of individual power has accelerated the turn toward politics by the energetic and more affluent. The political struggle is framed in the language of authority: There are high and historic offices to be won, momentous issues to be debated, grave social questions resolved. As alternative sources of social influence are consumed, belief in the large possibilities of government often appears the only alternative to an unacceptable impotence. And it is natural for the expectations of a fragmented populace, stripped of their ties to traditional, organic units of existence, to flow toward a central government which remains a visible symbol of social unity. Moreover, government is consequential. It is huge, an essential element in the economic process, and, as one of the largest of economic bureaucracies, it is also a powerful special interest. The actual importance of government as a support and substantial part of dominant private relationships is easily confused with a potential importance as leader and agent of basic social change.

We could multiply reasons like these without fully explaining the belief in politics as transcendent; not simply Oakeshott's "vast reservoir of power," but as power able to modify and redistribute all other claims to dominion. Many of us who worked in the White House during the early sixties may have been victims of the anxiety for place and recognition; but ambition also extended to the desire to "make a difference," to use this force—whose existence was an article of faith—in order to enhance human well-being.

Around the meeting and dining tables of the White House, those of highest influence reached agreement on still untried ideas, new approaches to public ills: The restoration of nature within the city so that contact with the natural world would be an aspect of daily experience; partial payment of rent to replace subsidized construction so those with little income might enter the housing market as consumers with some power of choice, thus eliminating forced segregation by age and income; the need to transform a historic under class, black Americans, through a cultural and economic integration which would provide content for legal rights. Yet somehow, always, circumstances and political realities, shortsighted colleagues, bureaucratic resistance and congressional opposition seemed to alter and weaken the boldest departure, flattening it into conformity with established patterns. Still, it seemed the power was there, if only . . . It was not then clear to me that the inability to exercise authority is almost infallible proof that it does not exist. Nor was this belief in the possibilities of achievement a personal arrogation. We were, by the almost universal consensus of ally and adversary, of fashionable belief and folklore, in the "center of action," counselors to the sovereign, at the temple's high altar.

Marx wrote that "the more a ruling class is able to assimilate the most prominent men of the dominated classes the more stable and dangerous is its rule." Politics does absorb much of the energy of discontent, the ambitions of those desirous to become agents of social change. Finally, however, Marx's statement is an echo from another world. It is not a ruling class and not politics, but the entire society which incorporates potential sources of resistance when, and only when, they acquire some measure of independent force and momentum. This assimilation is conducted through libertarian virtues—through social mobility, occupational fluidity, rags to riches, illiteracy to Ph.D., obscurity to celebrity. It is not a device contrived to maintain dominant relationships and institutions, it is an aspect of the process which creates them. "Every man a king" is mostly illusion, but it is also true that the chambers of social power are more accessible than ever before; except that, unknown to the occupants, the true sovereign does not wear a human face.

Our reliant trust in the political sustains the ascendant relationships of modern society, but this trust is not a wholly contemporary creation. It is an aspect of American tradition—as transformed by historical circumstances and by an explosive growth of politics—which has virtually obliterated rival objects of social mediation and influence. It is this tradition which has influenced historians to identify periods of important social change with the President of the time: the Age of Jefferson, the Jacksonian Revolution—and not just for convenience, for more precise or dramatic dating.

The Founding Fathers believed that political structure was a crucial support and protection for individual welfare and liberty. To secure natural rights, governments—not societies—were instituted among men. Although the framers were aware of the importance of social relationships, the emphasis on government was natural to those who were initiating a new political order. This stress on the forms of government departed from the political thought of Europe which tended to look upon government more as a necessary consequence of society or natural order (or of transcendence) than as an agent of human well-being. Even those Enlightenment philosophers who most influenced American ideas stressed the responsibility of government as the protector of rights; a difference of emphasis which was to gain in significance. The thought of those who studied Locke or Montesquieu was unavoidably imbued with a different meaning by American circumstances—inspired by confidence in limitless opportunity rather than by protest against unjust distribution and official lawlessness. And like the nation itself, American political theory was animated by defiance and rejection of the European order, as was the Marxist thought of a later century and the Russia which finally embraced it. Modern America and Russia both evolved in reaction against that Europe which was to be divided by their armies and, ultimately, by their social orders. Indeed, Americans expected the same liberating results from the people's "ownership" of government that Marx later anticipated from the people's "ownership" of property.

The repository of this American faith was not government itself, but the political process: the balancing of factions, dispersal of authority, confinement to prescribed powers and a variety of electorates with the power to renew or replace their representatives. This careful construction would permit government to function effectively while foreclosing those oppressions of the kind which, in a new continent and during the eighteenth century, seemed the greatest threat to freedom. The political process would protect social freedom from the state.

In our own century, traditional political ideology was reinterpreted. Government itself came to be regarded as a source of freedom, endowed with the capacity to redistribute social power. Elements of the political process inconsistent with this view were attacked or discarded as obstructions to freedom. This change cannot be justly attributed to "liberalism," or any other form of political attitude. To do so is to participate in the illusion that social changes have political causes. Politics evolved to reflect the imperatives of new economic relationships, and no change of government defied or even retarded the movement. The concentration and bureaucratization of economic power, and the consequent centralization of public authority continued undisturbed under "conservative" and "liberal" guidance alike.

Similarly, the degree of willingness to hinder or narrow civil liberties does not depend on party or ideological labels such as conservative or liberal. Any strong government will, under favorable conditions, try to intimidate acts and expressions which oppose its conduct or favor its adversaries. Men of power always resent obstructions, a resentment strengthened and rationalized by the inclination to regard any hindrance as self-serving opposition to the needs and well-being of the nation or, in a more advanced stage of megalomania, to the will and desires of "the people." Political liberty can only be protected by the legal process, constitutional separations and, much more, by the shared and accepted values and standards of society. To the extent citizens must rely on the good will, self-restraint or libertarian ideals of a strong Executive, liberty is already lost.

The modern rallying to politics is something more than an intensification of tradition, subject to correction by argument or analysis. When we bestow upon politics the power to guide and alter society by acts of will or decision we are engaged in mystical creation. An authority believed able to encompass and fulfill the interest of "society as a whole" is being invested with a quality of detachment from the social process, granted a vantage point without, or beyond or above society. It is made transcendent, and that element of transcendence reveals that we are in the presence of faith; a structure of belief which, as the corporeal translation of passions and revelations, is resistant to the contradictions of experience and logic.

In his report on the 1972 Democratic Convention, Norman Mailer concludes that to Americans their country is their religion in order to explain why the Miami auditorium, despite external sham, deception and naivete, was impregnated with a sense of high moment and ceremonial solemnity; why even trivial issues excited the passions of the serious and substantial. As a participant in such gatherings I know the exhilaration which occasionally intrudes upon the most practical and ruthless of actions and invades the keenest perceptions of cynicism, an exhilaration kindled not simply by the sensed expression of personal power, but by a consciousness that the nation and the future are contained in the same vessel which encloses the tangle of political ambitions and desires. Sixty-seven million people watched the final night of the Democratic Convention. That immense audience is far larger than the number even casually interested in politics combined with those who watched because they had nothing else to do or were fatally addicted to the electronic narcotic. Yet, the size of the audience is not surprising. For with rare exceptions the high moments of politics—the emergence or the death of leaders—provide the only experience shared across the divisions of our society.

However, politics is not the nation, nor the incarnation of the nation, nor the distilled essence of the nation. The faith which enfolds it is not a religion of the civil society of America, but of the political process. It is presaged in Lord Bryce's observations that "The Federal Constitution is, to their eyes, an almost sacred thing, an Ark of the Covenant."

The political faith allows the outcome of social conflict to be ratified by a process whose legitimacy is rooted in common belief. The law is passed, policy instituted, directive given. In this way, government provides sanction for social realities, power is robed in principle. Dissent can be unrestrained so long as the laws are obeyed; one can oppose the acts of the Church, but may not challenge the faith. In ordinary times the political creed is benign. After all, when the social battle has been decided, matters must be put to rest, defeat accepted, and the victors contained within the dimensions of their triumph. The alternative is forcible coercion with the prospect of continual turmoil. But these are not ordinary times. Our afflictions cannot be subdued by repairs or modifications, by those adjustments we call "reforms." For us, therefore, a political faith is not a useful and salutary illusion. It is an accomplice in oppression.

We are not the victims of perfectible weaknesses in the social structure. Our humanity is being consumed by the structure itself; by the ruling constituents—the institutions, relationships, consciousness and ideology—of the process which contains modern America. Our possibilities and our awareness of possibility are mutilated by the rising strength and effectiveness of that process. If we wish to be free, then we must reject a stable tranquillity—the calm acceptance of "realities" which are not real—in favor of defiance, outrage and conflict. Our condition will not be altered, alienation will not be diminished nor freedom amplified, by new accommodations with the dominant sources of social power. Power itself, the command over social resources, must be transferred and redesigned. This is not a task of destruction, but of displacement; a task which can only be achieved by merging the fragmentary claims and desires of multitudes into social strength adequate to claim dominion. This may not be a possible achievement, but if we seek it through politics it is surely impossible. The political faith turns us from contemplation of fundamental disorders, lures discontent and anger to the pursuit of the "practical," by which is meant the victories and rewards which politics can offer. This does not include basic social change.

Large and swiftly increasing numbers have lost their confidence that politics or politicians will respond to their felt grievances or enhance the quality of social existence. Their disillusion is often described as distrust or as a "loss of faith" in the institutions of democracy. Rather, it is an intuitive realism grounded in the congenital incapacities of politics. Yet, even the most cynical retain the assumptions of the political faith. They have lost confidence only in its worldly incarnations. This compels them to the conclusion that if the political process is inadequate, there is no hope for improvement at all. If this is what one believes, then we can also be persuaded that energies are best devoted to defending the present against further decline, while social action outside politics presents itself as a disruptive attack on the defended position. In this way the political faith becomes a source of resistance to necessary change. At the same time, the moving remnant, whose discontents and ambitions should fuel reconstruction, pour their energies into politics with mounting intensity. As bureaucratic structures congeal, as the sources of oppression extend their hold, this political fervor will increase. No other course will seem "practical," none able to compete with the yellow brick road leading toward the sovereign who can make us whole again.

Through the Middle Ages the Church was not an agent of oppression. At times it associated with injustice and abuse of power. But the world was poor, and no social structure could have kept most men from lives of harshness and material misery. Religion added a liberating dimension to existence by reconciling humanity with the inevitable. When material possibilities began to enlarge, the virtues of religion—acceptance of position, the insignificance of worldly enslavements compared to the rewards of immortality—no longer constituted a reconciliation with necessity, but became an ideology in the service of oppressive relationships. Today, too, the foundation has shifted. The possibilities of human freedom are so much larger than the reality, the gap between the two so great, that politics as faith seduces us to support the agents of our confinement, the mutilators of existence. Politics is not an opiate. It is speed; creating an illusion of command, causing an outpouring of energy and force for their own sake. But always it wears off, leaving the world and us as before. To the believer, politics is real war, summoning the commanding spirits of decisive battle. Yet, such struggles do not interrupt the purpose of material rulers, although their attention may occasionally be distracted.

CHAPTER 23

Self-subjugation appears in more naked and enslaving form among the bureaucracies of advanced communist nations. The necessary subordination of politics to private power still leaves some breathing space, allowing us to protect concerns and liberties which do not actually threaten the economic structure, even though the transient manager of economic institutions might regard them with distrust or fear. But where the economy and politics have been formally fused, there can be no politics; only bureaucratic struggles for executive positions. It is like merging a whale and a minnow.

Marx himself never thought that political power could check economic power. Rather, a change in the nature and distribution of economic power would change the state; and one day there would be no economic power as we know it—that is, no power to compel people to expend their energies for purposes which were not their own. Then there would be no state. The conclusion is true, almost a tautology. In a world without economic power, there would be no political power, only agents and spokesmen for community choices based on shared values.

In postrevolutionary Russia, and in the countries it conquered during and after World War II, economic power was largely concentrated within a central authority. As in our own system, formal ownership—in this case by the people—was not control. Instead, traditional ownership was fractured, and thus diminished, leaving economic power with the economic bureaucracies and their managers. Since the population did not have the control over resources necessary to the development of community, the community necessary to communism could not develop.

Where economic and political power are one, every expression of need inconsistent with the existing process appears a threat, not only to the production of wealth, but to the entire society. Americans tend to fear that radical economic change will make them poor; that it will endanger their possessions, their expectations and, in part, their social existence. In a communist society, radicalism in all its forms, even those most remote from the economic structure—literature, sex and rock and roll—is perceived as a direct threat to social existence itself.

One could maintain that such perceptions, enforced by political repressions, are compelled by Marxist theory; that art, ideology and personal behavior either serve the economic structure—in this case communism—or they subvert it. However, Marx explains that no state acts in obedience to theory. Concepts may govern amid the disorder of revolutionary beginning, but, finally, it is settled material conditions which create both theory and actions—in this case the fused economic and political bureaucracies of Western communism. In obedience to the nexus between "relations of production" and society which Marx uncovered, they have selected, distorted and reshaped Marxist thought to conform to material realities.

Even though the economic process contours values and beliefs, forms the culture itself, that does not mean that the economic process *is* the culture. It is incompleteness of control, inconsistency, which permits progress toward freedom. The bureaucratic fusion within modern communist states has stripped away the conditions for Marx's expectation that the socialization of capital would initiate an evolution toward true communism. The disciples of dialectic and change, servants of a faith in the creation of new historical possibilities, have acted to freeze the process, and thus, to obstruct any progression toward increased freedom.

In the Soviet Union and Eastern Europe, the abolition of private property was not Marx's "positive abolition" which would lead toward elimination of the division of labor under the guidance of a state no longer rooted in a dominant mode of production, a state which was an expedient of transition. Nor could it have been. For those countries were not wealthy enough—the productive forces not adequately developed—to permit full elimination of bourgeois economic relationships or substantially to reduce the division of labor. Yet, to Marx, these were the necessary conditions for the socialism from which communism would emerge.

Instead, the revolutions in Russia and Eastern Europe simply hastened progress toward an economy dominated by bureaucratic modes of production. Those ruling forces constitute far more formidable obstacles to communism than did the comparatively immature capitalism of the middle nineteenth century. To Marx, the socialization of property was a prelude to communism—the "negation of the negation." He could not have foreseen that this second negation would also require revolution against productive forces and repositories of power now firmly entrenched.

Marx could not have fully anticipated this danger because the nineteenth century was a time imbued with concepts of a mechanistic and sequential causation. It was, as Wittgenstein noted, a period of search of "essence," a primary condition, relationship or impulse which formed all others. Marx described the essence of social evolution, just as Freud defined the essence of dreaming and Darwin the essence of biological evolution. In the nineteenth century these were the forms in which truth itself appeared.

The changed awareness of our time teaches that in very intricate process—and none is more complex than human society—there is room for unexpected and inconsistent events without impairing essential function. This characteristic permits unpredictable change as distinct from changes which are inherent in known structure, e.g., the development of a seed into a plant. If economic relations produced a totally conforming culture, they would also produce the restraints and prohibitions which would prevent new economic relations from developing. The formal fusion of economic, political and cultural power has just this effect on the more liberating possibilities inherent in the abolition of private property. It tends toward virtual social stagnation, although it cannot easily exclude stimuli to change coming from outside the society or from a changing technology.

One cannot explain the evolution of European "communism" toward totalitarian bureaucracy as the result of a departure from

Marxist teachings, as the consequence of infidelity to the master. This is both true and irrelevant. Societies have established themselves on the foundation of Marxist ideology. The consequences of their actions, the resulting historical realities, constitute the inner meaning of the philosophy, even though that meaning contradicts the intentions of the philosopher. To think otherwise would transform Marxism from a materialistic system to a variant of idealism. It would return Marx to Hegel, from whence he issued.

These observations are intended for the advanced industrial countries. China is a far more hierarchical society. Individual consciousness incorporates the community and its values. These bonds themselves limit the scope, the power, of central authority, however authoritarian the legal framework of control may seem; and they provide some of the cultural conditions necessary for the evolution toward communism. Unfortunately, this kind of social structure also obstructs the process through which modern wealth is created, which is, in part, why Marx thought industrial development had to precede communism. There may be other ways to create wealth; but, within historical experience, technology and economic enterprise thrive upon a fragmenting individualism, the dissolution of human bonds. Thus, China and the West confront the same contradiction, except that the thesis of one is the antithesis of the other. But we cannot yet be instructed by the Chinese experience, for to the West, China is still a country in the mind.

PART VI

THE COERCIVE PROCESS OF THE
BUREAUCRATIC ECONOMY

CHAPTER 1

Social choices—values—beyond physical necessity are usually generated and supported by ideas and beliefs. Since these ideas and beliefs are related to each other through a common purpose, they form an ideology. Ideology and culture sustain the dominant elements of society at many levels of abstraction. For example, an effort to describe the relationship between sexual mores, art and ownership would require us to explore an immense number of ambiguous connections. At the end of such an exploration one could only show consistency, although one would know which features were dominant.

There are ideologies whose relationship to dominant forces is directly and openly avowed, such as the nexus between medieval theology and the medieval Church, the feudal code and the feudal system, the divine right of kings, nationalism and emerging commercial society. As befits so segmented an age, the elements of our own ideology appear isolated and distinct, inhabiting disciplines whose seeming autonomy conceals their common origins and social function. Earlier we looked at the ideological links between mysticism and scientific reason. But if these are manifestations of the spirit, economics is emblem of the body which contains them.

Not too long ago there was no "economics," only "political economy." (There has been an analogous progression from political philosophy to government to political science. However, political science doesn't work and rarely influences practitioners, but economics sometimes works and influences many.) Political economy descended from theology and political philosophy when historic unities—the structures of thought and belief which embraced all aspects of existence—began to lose their hold. It emerged from the gathering impulse to analyze and describe the mundane world; responding to new awareness more slowly than science or art because many of its concerns did not arise until increasing complexities of commerce and the market required more systematic explanation and justification.

Written before the final triumph of scientific reason, the descriptions of political economy were framed by a conception of human nature and the proper end of human society. Except for Marx, most of the political economists were not extraordinary philosophers and their work often lacks dimension. The elements which seem economic tend to crowd out all others, more completely from our perspective than from their own. But they were not economists. From the vantage of economic life they reflected upon the condition and prospects of the race, the secular counterpart of salvation or damnation. If they were among the first to systematically relate such concerns to the organization of commerce, resources and labor, it was because economic life no longer appeared as a fixed aspect of the landscape, but as a condition which had entered the process of history.

The transitions from political economy to economics were consonant with the changing world view, the new forms of description, which marked the passage to our own century. In the 1880s, Michelson and Morley performed the experiment which helped to overturn classical physics, Germans invented the automobile and Karl Marx died. In the first year of that same decade, Francis Edgerton, a British professor, published *Mathematical Physics*, a work which reduced economic behavior to equations, and used the differential calculus to prove that existing privileges of wealth and birth were just, sound and useful. Economics had arrived.

"Economics," writes Robert Heilbroner, "had ceased to be the proliferation of world views which . . . seemed to illuminate the whole avenue down which society was marching. It became instead the special province of professors whose investigations threw out pinpoint beams . . ." However, the fulfillment of the promise implied in this new discipline—economics as an instrument of management—awaited John Maynard Keynes, the combined Thomas Edison and Henry Ford of economic technology. By stripping modern economic thought of any concern with the entire social process or ultimate human ends, he made it a powerful instrument for regulating the economic machine.

Since bureaucracy is the logic of technology, it is also the logic of Keynesianism. Keynes helped construct the ideology of the modern economic process in response to its emerging imperatives. In order to strengthen the economic process, Keynesian economic management, public or private, requires bureaucratic controls. Analysis would probably reveal that the private economy has become more Keynesian than have the policies of government. For the economic bureaucracy, reinforced by the partial bureaucratization of capital, is now able, within expanding limits, to manage and plan investment, prices and wage costs.

In 1926, long before he had become an "ism," Keynes wrote that "progress lies in the growth and the recognition of semi-autonomous bodies within the states . . . [large business corporations which] . . . when they have reached a certain age and size . . . approximate . . . the status of public corporations rather than that of the individualistic private enterprise." His own work helped to materialize that bureaucratic vision, while his successful example has increased the dedication of economics to problems such as "productivity," "wealth," "growth," "employment"—terms whose content is imposed by a particular order of society. The determination that these constitute the issues, the appropriate subject matter, of economics, tacitly adopts and reaffirms the values and institutions of contemporary life. Not only does economics justify present limitations of social choice, but as a branch of technology it strengthens the barriers which confine our wants.

In one of his most famous statements Keynes proclaimed, "The ideas of economists and political philosophers, both when they are right and when they are wrong, are more powerful than is commonly understood. Indeed, the world is ruled by little else. Practical men . . . are usually the slaves of some defunct economist." It is the kind of modesty one might expect from a man who could condescend to both Marx and Roosevelt. And it is false. It is economics that has placed itself at the service of dominant economic institutions, and helped to increase their hold over our human possibilities.

The change from Smith, Ricardo and Marx is not a consequence of enlarged human thought and understanding, but of a change in economic institutions. There are modern economists such as Milton Friedman or John Kenneth Galbraith for whom economics is not a self-contained system, but the adaptable servant of human wants and values. Yet, they receive professional recognition for descriptions of the existing process, while their discussions of freedom or the public well-being are, at best, dismissed as the harmless digressions of generous spirits. If, for example, Milton Friedman could produce an equation demonstrating that wage and price controls would lower productivity and diminish real income he would provoke debate and concern in every center of economic thought. He might even win the Nobel Prize for "economic science," a category which effectively limits the award to technicians. When he objects that such controls interfere with freedom he is talking to himself and, perhaps, to a few non-economists. Even to raise such questions imperils the legitimacy of a discipline whose entire function is to support—with ideology and practical technology—the existing economic process. To ignore values, ultimate ends, is always to accept those which have been built into the structure. Although the relationship between economic activity and the necessities of human freedom may be ignored, it cannot be denied.

Power over demand is exercised to confine material resources to those uses consistent with the values and purposes of dominant economic relationships. Imputing "purpose" and "values" to social institutions should not be mistaken for animism. The same realities can be described in terms free from such ambiguous overtones. The structure and size of such institutions and the way in which they function have particular consequences for society. Substitute "consequence" for "purpose," "manner of function" or "process" for "values," and one can describe the power of material institutions without seeming to bestow those attributes of will and choice historically limited to human beings and their gods. The use of this more traditional vocabulary provides a greater precision of statement. But it does so at the cost of obscuring the relationship between humanity and economic institutions. Consequence and function, being inanimate, seem to be objects of choice, subject to the clash of human resolves, rather than forces which can influence, oppose and enslave the will of social man.

The categories of this analysis, "ownership," "market," "demand," are drawn from the terminology of economics, but they describe the conditions of life within society and they define the limits of human possibility. The phrase "patterns of demand," for example, is an arid equivalence—a counterfeit of analytical inquiry—for those social values expressed through the acts and choices of individuals. It describes what people will work for and spend for: the objects for which they exchange their powers, and the irreplaceable vitality which constitutes their humanity. Control over demand, acquired by choice or circumstance, maintained through decision or structure, is power over society.

In order to exercise that control it is necessary to coerce choice, and what we choose constitutes the social values we possess. For social values are those which govern relationships with others and the material world, not only in those activities we call economic, but in all expression of human attributes—in art and in consumption, protest as well as conformity. We may believe that in a certain situation we would make a certain choice, but that is only a prediction of what our social values will be. We may regret the choices we have made, but that is only a wish that our values had been different. Values themselves exist only in relationship, and external expression is their reality.

The "market" through which choice is expressed and satisfied is not simply a mechanism for establishing value through exchange. The structure of that market determines the historical content of the terms "wealth" and "value" themselves. To the extent the market occupies the realm of social interchange—is the forum for the external relationships between individuals, groups and institutions—it defines what we may choose and thereby regulates the possibilities of our existence. The present economic process imposes a market ideology whose rule is so extensive that some of the most important material necessities of freedom are not only unavailable, but are excluded from practical consideration: the desirability, for example, of constructing neighborhoods where the essential activities of life such as work, recreation and services are contained within an area small enough to permit human community; or the need to expand the possible, practical uses of free time in order to encourage the extension of our faculties. Instead, our inward sense of loss or incompletion is translated into those choices which the market provides, e.g., an increase in leisure time expands the demand for goods of personal consumption: for motorboats and campers and for more highways to permit a swifter and easier escape. To explain the production of these goods as a response to expressed desire implies the existence of a choice which the market denies.

The distinction between society's ability, its willingness, to meet public and private wants is not a distinction between sacrifice and indulgence, but between power and impotence. Even what we think we want—our desires themselves—is contoured by the existing social process; and not just our desires but our awareness, that consciousness of existence which relates our inmost selves to external realities. The structure of the market, the essence of the economic process, can thus be seen as strategy and ideology of the dominant relationships of society to confine the use of wealth—the distribution of social resources—in their own interest.

The analysis of our transaction economy and its governing bureaucracies which occupies the last half of this book is not intended as a critique of the American economy, a guide to more efficient production, or an argument for the fairer distribution of wealth. Like the parts which precede it, it is a pathology of society. To speak of "dominant forces" or "governing institutions," while accurate, tempts us to misconceive of the relationship as one between ruler and ruled; to regard economic power as an external imposition on society and, by extension, on life within society. Society, however, is not an object or a collection of objects, but a field of desires, claims and transactions. The rules and forces which prescribe assertion and response, and which regulate function—which seem only to define and limit the process—are the social process in itself. They are society. Just as the laws governing the strength and direction of magnetic attraction are the magnetic field; or the rules, explicit and customary, which govern the rights and conduct of courts, lawyers and parties are the legal process. Within the social process all causes are also, partly, consequences. The necessities of analysis which isolate one from another also change, distort and deceive.

Economic relationships dominate this social process because they bring forth material necessities and these objects of desire whose satisfaction, requiring most of our energy, become the social translation of our humanity. *By separating gratification from the immediate use of human energy, economic relationships acquire their power over society.* This separation can only be maintained if we value what we buy, if the objects of consumption make their appearance as the satisfaction of needs and desires. This is not equivalent to an assertion that the social dominance of economic relationships derives from power over consumption. Consumption is itself a process which contains the means through which we acquire the capacity to consume.

We can clarify this aspect of consumption by analogy to the relationship between supply and demand: Each party to an economic exchange supplies something which is demanded by another. Ordinarily, but not always, the one who supplies money is regarded as the consumer, and the value of what he exchanges enters into a calculation of demand. The categories also have more complicated uses, some of which, for example, underlie the continual debate over the best method of stimulating the economy—whether to transfer resources to individuals or to economic institutions. Nevertheless, the most elaborate analysis would reinforce the conclusion that "supply" and "demand" cannot be abstractly defined, but derive content from present methods of exchange and market structure and, therefore, from the current distribution of economic power. Similarly, one who consumes is also occupied with acquiring the means to consume, usually by work. The social values which sustain patterns of demand find expression not only as wants, but as submission to the process of production and transaction. Nor is that submission a subjective condition, being consistent with enthusiastic belief as well as the resigned acceptance of seeming necessity.

Although economic relationships are always an important constituent of society, that fact does not, of itself, mean that economic relationships control social life. They are oppressive only when they become external to the members of the society, when they are not the instrument of shared social purpose. Their power over human existence is a consequence of alienation, exercised to increase the alienation from which that power derives. Since society consists, not of elements but of function, its dominant forces and institutions, out of structural necessity, influence all the relationships which constitute that function—not only external circumstances and actions, but qualities of thought and feeling which we perceive as internal and autonomous. However, to dominate is not to determine. Economic relationships are an aspect of the process they govern, which is why we cannot end the alienation Marx described simply by modifying or destroying the institutions which are the current repository of alienated existence.

We have no experience of man who was not also, in some large measure, economic man. When human tribes first established settlements, it was necessary for them to submit to the process of growth. Soil and weather have requirements to which the farmer must attend, as do seeds and flowering crops. In this way the process of agriculture also ruled the lives of those who conducted it. Its restraints were manifested and effected by natural forces, but they were transformed into limitations by a social creation—the agricultural process. The necessities and rigors of agriculture were not, by themselves, alienating. They did not constitute oppression so long as obstacles and goals reflected shared community purpose, were imposed by a collective humanity on itself. When this was no longer true, when control became external to labor, those who worked the land were alienated, enslaved to the process and to those who owned it. They became helots or serfs or migrant workers.

One cannot set forth with any certainty the precise extent of contemporary alienation, establish a fixed boundary between external coercion and human autonomy. We are all contained by the social process we seek to understand; even the most resistant mind cannot fully sever autonomous thoughts and passions from the impositions of society. Hegel wrote, "It is just absurd to fancy that philosophy can transcend the contemporary world as it is to fancy that an individual can overleap his own age." Even the genius of Marx could not escape the assumptions which underlay the conflicts of his age, e.g., the materialism and scientific spirit of ascending industrialism. Had he done so his work would have refuted his own philosophy. Nevertheless, such a limitation is a barrier more to prophecy than to analysis. One need not establish a precise formula in order to perceive and understand the magnitude and sources of oppression. A slave may not realize that his religious convictions are an imposition of his slavery, but he knows he is a slave, even if by the will of God.

The oppressive power of contemporary institutions tends to reveal itself most clearly amid failure than at the height. Our experience in Southeast Asia, for example, has given us a glimpse of a military bureaucracy able to command the behavior of those who manage it. One need only observe the existence of attitudes and convictions which are distinctively military along with an inclination to adopt techniques and methods which are unsuited to the physical realities of a particular situation, in order to conclude that the military institution has a direction and purpose of its own.*

In the case of the armed forces, the functions and attitudes which are distinctively and traditionally military have little influence over society and culture. The defense structure is powerful because it has been largely refashioned to the image and purpose of economic bureaucracy; having become component of economic bureaucracy, our analysis has emphasized the ability of the ruling

---

* Compare the military leaders who emerged from the pre-World War II Army with current commanders. Men like Bradley, Eisenhower, Ridgway and MacArthur belonged to a tradition going back at least to the Civil War. Their "military" outlook was both more spacious and more focused than that of today. The integrity of the military calling depended on its separation from civil society and its dedication to the service of that society within the limits of specialized competence. It was not unlike the relationship of certain religious orders to the Church. To mingle with civil society, and especially with politics, would threaten the sense of mission and brotherhood. The principles of separation not only protected society from the military, but guarded military ideals and cohesion from the dissolving corruptions of society. Separation and the specialized nature of their service also intensified perception of the limitations of military power. As a dependent instrument of society, the military could be expected to deal only with problems that were of a military nature, and those only with the support, and at the command, of the civilian structure. This protective integrity was a casualty of the military's merger into the industrial structure, a merger which was made inevitable by the economic dimensions of our post-Korean defense forces.

economic bureaucracy to define the limits of choice, to regulate the allocation of social resources. In order to reinforce this ability, and as a consequence of the forms through which command over resources is exercised, economic relationships must influence aspects of social life which seem remote from the subject matter of economic exchange.

The foundation of this strength is bureaucracy's capacity to immobilize resources, to organize the ingredients of production in the service of its own function and purpose. The dominant institutions of our economy command concentrated resources on a scale that would have been unimaginable a half century ago. The resources so commanded include not only institutional assets and productive power, but access to principal sources of capital: to banks, insurance companies and the increasing accumulations of money held by funds—mutual, pension or investment. "Small" and "privately owned" business is increasingly dependent upon the bureaucratic structures, which, for example, often establish both price and product for local retailers whose ability to survive and profit is supported by centrally controlled mechanisms of transaction. No local dealer in high fidelity equipment, for example, can afford the national advertising which helps persuade a customer to purchase a Sony tape recorder. Often he becomes an authorized dealer, further integrating his business with the bureaucratic structure. The more threatening aspect of this control was vividly illustrated when major oil companies decided to reduce supplies to gasoline stations which called themselves "independent," demonstrating that the absence of ownership, franchise or contractual obligation does not permit escape from ruling economic structures.

The existence of this power to control social resources, the forms through which it is organized, and the manner of its exercise are the consequence of modern technology. The creation of new products (e.g., the mini-calculator) or of new means of production (e.g., the high-speed printing press) compose the dramatic facade of the technological revolution. It is, however, the modern technologies of organization, more precisely the technologies of control, which have transformed economic relationships—not only material structures, but manner of function, ideology and belief.

A recent economic projection foresees that by 1985 computer production will constitute 8.6 per cent of the Gross National

Product. But the computer is only the centerpiece and symbolic distillation of the numerous technological innovations which have made it possible to manage vast accumulations of capital maintained in widely dispersed locations; to construct a nation-wide, even global, machinery of transaction; and to exercise control over enterprises and resources which are neither owned nor implicated in legal obligation. The most visible of these innovations fall within traditional categories: communication and, to a lesser extent, transportation. (It is information and ideas, not goods, which must move swiftly.) Much of this new technology has less familiar names, resonating of complexity, certainty and scientific method: "Market research," "data processing," "systems analysis," "cost-benefit analysis," "productivity studies," "management consultancy," etc. And surmounting the technology of control is the clowning despot—television.

Through the capacity to accumulate and analyze information, to convey directions and enforce standards, managers maintain control, or the illusion of control, over the bureaucratic enterprise. Techniques such as market research, advertising and those devices which supply procedures and standards, all operate to reduce what would otherwise be an impossible burden of decision while, and not incidentally, shielding individuals from responsibility. It does not matter if the product of these technologies is wise, accurate or even relevant. The products work. Not in an older sense, as one might say the steamboat "worked," but they sustain the power of dominant economic institutions. They enable it to function. And that is the first necessity, desire and commandment of the bureaucratic economy.

The accumulation and concentration required by the scale of the modern economy could not have continued without this technological innovation. In part, that necessity created its own technology, but it is also true that technology shaped modern economic relationships. It is, therefore, meaningless to assert that technology is neutral—i.e., able to serve any set of values. One could as well say that industry or private property is neutral. Technology is a product of an economic process. It is born imprinted with the values of that process. It exists within a particular social structure, and its possibilities—the ways in which it will be used—are determined by the dominant relationships of that structure. Technology as a Platonic ideal may be neutral, as is wisdom or knowledge, but any particular technology is irrevocably dedicated to certain interests. And only particular technologies exist.

Moreover, technology is also a mode of thought which must enter the consciousness of any society which depends upon continued technological innovation. That mode of thought is essentially what we have described as scientific reason. It is orderly, precise and systematic; it leaves little space for the irrational and chaotic which, in the present and future state of knowledge, are essential to human freedom.

Almost every discipline, including the study of society, reflects an increasing submission to the technological ideology. That ideology influences the behavior of industry and government. It impels a search for the kind of certainty which numbers provide, although the numbers often measure nothing but the method from which they are derived. In this sense, technology may be inherently repressive, since it forces us to look upon individuals as subjects and objects of the measurements it can make. The type of thinking which makes it possible to develop an improved computer circuit is crippling when applied to human activities. Yet if technology shapes economic structure, its ideology cannot be confined to the subject matter of scientific inquiry.

The power of modern economic relationships is not only a consequence of size and reach, nor of market structure, exchange mechanisms and other relationships external to the economic institution. Power is also conferred by structure and manner of function, by the internal process which increasingly governs bureaucracy's relationship to the social process. Marx's statement that in every age the ideas of the ruling class were ruling ideas is an elaboration of alienation: human autonomy yielding to external coercion. The institutions which dominate our own society are not a "class" nor do they possess ideas. They have function—a term which includes both operation and purpose. The functional necessities of material institutions are inanimate, but they are internalized by the individual in the form of ideas, values and beliefs. They become an ideology. This transformation is required by the fact that modern society is governed by inanimate structures; while the necessity to transform strengthens alienation. One could, for example, readily observe that belief in social Darwinism—the survival of the fittest—justified and supported the capitalist. Function and idea, however, often seem unrelated, belonging to a different order of phenomena, thereby making it difficult to establish the connection between human behavior and institutional imperative, persuading us, at times, to strengthen oppression through actions and values which are perceived as an extension of freedom.

CHAPTER 3

The detail which has accompanied the description of contemporary economic institutions was intended to aid understanding of a process whose complexities themselves mask the source of social power. Our description also warns of the need to qualify any general description or indictment of economic relationships which are varied, incomplete and in continual evolution. But one must be wary of the modern inclination to accumulate contradictory detail or to assert the "scientific" inadequacy of demonstration in order to deny all general statements about society, even to deny the possibility of such statements. The disintegrative claims of specialization are themselves the intellectual companion and consequence of the process of social fragmentation. Despite justified qualification and ambiguity, the governing precepts of bureaucracy are undeniably in the ascendancy, and they continue to extend their domain.

The relative autonomy of large economic institutions, free from the claims of ownership, imposes a table of doctrine upon its alienated workers, which is enforced by a mechanism of economic reward, position and success. The voluminously described qualities of corporate life (enforced conformity and expected behavior, caution and office politics, the value of experience in Duz rather than in Jif Peanut Butter, diffusion of responsibility, committee decisions and the organization man) are the creation of economic bureaucracy, necessary to sustain the contemporary relations of production. Similar qualities are endemic in all advanced societies whatever their formal creed and in the governments which mirror the ruling forces of social life.

These forms of behavior manifest the bureaucratic structure. Unlike the capitalist, bureaucracies do not retire, nor do they enjoy the goods money can buy. They need not contemplate mortality, and they have no heirs. Although the nature of the capitalist was to accumulate wealth, no capitalist accumulation of the past approaches the concentrated resources commanded by the modern corporate giant. But the dominant purpose of corporate accumulation is to ensure the continuation and expansion of the organization itself. Some managers may not consciously regard that as their priority, but it is the consequence of bureaucratic structure; it is of the "nature" of bureaucracy. If other objectives become inconsistent, they will be displaced. The imperatives of continuity and growth require a continuing effort to eliminate hazards, and to minimize uncertainties which nearly always appear as potential danger to established power. Many of the techniques for reducing perceived threat or instability have been discussed: reduction of competition, present market structure, dispersion of ownership, the obstruction of technological innovation, etc.

Since changes within society or in the bureaucratic structure itself are inevitable, they must be incorporated within established relationships. The highest of bureaucratic virtues is to contain energy within order, and expansion within the familiar and established. This requires control over social forces which might impair or disrupt bureaucratic function. The impulse toward control dominates modern economic relationships. Bureaucracy is a mechanism of control. And the bureaucratic process is a coercive process.

Modern enterprise has established extensive internal control, designed to ensure uniform behavior by its human and material components. The quest for statistical methods of measurement and techniques of scientific analysis, for example, infuses every stage of the productive process, from analyzing the handwriting of job applicants to polling of consumers. Such objective measurements provide a comforting illusion of certainty and change the process and responsibility of decision into the proper application of procedures. As constituents of the bureaucratic process, methods of internal operation tend to become ends in themselves. Individual success, promotion and reward, is increasingly based on achievement in relationship to the structure. Violation of procedure—to whatever end and no matter what the result—is discouraged and punished. The mechanism designed to shield the institution from individual misjudgment also minimizes the possibility of individual judgment. Finally, it becomes a protection against individual responsibility. Through this form of alienation oppression enslaves the oppressors, for the escape from responsibility is an escape from freedom.

Since governing structures form social ideology, the necessities of bureaucratic function are imposed on the general society. They invade the promotion policies of university departments and the editorial decisions of publications, the restrictive specialization of garage mechanics and the attitudes of airline stewardesses. Advertising agencies, law firms and hospitals are among the innumerable mini-bureaucracies which have been conformed to practices neither justified nor required by their own scale and function. While the new office buildings being constructed in every large city are architectural testimony to the hegemony of the bureaucratic spirit.

The greatest potential danger to bureaucratic stability and expansion is not internal malfunction; it is latent in the market, government, competition, technology and, most important, the shifting desires of the population. The exigencies of structure thus compel a continual effort to extend control into all aspects of social life, while the technology which is part of bureaucracy has increased the reach and capacity of social control. Control is not only directed to determinations of production and demand, but, consonant to the internal priorities of bureaucracy, to regulate the manner and forms of social assertion and decision.

This form of control is most openly displayed through the relationship between economic institutions and government. In the capitalist period, that relationship was primarily one of a conspiracy to steal—the theft of land, timber, oil, etc., from the public. Today's relationship is one of regulation. The machinery of government is used to protect business against general economic conditions, or from those hazards of competition which enterprise itself cannot fully eliminate. Regulatory agencies serve to tame and control market forces not yet under private domination or which take an unforeseen turn. The "discretionary authority" of regulators and government attorneys protects institutions from a hampering enforcement or "interpretation" of existing law. The difference between the attitude of business toward Roosevelt and toward the far bigger government of today measures the distance between capitalism and bureaucracy.

Law is the most traditional form of direct social control. The characteristic of law is that it is abstract and of general application; i.e., it is not directed at a particular individual or incident, but establishes rules for the general population or for classes of individuals and activities. Domination of the formal legal structure is inadequate to the necessary extension of control, compelling bureaucracy to assume a large legislative role of its own. Computerized central credit systems, for example, evaluate "creditworthiness" by general criteria which are neither debated nor published. An adverse decision can foreclose an individual's access to credit almost everywhere, stripping him of an asset which is increasingly important to participation in the modern economy. This judgment is made in secret, according to hidden regulations, without hearing, and with little opportunity for protest or appeal. It bears a closer resemblance to the legal system of Kafka than that of Blackstone. Marx wrote that credit was the economic judgment of a man's morality. A centralized national credit structure is an imposed and enforceable moral system, i.e., a law.

Similar legislative authority is exercised in other fields. The denial of insurance—a verdict of "uninsurability"—can seriously restrict individual activity and opportunity. With insurance as with credit, closing one door can close them all. The requirements established by pension funds limit the mobility of a worker. The ability of economic institutions to pass on costs is equivalent to a private tax system, whose revenues support credit structures, technological research, pension funds and a host of activities whose purpose is not productivity, but the extension of control. The imposition of formal, general standards on private life by economic bureaucracy is now larger than the output of legislatures.

In the modern economy the large majority have an income beyond necessity, giving them an increased possibility of economic choice. The mass market, which is the source of bureaucratic concentration, is also a danger, since it makes economic control potentially vulnerable—not only to competition, market changes or resource scarcity—but to the choices, and therefore the values and life style of the entire citizenry. Thus, effective control can only be established by extending the process of coercion to individual social behavior and values. The technologies which enforce this coercion are those which created the structures which contain the impulse to control. Consonant to the bureaucratic ideology which views the organization as an end in itself—the means create the end.

The recent events labeled "Watergate" have given us a rare public view of the bureaucratic spirit, in which the boundary to control is established by the available instruments of coercion. It is not that the means are thought moral, but that the issue of its morality does not arise. Nor is there any natural or intrinsic culmination to the extension of control, since control of a process—the state of always becoming—must always be incomplete even as it must continually strive to complete itself. The more successful present economic relations are in extending control over social resources and, thus, their ability to exclude the satisfaction of inconsistent wants, as the purposes of the rulers further diverge from the freedom of the ruled—the more urgent the necessity of coercion becomes.

In American society control over the means of production and transaction cannot be maintained in conflict with the will of the members of society. To prevent such conflict, inconsistent choice and values must be suppressed. This suppression is not achieved by conspiracy, and only occasionally by the direct application of coercive force, but predominantly through the ability of external authority to increase the alienation which supports it.

A complete anatomy of the structure of control, of the constituents of modern alienation, is the subject matter of a further work. It requires an exploration of the entire society—a multitude of connections which are ambiguous, evasive of rational analysis, and whose dominating elements are also influenced by that which they govern. One can, however, set forth some illustrations which, when added to the discussion of preceding chapters, indicate the range and variety of a coercive process which deprives us of choice and the power to choose, thus shriveling man's ability to establish the purposes of his life—that ability which is the condition of freedom.

CHAPTER 4

Our description of contemporary alienation disclosed the extent to which the economic value of unions and workers, managers and investors had become dependent upon the present economic process. Partially absorbed by that process, their own felt interest merges into that of the institutions which they serve. The values of the institution appear as supports of their own welfare and, more than welfare, of their economic value and hence a portion of their existence. They comprehend themselves as being, in part, creations of the economic process. Of necessity, its social values become their own; those values consisting of choice and the machinery of choice, of the entire process of transaction and the aggrandizing ends to which it is devoted. Nor is this the plight of deluded masses. Nearly every movement of protest, liberal or militant, of the excluded or elite, demands power over the existing social process. It is the radicalism of redistribution. In isolation, such goals can be benign. But justice is not freedom; and discontents which seek redress through redistribution are no threat to the process.

Redistribution of authority over alienating structures does not necessarily lessen the power to oppress. "Participation" is often a euphemism for that fragmentation of human control which increases institutional autonomy. Nevertheless, social goals are unavoidably framed in such terms, because discontents can rarely appear in any organized and effective form unless they can be satisfied without basic alterations in economic institutions. Commanded by the process to which he is alienated, the worker is an accomplice to limitations on choice and protest. (By "worker" is meant not just the proletarian worker or the blue-collar worker, but all who exchange energy for income—the entire middle class.) Americans have unsatisfied needs whose fulfillment would impair the process. But any fundamental attack on the nature or structure of economic demand is experienced as a threat to the individual's value, well-being and identity. It is made to seem that the act of choice will destroy the power to choose; that to choose freedom is to receive slavery. In this fashion we are persuaded and coerced to tyrannize ourselves.

Hardly a year goes by without fresh evidence of this imposing social reality. Most of the time, for example, the "movements" known as "environment" or "consumerism" concentrate on abuses or outrages of the existing process: dangers to life and health, imperfect commodities, corruption, momentary relapses into predatory capitalism. Occasionally, groups within these movements begin to infringe upon the process itself. A handful of zealous environmentalists not only wish to increase the cost of production, but to limit its expansion. A few consumerists glimpse flaws in the structure of corporate control. At this point there is a collision, or at least a brush, with dominant power, and, as one would expect, the assault is readily halted or repelled. The disparities of power are too great.

Most revealing is the fact that such "extreme" positions force a withdrawal of support by the general public. Should important elements of the economic process actually seem to face serious challenge, the overwhelming majority would turn, not on the sources of their oppression, but on the proponents of change. For the content of social conflict is itself defined by the existing structure. For example, if one ends pollution, sets aside open land in and around cities, and requires that new construction enhance the quality of human experience and the possibility of community, the result will be to destroy jobs and drive up prices. The people most directly involved are being asked to divert concrete resources for the sake of an abstraction and probably an untrustworthy abstraction. Moreover, within our present economic structure such a definition of the issue is accurate. The issue can be resolved only if it is redefined, eliminated, through a structural transformation. In the abstract, that is, in a different society, a new and innovative pollution industry would increase investment and income; while large quantities of high-cost housing would create greater wealth than the same amount of low-cost housing. But we cannot distribute such increased wealth in a manner which would create the necessary large-scale market, or, more accurately, we are kept from creating wealth in those forms by the absence of a market.

New choices can only be provided by new structures whose existence will not be compatible with those which exist. They must have the ability, for example, to command and redirect resources which are now in the hands of others. All the products of the economic process are consumption goods: cars and television sets, polluted air and crowded cities. They are all paid for. Chemicals pollute the air. We purchase these chemicals directly, e.g., gasoline, or they enter into the process of industrial production and their cost is reflected in the prices of the finished goods. We buy pollution. Unlike a television set, this purchase is usually available to purchasers and non-purchasers alike, but it is paid for. Most people who buy a car or a ream of typing paper do not want to purchase pollution. They have no choice; it comes with the product. Their inability to choose is not an aspect of natural order, but an imposition of the economic structure and its political satellite. One cannot expect current economic bureaucracies to change this. Exhortations to "social responsibility" are equivalent to having advised the medieval Church to abandon the concept of salvation after death in order to encourage more vigorous pursuit of happiness in this world. This is not because the managers of great enterprises are callous, obtuse or selfish. They are bound to institutions whose behavior is a consequence of structure—their own, and that of the economic process wherein they flourish.

CHAPTER 5

The control imposed by the alienating relationship to institutional process is reinforced by the nature of work within that process. The labor consistent with freedom is experienced as an extension of inward faculties and powers; its principal object is the product itself: either as personal achievement or as a contribution to a social purpose which is an attribute of the worker's own existence.

Public dialogue now assumes that only a dwindling fraction of workers experience work as an expression of self, and that an even smaller minority take satisfaction in the belief that their efforts make an improving difference to the life of others. This awareness has stimulated a search for ways to make work more fulfilling, to "humanize" labor. Such efforts may meliorate conditions, but the important obstacles to fulfillment are not subject to reform, being creations of economic process and bureaucratic control.

Work is largely a process in which the individual exchanges his humanity for inhuman rewards. He comes to believe in the worth, even the necessity, of the money and position which are the object of his toil. At every level of income, the worker must experience an urgency of desire to maintain or improve his "life style"—which consists primarily of the goods and other benefits produced by present economic structures. Since these satisfactions are bestowed by economic institutions, the values of the institution are absorbed by the worker.

One manifestation of this control is a phenomenon which might be called "the urgency of possession." Its objects are not "necessities," even in the most expansive modern use of that term, nor the acquisition of luxuries in the traditional sense. Such acquisitions are often simply the objects of desire, destined to yield little pleasure beyond that of possession itself. Yet they are a national narcotic far more powerful than anything dispensed in the back corridors of the country's high schools. This urgency of possession is a disease of our present economic process and ideology, including the enforced belief that private consumption and private pleasure are the same thing.

The very existence of this disease informs us that the wants which individuals feel and express are not the fixed or inevitable needs of human nature. Thus, a different structure, an awareness of changed possibilities, might direct desire toward objects more closely related to the enhancement of existence. Should this happen we will find that demands for parks and schools, for nature and the associations of community are also "economic" and a stimulus to the creation of "wealth." It is not necessary to forgo the pursuit of pleasure, only to understand what pleasure is and liberate ourselves to pursue the true source of happiness, which is freedom.

Income and goods, even "life style," are not the only rewards which strengthen external control. The ambiguous word "success" is not an equivalent for money or position, although it can be accompanied by both of these. It has no necessary relation to concrete achievement, to any increase in the wealth of either the enterprise or society. It is a synonym for recognition by the social process, a title of reward for service to the purpose of institutions. To exchange oneself for recognition, for an abstraction, is an alienation more subjugating than an exchange for material necessity. It tells of submission, not to goods or owners, but to a process, to an entire world of beliefs, hierarchy, commands and procedures.

The difference between the pursuit of success and the pursuit of excellence is a difference between freedom and slavery. Belief in success is maintained through fear. The striving for success, explains R. D. Laing, "forces every man reared in our culture, over and over again, night in, night out, even at the pinnacle of success, to dream not of success but of failure." That fear of failure haunts every aspect of American life. Since we pursue that which we do not need, we must endow the objects of our pursuit with value. Otherwise what we are doing is worthless and, insofar as we are what we do, so are we. The needs so created, being external, are turned against us. Not to succeed in their attainment is to be unworthy, and failure is more than failure, it is annihilation. We do not advance to the "realm of freedom" because the process which enabled us to conquer the "realm of necessity" now imprisons us within it. Compelled to expand our needs, we annex the unnecessary, replenishing fears that further strengthen the process.

The increasing fear of failure is counterpart and consequence of the bureaucratic structure we have described. In the course of reducing its own vulnerability to individual mistake or incompetence, bureaucracy appears to shield the individual from the prospect and consequences of failure by a structure designed to minimize personal responsibility. Bureaucratic function is sustained by the fear of failure, as the Church was once supported by the fear of damnation.

But the protections against competitive judgment are illusory. The fear of failure is built into the system, instilled by the needs it creates. The most sheltered levels of the most tutelary of bureaucracies are inhabited by men for whom the daily routine is a source of dread, whose very security is experienced as failure since it confines their capacities and limits their achievements. No modification of existing structures, no new standards or work procedures, can eliminate the fear of failure within structures designed to maintain it.*

When work is more than work, when it becomes a system of belief, it cannot readily be laid aside. The leisure hours become an extension of the working day. The pursuit of success is continued in other forms: reading documents, participating in professionally

* It is not necessary for the purpose of this analysis to summarize the extensive literature of the current movement for women's liberation. The assertions of that movement will persist and gain in force. They are made within a society that has the capacity to respond—a fact which is also a cause.

However, liberation from an imposed and subordinate social role will not strip away the general oppressions of the time. Equality is an expression of symmetry. It does not determine the content of the elements it equates. Women's right to equality is undeniable, but liberation must attend the general enlargement of human freedom.

advantageous clubs or civic activities, and in social life with those we might impress or use. But contact is not relationship, as touching is not intimacy. Or these same hours can be used to relieve today's tensions, to "recharge" and prepare for tomorrow. We speak of leisure time, not free time; "recreation," not "play." How wonderful a word is recreation, telling us of the fragmenting toil which requires us periodically to re-create ourselves.

The development of skills, the acquisition of knowledge, the heightening of sensual response and the cultivation of love require time and systematic effort. They are not possible without commitment. The more our work is "unnecessary" and devoted to purely external rewards, the less we are able to pursue outside of work those achievements whose rewards are internal. Since alienation is a transformation of existence—of psychic structure—all rigorous and challenging activities become assimilated to the idea of necessary work, while the fear of failure infiltrates every serious and sustained effort. Yet the concepts of success and failure are not relevant to the free extension of inward powers, which is not a competition for external reward but the attempt to be as much as one can be. In the pursuit of freedom man measures his achievement against himself.

All the varied controls upon demand and the process through which they are exerted reinforce a common function: to shape inward desires to the actual and potential products of the economic structure. Desire is an attribute of belief. At one time a sinner could reduce punishment by purchasing an indulgence from the universal Church. The possibility of exchange meant that there was an economic market in indulgences; a market which created employment, added to income and helped to accumulate capital for investment. This monopoly of forgiveness was dissonant from the structural imperatives of ascending commercial societies, which included national autonomy and the dedication of economic resources to the ever more abundant things of this world. The sale of indulgences and the construction of great cathedrals alike were the inevitable victims of historical evolution. One cannot restore the market for indulgences, even though it would add to the Gross National Product, as do purchases of services from massage parlors, astrologers and psychiatrists. The culture which created that market no longer exists.

The beliefs which underlie economic choices do not require spiritual or intellectual authority. Nor must they be part of some systematic body of thought. We may only believe that a particular choice will bring us pleasure or benefit, or discharge a responsibility to family and children. The belief itself may be rooted in rational calculation, fear, madness, greed or the desire for self-destruction. Whatever its object, the belief is real and its sources constitute a description of the society.

Although choice is always limited by available alternatives, the beliefs which impel choice are largely the creation of experience. People are born with a need to eat food and to extend their senses. They are not born with a taste for barbecued hot dogs, caviar or television sets. It is through experience that the elements of our humanity become linked with the output of the external world. To dominate the organization of production is to decide what shall be experienced. The increasing centralization and autonomy of this power to decide reduce the clash of competing wills and purpose which was implied and permitted by the spirit of enterprise.

The power to limit experience does not merely confer authority over the choice between hot dogs and health foods, television and theatre. It is the power to strip away essential elements of human freedom. If we are denied community life and contact with nature, the fulfillments of play and the satisfactions of work, our belief in the exigent necessity of these generative experiences is enervated, made abstract. We cease to demand them. Our choices are confined to objects we have come to value through the experience which is itself a creation of our present social structure and the institutions which dominate it. The belief that one no longer needs food, however sincerely held, will bring on starvation; the failure or inability to believe in the conditions of life necessary to freedom leads to enslavement. In this fashion one of the supreme gifts of evolution, the social adaptability of the human race, is turned against us.

We have developed a technology of the senses, able to master experience at the organic juncture between man and his world. Increasingly, what we hear and see, touch and even feel is the product of manufactured goods: the "media" and street noises for ear and eye, chemicals for the perceiving mind, concrete and plastic for the fingers. This manufactured sensuality numbs awareness and guides our choice toward the service of the process which has produced the materials of experience. Through television, for example, we experience a link between pleasure and passivity, which dulls our demand for more active, creative, enlarging opportunities for play. Once established, that link stimulates an entire industry of the passive. Its influence now extends even to the means of individual, sensual satisfaction—to much of the drug culture, for example, and among the practitioners of a sexuality whose intensities are not shared but exchanged.

Modern production includes goods whose contribution to Gross National Product and income is trifling alongside the transforming strokes of the goods themselves. Automobiles, televisions and computers have compelled new connections between home and work, city and city, managers and their industries, citizens and institutions, parents and children. And these sizable alterations of experience always serve the productive process which causes them. Such goods constitute a technology of consumption, whose end is not to change methods of production, but ways of life. Unlike factory machines, they absorb directly that portion of human energy not consumed in labor, thus extending the grip of production and enlarging alienation.

CHAPTER 7

In 1611, responding to the new astronomy, John Donne wrote: ". . . this (world)/Is crumbled out again to his Atomies/'Tis all in peeces, all coherence gone/All just supply, and all relation." From our vantage the poem seems premature as description, but it has been vindicated as prophecy. In Part I we sketched the development of the consciousness of individualism and its modern culmination in a social fragmentation which has weakened or destroyed most of the bonds and institutions of shared existence.

Place an iron bar a small distance from a magnet whose attractive force is slightly too weak to move the bar. If the bar is then shattered into a multitude of tiny filings they will be swept toward the magnet and confined along the lines of force.

The relationship between coercive bureaucracy and social fragmentation is more complex and ambiguous than our metaphor of the magnet implies. The modern condition is the result of a process which is neither recent nor American in origin. Nevertheless, the deterioration of social existence has been accompanied by the growth of continually more powerful productive forces and has taken place more slowly, or not at all, in countries where these productive forces did not evolve. It is a condition for the coercive power of economic relationship, although coercion was given its modern bureaucratic form as a result of the preceding growth of productive forces, the weakness and virtual collapse of capitalist relationships, the intervention of new technology and, perhaps, the impact, or at least the timing, of World War II. Nevertheless, social fragmentation is necessary to the domination of the present economic process and stimulates the extension of control, which is an attribute of bureaucratic structure.

The multiform connections between coercive bureaucracy and the loss of social existence are a major theme of this work. Let us, by way of summary and example, extract from the previous discussion some of the links which compose and justify these major categories of analysis.

No individual or group of individuals can buy or compel an end to pollution of the ocean, the construction of neighborhoods or a reduction in the amount of necessary labor. This requires a society with shared values, a common awareness of needs so strongly and concretely felt that the same demand arises from a multitude of unco-ordinated centers, powerful enough to transform or redirect the economic process and enter into the dominant ideology. Collective demand requires collective existence. Individuals, even though they may be liberated to pursue the objects of private desire, cannot attain to mastery over productive forces or determine the allocation of social resources. Since that control—which is the power to determine the material conditions of society—must be exercised, it is necessarily transferred, alienated, to the dominant forms of social authority.

The alienating consequences of the structure of demand demonstrate that only through association can human beings acquire and exercise power over their own social existence. We have seen that accepted values and morality of right conduct can only arise within a human community; that sanctioning authority, even if it assumes divine forms, is the creation of a collective humanity. Moral codes, themselves, are among the bonds which constitute, make possible, a shared existence. Their dissolution compels the establishment of external authority. Morality becomes regulation.

The inability to establish values and a morality of right conduct is also an inability to select or control the sources of authority. Alienation includes loss of choice, and the power lost to human beings is inevitably absorbed by the ruling forces of social life.

Values and codes of conduct are made consistent with the purposes of economic bureaucracy, thus becoming the purposes of the citizen. We value the goods it produces, the highways it builds, the opportunities it affords. Even when we are apprehensive about extensions of control—e.g., the use of television, the centralization of credit decisions, the increasing autonomy of the military bureaucracy—we lack the internally shared principles of value and conduct which would provide a restraint and a source for collective opposition. We tend increasingly to discuss such matters as "practical" problems instead of problems of principle, which means that the scope of discussion has been confined by the dominant ideology. Since function in itself is a pre-eminent value of the bureaucratic ideology, the concept of "effectiveness" overshadows considerations of ultimate purpose and product.

Institutions and activities, which in a different social structure might afford self-mastery and fulfillment, are made coercive by the process of social fragmentation. The inability to find fulfillment in work, for example, is a consequence of the social fragmentation which severs the individual from his co-workers, the enterprise which he serves, his task and his own talents. Work which is not experienced as a contribution to shared goals, whose purposes are not those of the worker as a social man, is alienating and imposes the requirements of economic process on one's own existence.

Once the national society which contains us is no longer experienced as a vehicle of shared social purpose, its authority over our lives also becomes external, is made coercive. It becomes a source of alienation. The consequent sense of impotence feeds on itself, increasing the withdrawal which strengthens the autonomy of the state. The same is true of our relationship to all ruling institutions. The requirements and obligation of shared social existence are not coercive. They are aspects of a natural order. The relationship of the individual to that order is not one of participation; it is an aspect of self, a constituent of his human nature. As a consequence of social fragmentation, power which, being shared, was also personal, is externalized. External relationships are substituted for human connection. No longer ruled by one another, we no longer rule ourselves. This loss of power intensifies the necessity and felt desire to rely on an external authority whose growing autonomy persuades us to the behavior and goals which may still appear to be personal choice, but which are only those choices permitted us by dominant ideologies. The pursuit of those goals reinforces coercive power or, at least, is not inconsistent with the extention of control.

Modern economic relationships have hugely accelerated the social fragmentation which had seemed to be approaching the limits of possibility even before the bureaucratic ascendancy. During the industrial age some of the most important decisions of the Supreme Court prohibited states from enacting regulations which might interfere with a commerce increasingly national in reach. If, for example, each state could enforce different requirements for the size, weight and load of trucks the burden of distribution might become intolerable. A doctrine called "pre-emption" was evolved, meaning that in certain areas of activity, the passage of a federal law or regulation would displace, i.e., repeal, state laws on the same subject. This centralization of authority was a response to the economic interests of expanding industry, although, as is traditional, those interests were called "economic necessity."

The interest, the intrinsic purpose, of modern economic structures is not simply the accumulation of wealth; its manner and scale of operation are ends in themselves. Because control adequate to guarantee this function—to protect against all present conflict and future change—is a mirage, the impulse toward control is insatiable. It directs a continual attack on all authority independent of the economic structure; not just state laws or legal authority, but alternative repositories of social power; principally on forms of social cohesion which might give expression to human wants inconsistent with the present structure of society.

Our entire analysis of the economic process describes, if often indirectly, ways in which this purpose is forwarded. Many involve a displacement of function. Community is not a willed condition. Shared existence rests on the realities of shared responsibility and the power to determine the conditions of the human life. Community cannot be maintained if confronted by forces which determine economic activity, the objects of production, and the method by which material goals can be attained; by forces which can even decide the forms of play and entertainment. One might like

McDonald's, but one can have a relationship with the corner store.

An economy on the American scale, dependent upon mass consumption, relies upon the general willingness to labor and spend for the gratification of private desires. This ideological necessity is internalized as a moral principle which equates the pursuit of individual desires with freedom. Forms of collective existence are made to appear as obligation or duty and, finally, as oppression. Moreover, the reach of modern economic relationships, and the affluence it has produced, has reduced the link between particular forms of social existence—such as community, family and economic necessity. Commitments which are willed and easily escaped lose their binding force. Many of the most radical forms of modern social behavior—freedom of sex and dress, drugs and pornography, the quest for pleasure and for new forms of self-realization, from consciousness raising to meditation—can all be seen as manifestations of a belief that fulfillment is to be sought in the gratification of private desires, through internal states or "self-realization" rather than through social bonds. Much of this behavior has little economic consequence; some of it may be beneficial; but it is consistent with dominant economic relationship. Were this not the case, it would not be allowed.

CHAPTER 8

Laws of nature and society are descriptions, not mandates. They are nullified when demonstrated wrong or inadequate, or when the conditions they describe have changed. Those conditions always consist of both external events and historical consciousness.

Every age has a science consistent with the social process of the time. This conformity is obscured by the scientific claim to continual progress, meaning that earlier laws and theories have been discarded or displaced. Naturally, there is no way to demonstrate that present theories are not equally in error. We can only be sure that we know more facts, in part because increased powers of observation have converted theory into fact, i.e., the motion of the earth. To move from one error to another which may be equally remote from reality is not progress. It is change. Some of these laws of nature work. They predict observable consequences, yield experimental or technological results. But no such result can "prove" a basic, underlying "law" of nature. The law may successfully predict a result which is consistent with no other explanation. But that only means we are presently unable to conceive of any other explanation.

Our conceptions, our capacity to conceive, are liberated and bounded by our history, by the social process which saturates every mind. The physics of the Middle Ages, received from Aristotle, regarded function and behavior—motion and velocity—as inherent in the nature of matter, and which differed according to that nature. This was the science of a humanity inhabiting a social order which was the earthly manifestation of a divine order. The behavior of men, as well as that of fire and water, was emanation and aspect of the nature of things.

No modern physicist will uncover a handful of coherent, fixed and orderly principles which specify the nature—the structure, motion, location, effect—of the material world. We do not live in an age suited to such a physics. Newton did, and such a time may come again. If it does, then today's complexities and uncertainties, a reality compounded of statistics, will dissolve before "advancing" knowledge.

The conclusions of science are the consequence of agreed judgments about the methods which can validate decision; what shall constitute scientific method. That method is a way to think about reality, and the way in which we think about reality prescribes the questions to be asked and sets limits to the conclusions that can be reached. Aristotle did not conceive it necessary to seek physical verification for the physical principles which Galileo displaced by applying newly conceived methods of observation and experiment. In our own time mathematical demonstration is accepted as proof of phenomena which, only a short time ago, would have not been accepted without some physical verification.

Often it seems that the only limit to choice is actual possibility and not the ways we think about reality. Physicists and astronomers strive to decide if the universe is bounded or infinite. Yet these cosmological possibilities are not defined by physical necessity, but by the nature of scientific thought and, perhaps, by the structure of the human intellect. For the universe might be both confined and limited, trapped in a single soul and depthless as the thoughts of God. Or it might be a dimension which knows neither time nor space.

So too the way in which we think about society and ourselves determines the conclusions we will reach or—because social method is broader and more imprecise than science—the range of conclusions from which we can select. Those social choices, which are the outward form of social values, often seem to exhaust social possibilities because the premises of thought are so widely shared that they seem to be part of the natural order. Yet those choices are the creation of the ruling social process which, in defining the manner and objects of decision, makes manifest the perception and awareness of the time. Indeed, the economic relationships which constitute the method and form of social choice are themselves values or systems of values. Since they dominate the society whose conditions shape perception, they fortify the historical consciousness which sustains their coercive power, and strive against changes in awareness which might threaten or diminish their authority.

It is difficult to glimpse the possibilities of an enlarged awareness from within the society. Indeed, almost by definition, one cannot know that his awareness is artificially constrained. One can only suspect it. Yet, we can know that the structure we have been describing can only attain its impersonal ends by limiting that awareness, by making us believe that the choices it contains define the limits of possibility. That difference between historical possibility and perceived possibility is the measure of oppression. We are thus persuaded to accept the inevitability of growing restraints on freedom, to insulate our will from a resolve to use the resources of society to enlarge freedom. So powerful are these distortions of our perceptions that any attack on the existing economic structure is felt as a danger to the power of choice, to possibility, even to economic existence.

Most of the afflictions we have described—the dissolution of moral authority, community and shared social purpose, the crippling of inward power by miseducation and work—are imposed by institutions, ideas and patterns of behavior which we create and endow with power over our lives. As we are necessarily contained in our creations, modern man is engaged in an unprecedented project of self-destruction: The end of alienation is alienation from oneself, a terror of freedom; the end of impotence is cruelty; the end of individualism, of social fragmentation, is the dissolution of moral responsibility; the end of technology is technology.

One cannot, in the manner of a journalist traveling to a foreign
country, describe the life of a society which has attained to freedom: The manner in which people behave and conduct public
affairs, the nature of work, the forms of play, and the way in which
energy is distributed among varied activities. The fulfillment of
our humanity requires the extension of individual faculties which
are given specific form by the social process. Freedom itself, however, can only be described as a relationship. It is unalienated
existence, wherein the institutions and relationships of society are
the instruments of human will. Within such a society the specific
constituents, the daily life of a free existence will materialize from
a range of possibilities restricted only by the physical capacity of
society.

Unalienated existence is a description of social relationships, but
the possibility of unalienated existence arises from historical consciousness. We have described the limitations on awareness imposed by present economic relationships. Those limitations not
only circumscribe our perception of external possibility, but our
perception of ourself. William James once wrote of the need to
discover a moral equivalent for war. All soldiers are subject to some
amount of coercion. But in some circumstances they have also
experienced combat as participation in a common purpose; for the
survival of their society or the protection of human liberty. They

did not simply serve this purpose; it was also their own. We cannot be certain that alienation was absent until we know the source of that social purpose; whether, for example, the war itself had origins in economic interest or was a response to a real danger of enslavement or extermination. Nevertheless, the soldiers' state of belief and behavior helps to clarify what is meant by historical consciousness.

The consciousness of individualism means that we perceive ourselves in isolation, of humanity itself as a collection of individuals. Our relationships with others are sustained and dominated by the need to satisfy wants which arise from that consciousness. Such relationships are external. They are purpose or desire rather than condition or attribute of existence. This externalization of relationship is the engine of alienation, which, therefore, contains the attribute of awareness. A worker, for example, may through his labor, contribute to the well-being of his community. He may even be glad of it. But since he does not regard that well-being as his own, as an aspect of his own condition, it is not the purpose of his work. And even should it be among his purposes, its source is external. The ability to decide one's own purposes and the requirements of society appear to conflict because we are dominated by a consciousness which excludes social existence. The consequence of that consciousness is always coercive authority. Were that not so then we, the most liberated, unbound, isolated individuals in history would also be the freest.

Although consciousness is an inward state, it is the product of material institutions and relationships; in our time the modern economic process and the bureaucracies which dominate it. Those structures are continuing to expand and to extend their coercive process. Bureaucratization is imposed on activities hitherto exempt: e.g., agriculture and construction. More recent technologies of control—such as the "franchise" and "the chain"—have extended bureaucratic function to nearly all aspects of consumption: hamburgers and fried chicken, hotel rooms and high fidelity equipment. The largest institutions are crossing national borders through investment in foreign concerns and the construction of plants in other countries. Major industries in different nations sign agreements to manufacture various parts of a single product, which is then marketed under different names in different markets. Trading companies and investment funds owned and managed by nationals of different nations are internationalizing the control of capital, a necessity for the globalization of bureaucracy. The end of this movement is not merely expansion, but to reduce those hazards of competition and technological innovation which still elude control.

The subordination of politics to dominant economic structures is also increasing. It is best illustrated, not by the dramatic revelations of Watergate, but by the virtual transfer of regulatory bodies to the representatives of industry, the overt bias of new legislation, failures of enforcement and, most powerfully, by economic policies which have permitted inflation—a tax on the citizenry—for the purpose, successfully fulfilled, of increasing corporate earnings.

At the same time the public temper indicates growing adaptation to the present structure and a willingness to accept coercion as necessary to efficiency and even prosperity. The bureaucratic danger to liberty does not take the form of direct and overt repressions by government. It manifests itself in subtler means of coercion, a system of rewards and penalties which dulls the urge toward individual expression and which makes the inability to exercise liberty appear as a consequence of individual and institutional choice. It may have been easier to resist earlier and more direct attacks on civil liberty than it will be to withstand the advancing bureaucratic spirit with its inclination to reject and penalize all forms of conduct inconsistent with function. So rooted a repression is further strengthened by the willingness to allow unlimited individual assertion in all aspects of social life which do not endanger bureaucratic function.

Since material realities dominate the social process they are able to enforce consistency. The merger of two sound waves which are in phase—whose structure is symmetrical—will produce a signal stronger than either of the components. The new signal is not the result of either signal, but of their consistency. So, too, economic structure and awareness reinforce one another. Yet unlike the world of the physicist, society is always changing. There are always inconsistencies between structure and awareness, and within each of them. Moreover, even the most autonomous of structures is continually threatened by human fallibility and unanticipated interventions, while the inward impulse toward freedom will try to assert itself against the most rigidly enslaving beliefs. However, social change is an idea without moral content; its inevitability is not the inevitability of freedom. And once the idea of causation yields to process are we not even more the prisoners of fate? Where does one strike from within a process whose elements are continually reinforcing and re-creating each other? The question is unanswerable in terms of the description. Yet we can also be sure that the description is incomplete; accurate perhaps, but incomplete in its attempt to analyze a process whose complexities exceed the reach of understanding, whose alterations are swifter than the act of observation, and which, moreover, contains the observer himself.

Marx perceived that all social structures contained contradictions which, through displacement and merger, created new economic relationships. The term "contradiction" is misleading, however, for it imposes the fact and nature of change upon the process of its creation. The interventions which lead to change can make their appearance as implication, achievement or event. Even if one could determine present contradictions—and Marx did so more successfully than anyone else—their resolution will be in terms established by the future, whose possibilities are so varied that historical prophecy is an exercise of intuition, even if it is couched in the language of analysis. As Marx predicted, "new, higher relations of production" have evolved. However, "higher relations of production" do not necessitate a higher, i.e., freer, social order. And many of the undermining contradictions of capitalism, such as the tendency to reduce free competition, are among the strengths of the modern economy. The dialectic is a powerful instrument of thought—the most fruitful way to think about ideas and the historical process. But it cannot predict its own movement, nor transcend the possibilities of rational process which in society are accompanied by the chaotic, non-rational and the mad.

One can anticipate, with varying degrees of accuracy, the effect of reforms within the existing structure. But proposals for fundamental change, a manifesto for revolution, is social prophecy. A purposeful alteration of structure anticipates the entire social process. To Marx socialism was the negation of capitalism, leading inevitably to the negation of the negation called communism—the true community necessary for the existence of freedom. It has yet to appear.

This does not mean one cannot conceive measures able to reduce the coercive power of modern economic relationships. The basis for many such proposals is contained in our analysis. It would be necessary, for example, to establish public control, to nationalize the major sources of capital. Power over wealth is power over investment, to determine what shall be produced. Many of the institutioned repositories of concentrated wealth which we described have divested the citizen of all authority over use of his money in exchange for services, protection, reassurance and hope, which involve no risk of loss.

Economic relationships should be decentralized, not only production, but the machinery of transaction. Present structures are hugely uneconomic and inefficient, even by present standards of measurement. More importantly, their influence on most significant economic activity is the source of their coercive power over social life. The new technologies of control themselves make it feasible to create a decentralized form of economic organization which is also consistent with the need to plan and allocate social resources. The technological contributions of bureaucracy allow us to fragment economic activity, without requiring us to sacrifice a larger social purpose. Decentralization would also strip economic bureaucracies of the legislative authority we have described, which is exercised through power over credit, insurance, etc., while public control over production could be exerted through a mechanism similar to that of the NRA, substituting participation for production. Socialism is another possibility. But it is control of resources, not ownership, that constitutes economic power. Bureaucracies whose managers are paid from the public treasury are still bureaucracies, as the most casual observation of foreign socialisms or the domestic Defense Department will show.

Since modern technological innovation is less a product of fortuitous genius than of decision backed by investment, authority over choice should belong to the society. Because a supersonic transport could not be constructed without federal financing it became the subject of a congressional debate which chanced to coincide with a rising public concern over deterioration of the environment. The SST was rejected—at least for the moment. This isolated event stimulates the prospect of public structures responsible for weighing technological development against social consequences and needs, and with authority to determine the direction of research and innovation.

No more serious blow could be dealt to economic coercion than a substantial reduction in the necessity to work. Marx wrote that "all economics is the economic of time." The need to use one's energies in labor is alienating in itself, and it deprives the individual of the will and the opportunity to cultivate other faculties and seek alternative sources of gratification. The technical foundation for increased automation already exists and can be greatly extended within the frame of existing scientific knowledge. Reducing the need for labor—decreasing the hours of work—would, however, necessitate drastic modification or elimination of the wage system, substituting new methods for distributing socially created wealth.

These proposals are not forwarded for the consideration of political platform committees or for serious public debate. They illustrate the possibility of concrete action to reduce coercive authority, in the hope of restoring alienated power to social man. Except that social man does not exist.

A society whose inhabitants lack the shared values and purpose necessary to freedom will not make radical changes in economic relationships, and should such changes occur they would only change the sources of oppression. At one point Marx writes that although men are changed by circumstances, "circumstances are changed precisely by men . . . the educator must himself be educated"; hinting at the dilemma which was to undo so many hopes. The wisest and most radical of economic revolutions cannot immediately enlarge our existence beyond our perception of that existence. Revolutionary awareness is itself formed within a historical consciousness which can nullify the expected evolution toward freedom by distorting or transforming new economic relations. Nor can a new awareness, an enlarged sense of human existence and relationship, be imposed on the material realities which are the source of consciousness.

The analysis offers no escape. Yet the modern consciousness is not the same as that of other ages. Consciousness does change, but only when new material conditions evolve from the weakness and achievements of earlier relationships and, we are forced to believe, as a consequence of human resolve. The germinating energies of change exist in all economic relationships, and to analyze them is a large and separate task. Implicit in our description of the modern economic process, however, are some of its vulnerabilities; touched on here not for purposes of prediction, but as evidence of incompletion.

Those attributes of scale and control which compose the bureaucratic process also weaken its productive power. And the presence of a productive potential larger than acutal performance is itself a social force, continually pressing against existing economic relationships.

Large resources are diverted to the machinery of transaction—to internal organization, distribution, sales, advertising, etc., and to the technologies of decision, control and management. Since bureaucratic function is exercised on a scale far beyond that necessary to optimize production—indeed, a scale whose limits are neither established nor defined by considerations of productivity—the result is an inefficient and wasteful use of resources. The instruments of production generate an internal demand whose requirements subtract from the resources of society. Added to this is the waste or misuse inherent in an economic process and market structure which has greatly reduced the pressures to cut costs and maximize efficiency; whose institutions are forced to rely upon methods of internal organization which prohibit effective management.

The same values which result in the uneconomic use of resources —e.g., continuity and control tending toward stagnation—enforce a hostility to technological innovation which might create new investments and markets. Entire industries have been built on new technology, e.g., IBM and Xerox; but established enterprise resists, and with remarkable success, important changes in product or methods of production. (The compact car and Wankel engine were forced on the automotive industry by foreign competition.) The relative inflexibility of bureaucracy—the rigidities built into structures of such impersonal complexity—reduces the ability to respond to changing conditions, to shifts in demand, changes in the nature, quantity and source of raw materials, and to general economic conditions. These same immobilizing tendencies are illustrated by the persistence of large-scale poverty. Modern economic structures achieved ascendancy through the creation of a mass market. Now, dominance secured, they are no longer impelled to end the exclusion of those whose participation in consumption would strengthen the economic process.

We can also glimpse portents of change in the incompleteness of control, a result of the increasing rigidities of institutions whose power is established. For example, we have already examined the failure to absorb unsocialized labor into the bureaucratic structure, and the ways in which this failure weakens the worker's identification with the existing structure.

The unprecedented creation of a large population with income beyond necessity—the foundation of modern economic relationships—contains the possibility of a shift in economic power. Since consumption is the engine of modern production, power over consumption is power over production. Most contemporary social protest—e.g., environmental protection, Naderism—comes from the consuming middle class. Both the existence and achievements of these movements are a consequence of changed economic realities. None of them, however, yet seek important change in power over resources. They represent a continuation of the regulatory philosophy, whose ultimate consequence has been to confirm the existing distribution of social power. The potential power of consumers— like that of shareholders—cannot be exercised because it is widely dispersed. The concentration necessary for effective exercise is not possible without those changes in awareness which are obstructed by the entire weight of the social process.

If an enlarged awareness does evolve its source will be the immense and increasing gap between our physical capacity to increase freedom and the conditions of modern life. There are some signs, isolated symbols, of an urge to reconstitute social existence. Continued discussion of the need for community and the creation of new forms of association—from street gangs to consciousness raising—all manifest an awareness of loss. This book could not have been written in a society devoid of that awareness. But awareness of loss is not awareness of self, and the expressed urges toward association remain, at most, isolated pockets of uncertain resistance to the continual progress of coercion and fragmentation, presided over by structures whose scale, reach and capacity for control are unprecedented.

The instabilities we have mentioned hint at the sources of inevitable change; they do not prescribe its direction. To the extent this book has a purpose beyond description, it is to contribute to an understanding of the necessities of freedom and sources of oppression—an understanding which must both precede and accompany any struggle to reshape society to the service of human ends. If some find this work cheerless it is only because analysis unveils the unprecedented magnitude of the coercive power which confronts assertions of the awareness of human possibilities which, although suppressed, are fixed attributes of human existence. Cheerlessness, therefore, is not a conclusion but a preparation. To be cheerful is to accept, and one who accepts is forever without hope.

*   *   *

Among present cosmologies is a theory that the universe originated when all created matter collapsed into a borderless mass, which then violently scattered fragments of stars, moons and planets across a vacant eternity until, the impulse spent, they will once again fall toward momentary rendezvous. Were this not science and thus subject, we are told, to rational emendation, it might stand as a lovely primordial myth, an allegory for the recurrent theme of human society: the alternation between hierarchy and individualism, unity and fragmentation, fusion and solitude, community and isolation. All societies are dominated by one or the other; in all societies the dominant consciousness must fight off challenges from the hostile vision; most societies are in transition from one to the other; and the most memorable flourishings occur during those brief periods when a particular society holds both views, both conceptions of existence, in an always precarious and transient balance.

Bureaucracy does not contain the seeds of its own destruction—the restoration of unalienated existence. One can also glimpse within its hardening structures the possibility of an evolution toward a new form of hierarchy, one in which economic structures are themselves the "bond of unity" and whose mandates infuse and mantle all of social life. A hierarchy which, being inhuman, is coercion itself.

INDEX

Absolute ("eternal"), the, mysticism and scientific reason and, 54–60, 64
Absurd, the, philosophy of, 114, 124
Abundance, 19, 95–96. *See also* Affluence
Adam (biblical), 126, 131–32
Adams, Henry, 33, 114
Adams, John, 208
Advertising industry, 182, 209, 232–33, 294–97, 362, 367
Aesthetics, 65
Affluence, 206, 213, 297, 384. *See also* Abundance; Wealth
Aggression. *See* Destructive (aggressive) instinct; Militarism (war)
Agriculture (agrarianism), 35–38, 43–44, 80, 190, 310, 329, 359, 389
Airlines, 332, 393
Alienation, 26–30, 71, 72, 102, 108, 141–48 (*see also* Fragmentation, social); development of modern consciousness and, 41–67, economic process and bureaucracy and, 157–65, 220, 226, 227–28, 235–36, 245–49, 303, 305, 326, 351–64, 365ff., 370–76, 377–79ff.; existentialism and, 118–25; failure to use capacity and, 172–88, 190–95; of labor (*see under* Labor); loss of individual freedom and power and, 151–56, 157–65, 220, 226, 235–36, 357–58; political process and, 336, 343–48; racism and, 108; sources of, 26–30, 153, 157–65; unalienated existence and, 388–96; values and freedom and, 26–30, 113–25
American Anti-Imperialist League, 97
"Americanism," issue of, 101–2
American Revolution, 16, 17, 92–93
American society. *See* United States (American society)
Anders, John, 251
Anselm, St., 52
Anti-trust legislation, 279–81, 288
Aristotle, 45, 64, 144, 385
Art, 147–48, 351
Association (groups), 84–89, 97–102, 103–10, 143–48, 395–96 (*see also* Community; Interest groups; Unity); exclusion of blacks from, 103–10; labor and, 232–33, 235; shared social experience and existentialists and, 119–25; and social action, 371–73
Astronomy (astronomers), 42–43, 49, 50–52, 63–65, 386
AT&T, 186, 218, 251–52, 265
Augustine, St., 78
Authority, 140, 149–56, 157–65, 258; alienation and freedom and, 26–30 (*see also* Alienation; Freedom); divine (*see* God; Religion); economic bureaucracy and, 183–88, 189–95, 203–20ff., 247, 282ff., 285, 307ff., 312ff., 325–26, 337–48, 351ff., 370ff., 380–84, 385–96; government and

bureaucracy and, 312ff., 325–26, 337–48; modern consciousness and, 41–67, 69–76, 78, 89, 90, 99, 102; moral (*see* Morality); values and freedom and, 112–15
Automation, 164, 224n, 227, 393
Automobiles (automotive industry), 73, 74, 138, 163, 178, 183, 186–87, 206, 217, 230, 231, 232, 251, 280, 282, 287, 288, 299–300, 307, 336, 379, 394
Autonomy, 27, 151–56, 228, 358, 359–64, 365ff. (*see also* Freedom); coercive process of economic bureaucracy and, 351–64, 365–72, 373–76, 377–79, 380–84, 385–96
Awareness. *See* Consciousness (awareness), historical and modern

Bank of America, 265, 266
Banks (banking, finance), 190–91, 206–7, 261, 265–74
Baron, Robert, 251–52
Beckett, Samuel, 147–48
Beliefs (*see also* Consciousness; Faith; Values; specific aspects, kinds): bureaucratic process and, 342–48, 377–79; values and moral conduct and, 113–25
Bellow, Saul, 69
Berle, Adolf, 183, 209
Bible, the (Gospels, Scriptures), 42, 46, 52
Biology, 142, 150, 171
Black Americans (Negroes), 39, 48, 189, 191–95, 318–19; government and, 313–14, 318–19, 339; militancy of, 85, 100, 106–10, 155, 310, 337n, 339; Panthers, 84; racism and, 39, 48, 85, 100, 104–10, 155, 189, 191–95, 313–14, 318–19, 339
"Black death" (plague), 40
Blake, William, 93–94, 197
Blundeville, Thomas, 43
Bonds of unity. *See* Unity
Bourgeoisie. *See* Middle class
Bradford, William, 78, 86, 94
Brandt, Heinz, 44
British. *See* Great Britain
Brown, Norman O., 262
Bruno, Giordano, 42, 51
Bryant, William Cullen, 94–95
Bryce, Lord, 342
Buber, Martin, 143–44
Budget (spending), federal, 328–29
Bureaucracy (bureaucracies), economic, 27, 62, 75–76, 146–56, 157–65, 169–88, 189–95, 201–20ff. (*see also* specific aspects, developments, kinds); coercive process of, 351–64, 365ff., 373–76, 377–79, 380–84, 385–96; defined, 183; domination of social process and, 201–20ff., 229ff., 245ff., 250ff.; and political process, 307–11, 312–20, 321–24, 325–36, 337–48; and racism, 107–10; and satisfaction of